# RIDING HIGH

**To Molly,**
**for smiling when I came home**

# Riding High

*SHADOW CYCLING THE TOUR DE FRANCE*

## PAUL HOWARD

MAINSTREAM
PUBLISHING

EDINBURGH AND LONDON

Reprinted 2007

Copyright © Paul Howard, 2003
All rights reserved
The moral right of the author has been asserted

First published in Great Britain in 2003 by
MAINSTREAM PUBLISHING (EDINBURGH) LTD
7 Albany Street
Edinburgh EH1 3UG

ISBN 9781840188943

This edition, 2004
Reprinted, 2004

A catalogue record for this book is available from the British Library

Typeset in Berkeley and Gill Sans Condensed

Printed in Great Britain by
Cox & Wyman Ltd

# ACKNOWLEDGEMENTS

If I'm to start where it all began, the first person to whom I must say a big thank you is Lino Lazzerini in Cavaillon, France, for his enthusiasm and passion for cycling that was just bound to rub off on me. In effect, it was Lino who started the ball rolling 11 years ago. Then there's C.S. Cavaillon, under the stewardship of Guy Chabert (M le President), the club which nurtured my enthusiasm and accommodated a novice English cyclist like it was the most normal thing in the world. I have many fond memories as a result.

It would also be remiss of me not to mention Mmes Lazzerini and Chabert, whose tolerance allowed their respective husbands to spend more time out on the bike with me than perhaps they ought, and who were integral in helping Catherine and me enjoy our stay and feel at home.

Back in the UK, I should thank all the usual suspects at V.C. Etoile for their unqualified support – and especially for devising the sweepstake as an extra motivational tool. I just hope they remember how slow I was before I went so that if I start doing well they'll notice the improvement, but if I remain an also-ran their expectations won't have been raised to unrealistic levels.

Thank you also to all those I met en route, who added wholeheartedly, if at times inadvertently, to the experience. I should also thank Stephanie at Giant for arranging the loan of a bike, which made the trip more comfortable than it otherwise might have been.

When it comes to the actual undertaking I must, of course, say a thousand thanks to my support team for the Tour itself. To Paul Grogan, for taking some excellent photos, many of which add greatly to this book, and for providing invaluable assistance and encouragement when riding with me. To Jon Clark, not least for having shared the dream and for having kept me on my mettle through the long winter months of training. To Jon also for having come to provide moral and practical support in spite of suffering the misfortune of not being able to ride with me as planned. To Dad, for undertaking to support me right from the outset and for perceiving this support as an adventure rather than a chore. Without him, none of this would have been possible.

Finally, I must say thank you to Catherine and Molly for coping so admirably with my lapses as a husband and a father that this endeavour has induced.

# CONTENTS

# PREFACE

Eddy Merckx, Lance Armstrong, Paul Howard. If I am to be honest, this is what I would have really liked this book to be about. About how I became the greatest-ever cyclist to come out of the British Isles. About how I became the first British rider to win the Tour de France, and how I earned the right to be spoken of in the same breath as such greats as Merckx and Armstrong.

You can keep Wimbledon and the FA Cup final. Although I used to have the same make of tennis racket as Björn Borg and remember being mesmerised by John McEnroe's tantrums, becoming the first home-grown player for millions of years to win at the All England club is someone else's dream. As for winning the FA Cup, these days it's enough for me to say that I'm a fan of Leeds United to understand why that was never a realistic possibility (although I can't deny that the Elland Road faithful chanting my name after I complete my hat-trick against *that* team from Manchester has a certain appeal).

For me, the greatest sporting dream was to ride, and then win, the Tour de France. The only problem was that I didn't realise the extent of this passion until too late. I was at sixth form before the intrigues and allure of bike racing inspired any real interest. Even then it wasn't for several years until I began to appreciate what was really happening: how Miguel Indurain imposed his will on the Tour for five consecutive years, how his achievements made him into the kind of star I dreamt of being. Now, at the age of 30, it seems to me that I have surely swapped 'promising' for 'past it'.

I say the only problem – it is of course not just age that has made the fulfilment of this dream such an impossibility. The biggest obstacle is perhaps the fact that I am nowhere near good enough a cyclist to become a professional. Certainly nowhere near the kind of youthful prodigy needed to make sceptical sponsors from the continent think of recruiting an unknown from a cycling backwater like the UK.

Even if I had the physical ability, which my amateur racing record makes quite clear I don't, my inherent laziness would have scuppered my plans: although I'm quite likely to train on a cold, rainy winter's day, the warm feeling of self-righteousness this engenders will then probably keep me off the bike for a couple of weeks, often when conditions are more clement.

Added to this I must also confess to the ease with which I can be distracted from my goals. Even when I was racing relatively seriously as an amateur (and occasionally showing signs of some latent ability), I'd often lose interest just at the moment when a bit more application might have seen me make some progress. Instead, I'd find articles of great interest in the Sunday papers that just had to be read. Or I'd surprise my wife with my sudden enthusiasm for family life and domestic chores when for the past two weeks all of these had been subjugated to the 'needs' of my training.

I like to think this is an endearing inability to take things too seriously, although a sports psychologist might demur and point out it could just be me hiding from the fear of failure: if I haven't trained that much it doesn't matter if I lose, but if I've prepared thoroughly and still lose then the blow to the ego will be serious. I think I prefer the first analysis.

Yet in spite of this litany of reasons why I was never going to be the next cycling great, the passion for cycling and the Tour de France has remained. In particular, the physical challenge that the Tour represents has always been compelling. It's been called the toughest sporting event in the world and it is difficult to disagree. Three weeks of riding upwards of 100 miles a day – often much farther – and sometimes more than 200 miles. Throw in the terrain covered in the

Alps and Pyrenees, with climbs to over 2,500 metres in altitude and some more than 15 miles long, and then add the weather the riders are likely to face (from almost unbearable heat in the south to the occasional snow, even in July, of the mountains; from the dismal rain that can plague the north to the strong winds of the west coast) and you begin to have an idea of the scale of the undertaking.

In fact, the enormity of the challenge is such that to my mind it always seems more akin to accounts of scaling Himalayan peaks and trying to reach the North or South Pole than more immediate sporting comparisons. It may be a remarkable achievement to hold your nerve and hole a six-foot putt to win the Open, but the physical requirements are not on the same level as riding, let alone winning, the Tour de France.

Some of this physical aspect is inherent in professional cycling. The famous one-day races, the 'Classics', are all epic endeavours in their own right. The distance covered – up to 180 miles in a day – and once again the terrain and the weather make for thrilling tales of human endurance as much as anything else. The cobbles and steep hills of northern France and Belgium, home to some of the most prestigious of these races, can be inhospitable places in March and April.

In the Tour de France this is magnified by a factor of 20. The result is a sense that a significant part of the event is competing simply to get round, completing the course. This is confirmed by the sentiments of the race's founder, Henri Desgranges: 'The perfect race would be the one where only one rider finished' was his infamous declaration, demonstrating just how important the difficulty of the task is to the fabric of the event. Hence also the affection reserved by fans and aficionados for those – the majority – who make no impression on the race and whose greatest achievement is simply to complete the course.

I think it is this epic challenge, these similarities with great feats of exploration and adventure, that kept my passion for the event alive even after the initial dreams of participating in it had lapsed. Even if I would never be able to take on the pros in the Tour proper, the question 'Is it possible to take on the Tour itself?' became embedded in my brain. The question was rhetorical to start with, aimed at other people with more cycling experience and ability than me. Nonetheless, as my cycling horizons shifted – after my first cycling tour, after the first time I rode more than 100 miles in a day – so the question seemed to become more pertinent, more personal.

What's more – let's be honest – here was a challenge that held the same attraction as following in the footsteps as Scott or Hillary but didn't have that awkward element of putting your own life on the line. Cycling has had its fair share of tragedies, and simply riding a bike carries a certain risk, but the prospect of being swept away by an avalanche or freezing to death in the wastes of the Antarctic doesn't come into the Tour de France equation.

The more I thought about it, the more it became apparent that here was an undertaking designed perfectly for a physical coward and a family man like myself (with responsibilities, as my mum would like to remind me). Without having to contrive a motive – like being the first person to roller-skate blindfold to the North Pole – and without the fear of not seeing my wife or daughter again when my folly caught up with me, I could satisfy that long-held desire for challenge and adventure.

And so I decided to see if it were possible to ride the Tour de France route; possible for a mere mortal like me, that is – each year hundreds of professionals prove it is quite within the scope of human achievement. The next question was 'how?' and then 'when?'.

Once I realised that 2003 coincided with the Tour's 100th anniversary, it became clear that this was the year I should try and achieve my aim. But should I ride that year's route, or a previous one? Should I ride it before the event, or after it? The answers to these questions would be different according to the different people who asked them, but the overriding aim for me was to emulate as closely as possible the achievements of the professionals. It is they who set the standard and who make of the event what it is; it is they who provide the epic tales of courage and endurance that reveal the scale of the challenge.

I had no option, it seemed to me, but to ride the current year's route and to try to do it as much as possible at the same time – and therefore in the same conditions – as the pros. This meant doing each stage on the very day of the race itself. I could do it a day earlier, or a day later, but a lot can change in a day. Besides, the schedule for the pros (dictated by the desire of television to have the stages finishing at popular viewing times) offered the tantalising possibility of being able to tackle the stages ahead of them, as long as I was prepared to rouse myself early enough. If they didn't start racing until 11 a.m. at the earliest, surely I could complete each stage before them if I set off at 6, 5 or 4 a.m? And after all, what's a few weeks getting up in the wee small hours in the grand scheme of things?

So that was that. The timetable had been set and the route was decided for me. All I had to do now was ride it.

DIEPPE

CHARLEVILLE-MÉZIÈRES

*Stage 2*

SEDAN

*Stage 3*

PARIS

MEAUX

LA FERTÉ
SOUS JOUARRE

ST-DIZIER

VILLE
D'AVRAY

MONTGERON

*Stage 4*

*Stage 1*

JOINVILLE

*Stage 20*

TROYES

*Stage 5*

NANTES

NEVERS

PORNIC

*Stage 19*

ST-MAIXENT-
L'ECOLE

TOUR
DE
FRANCE
2003

*Stage 18*

*Stage 6*

MORZINE-AVC

SALLANCHES

*Stage 7*

*Stage 8*

LYON

L'ALPE
D'HUEZ

BORDEAUX

BOURG
D'OISANS

*Stage 9*

GAP

*Stage 17*

*Stage 12*

GAILLAC

CAP' DÉCOUVERTE

CAVAILLON

*Stage 10*

DAX

TOULOUSE

BAYONNE

*Stage 16*

*Stage 11*

PAU

BAGNÈRES
DE BIGORRE

MARSEILLE

*Stage 15*

ST GIRONS

*Stage 13*

NARBONNE

LUZ-
ARDIDEN

*Stage 14*

LOUDENVIELLE-
LE LOURON

AX-3
DOMAINES

# MY MOTHER-IN-LAW DOESN'T TAKE DRUGS AND I DON'T HAVE A DOG

I think Catherine, my wife, initially thought my plans to ride the Tour were just another of the 'big ideas' that I occasionally come up with to enliven rainy days and Sunday evenings in front of the telly. She no doubt also thought that, like all the others, they were destined to be shelved quite soon when something more appealing came along to distract me.

Her confidence in this not unlikely outcome was probably enhanced by the arrival in September 2002 of Molly, our first child. Although supportive of my whims (we'd already spent a year in France so I could cycle in the sunshine), it must have seemed reasonable to assume the challenges of parenthood would soon put paid to this particular fancy.

In fact, I think neither of us realised just how deep-seated my desire had become until, in January, I started booking hotels throughout France – which was interpreted as a significant degree of commitment. This was a fairly thankless task, with small mountain towns like Bourg d'Oisans and Gap already claiming that all hotels were full for the days surrounding the visit of the Tour.

I began to worry that I would fall at the first, logistical, hurdle even before I got anywhere near to riding a bike. I also grew concerned that as the staff at the tourist information centres in deepest France became more and more irritated by my insistence that 'there must be somewhere' I would end up in the French equivalent of *Fawlty Towers*. Visions of Manuel inadvertently putting the bike out with the rubbish, or of Basil spitefully deflating the tyres after he'd tripped over it once too often, flashed repeatedly across my brain, already addled by hours of futile French conversation on the phone.

Nevertheless, all the hotel rooms in the right towns at the right times were eventually reserved, and the first step on the journey was completed. The next thing to do was to make sure my training was up to the mark. I'd already managed to fit some rides in before Christmas and then started in earnest, if somewhat aimlessly, in January. To try and give myself a sense of focus and perspective I drew up a training schedule, something I'd never done before. It was a bit like being back at school and compiling a revision timetable, although I hoped it would prove more successful than those, which were never followed but were often modified in lieu of doing any real work.

Working on the assumption that I only ever do two-thirds of whatever preparation I intend to, I saw the actual schedule as something to aspire to rather than a plan to follow to the letter. I figured that if I set my targets high I wouldn't be disappointed when I inevitably failed to reach them: after all, two-thirds of a lot is better than two-thirds of a little.

The end result was that I worked out a way in which I could fit in 6,000 miles in the first 6 months of the year through a combination of riding at weekends, riding to and from work and using public holidays. I'm sure there are amateur cyclists who think nothing of doing this every year, but when Catherine and I looked at the schedule it seemed to leave little time for other activities. Apart from being concerned at not fulfilling my family responsibilities I was also worried about the effect such an intensive regime would have on my morale. I've never been very good at focusing on one thing to the exclusion of others, always relying on variety to keep my appetite whetted for the things I really want to do. Yet here I was effectively giving over all my free time solely to cycling.

Still, with the Tour de France as an objective I decided I ought not to be lacking in motivation and set about with some relish the task of following my schedule. At least initially, anyway. January wasn't bad, February was a bit worse and March was a bit of a write-off, not least because we moved house. In fact we moved into a wreck and a degree of emergency DIY was added to the unpacking (still not finished) and sorting out (definitely still not finished), both of which reduced the opportunities for cycling.

By mid-March things were looking bleak, although I was feeling fit. Then the arrival of spring and the clocks going forward brought a new lease of life. For a start I could now cycle all the way home from work in Sutton – 35 miles – which I managed to do on average twice a week, sometimes more. Then there was the growing enthusiasm of my friend Jon to help maintain my motivation.

Jon and I have cycled thousands of miles together on a variety of trips at home and abroad, and as soon as I'd decided to try and ride the Tour route I asked him if he'd like to join me for some of it – maybe the Alps or the Pyrenees, when the riding's exciting and challenging. I was initially disappointed to hear him say no, but then I realised it wasn't because he didn't want to do any of it, it was because he wanted to do all of it. The prospect of there being two of us was a great boon, and by the time the days were getting longer we were managing to motivate ourselves successfully to maintain a healthy weekly mileage.

We also goaded each other into going out when we otherwise might not have, including several Audax rides across the south of England. For some reason these organised events have quite a poor reputation amongst racing cyclists, who seem to be a bit sniffy about the activities of their non-racing cousins – maybe it's the notion of a maximum speed and the traditional requirement to have mudguards and lights. For us, however, they provided a wonderful, cheap, local alternative to an expensive warm-weather training camp. They also provided the sense of obligation that was needed for us to make the transition from comfortable rides of 60 miles that could be fitted into an afternoon to day-long rides of 100 miles or more. After all, it was this kind of ride with a long time spent in the saddle that we had to get used to.

And so it was that I spent almost all my free time in March and April riding around the lanes of Sussex on my bike. The more I did this, the more my friends and acquaintances become aware of what I intended to do, and the more they started to ask questions. 'Why?' was the most frequent, but the most uncomfortable was 'Why do you want to pay homage to a bunch of drugs cheats?' In fact, in a variety of forms, some more subtle, some less so, this had been raised with disconcerting regularity ever since I'd set my heart upon the trip.

In some ways it's not an easy question to answer – the prospect of being labelled an apologist for any kind of doping is not appealing. Why indeed should anyone be so keen to celebrate such a tarnished institution as the Tour de France?

At least spending long hours alone on the bike gives you a chance to think things through. Non-cyclists may be forgiven for their scepticism, given that their knowledge of the sport is perhaps influenced by the recent grisly tales of doping and suspensions. But even the keen cyclists I know who are aware of the scale of the achievements of the pros find it difficult to lavish unfettered praise on today's champions. So frequent have become the tales of 'institutionalised' doping that even those who still admire the sport and its stars remain unconvinced by some performances.

And, let's face it, cycling hasn't exactly helped itself in the credibility stakes. If the best excuse you can come up with for being found with a stash of dodgy substances in your fridge is that they're for your dog, it seems unlikely that more legitimate denials will be readily accepted by the sporting public. How often does a dog need asthma drugs kept in the fridge?

Or what about saying the comprehensive supply of illicit products found in the back of your wife's car after finishing third in the Tour de France was destined for your mother-in-law? 'If my mother-in-law had taken all this stuff, she might have had a chance of making it to the winners' podium in the Tour de France as well,' was the response of one prosecutor.

It's hardly surprising that legitimate exploits are greeted with a degree of caution. Mind you, I've always thought that cyclists had some quite reasonable excuses for illegally enhancing their performance simply as a result of what they were required to do, at least historically. In the early years of the Tour, Henri Desgranges was as good as his word in trying to make it as hard as possible, with routes averaging more than 3,000 miles – over 1,000 miles more than this year. The longest Tour on record, in 1926, totalled 3,590 miles. With bikes weighing maybe twice what they do now, unsurfaced roads and stages of nearly 300 miles long necessitating pre-dawn starts it doesn't take much imagination to appreciate the need for a little extra help.

And at a time when most of the now 'illicit' substances that they used to keep them going weren't necessarily illegal or even condemned (amphetamines were available to naval captains and pilots during the Second World War), cyclists weren't coy about their habits. In the 1920s Henri Pelissier shocked journalists by revealing the contents of his pockets; in the early 1960s Jacques Anquetil, the first man to win five Tours, infamously declared that you couldn't ride the Tour just drinking water (he was reputed to be a fan of champagne, of all things).

I suppose, though, that these justifications cut less ice now, as bikes and roads have improved and the Tour has been shortened. This legacy must even be quite galling to those who complete the Tour without artificial help. If you've just cycled more than 2,000 miles in three weeks and then have people saying you couldn't have done it without cheating, you might quite reasonably feel a bit miffed. It's no wonder Armstrong – among others – is exasperated by constant questioning about doping.

The trouble is that the lame excuses and appalling scandals mean that the trust required to take people like Armstrong at their word – even when there's no good reason to disbelieve them – is now missing. This inability to trust in the honesty of today's riders (and even those of past generations, for the misdeeds of others reflect badly on them as well) risks undermining the whole sport. If those who participate cheat, those who encourage and support lose faith and everybody loses out in the long run.

And I suppose this is one of the reasons I want to ride the Tour route myself. Not just to see if it's possible, or possible to do it without drugs (you only have to meet my mother-in-law to know that she certainly doesn't take drugs, and I don't have a dog), but to demonstrate the magnitude of the Tour de France and how much those who complete it deserve to have their achievements applauded. What's more, I don't want to laud the event and the riders and look like some naive fool who isn't aware of the dubious practices that are indulged in. In spite of the lame excuses and appalling scandals, I want to believe that these are sportsmen worthy of our approval – even if by and large it's their own fault that the scepticism exists in the first place. Otherwise it's like discovering Hillary didn't actually climb Everest and just told a big fib because he knew he could get away with it. Or that Scott didn't die a heroic death, fighting the elements on his return from the Pole, but in reality got a fishbone caught in his throat.

These were the thoughts that occupied my mind as I spent the equivalent of several weeks out on the bike. It's hardly surprising that people say I looked distracted when they saw me toiling away through the Weald and over the Downs.

Not that these were my only concerns. For a start, the rather more immediate issue of 'saddle sore' frequently attracted a considerable amount of my attention. I managed to get off quite lightly to start with, but as my training built up I began to appreciate the need for some sort of balm. What should I use? My V.C. Etoile clubmates were divided as to the best strategy. Pete swore by baby's nappy-rash cream. 'Never had a problem since I started using it,' he said. With Molly's recent arrival this was something I had plenty of, and if it was good enough for her, it should be good enough for me.

Clive, however, was scornful. 'Vaseline's the only thing you should use,' he said. 'Use surgical spirit to keep clean' – I winced at the prospect, but he told me not to be soft – 'and Vaseline while riding'. His reference to a Radio 4 dermatologist's assertion that anything other than Vaseline does more harm than good was the clincher. Indeed, the way he implied the presence of unpleasant additives in anything else – including nappy cream – I began to wonder whether or not I would pass a drugs test if I were to use it. Then I started to think I ought not to be so lavish with the stuff when I was changing Molly's nappies . . .

Another frequent topic was trying to decide whether or not to ride the neutralised sections of the Tour that the professionals ride each day before the real racing starts. Often this is simply a question of a couple of miles from the centre of town to the outskirts where the roads are clear. Sometimes, however, particularly in the cities, this can be up to eight or maybe ten miles, and this year's first stage had a neutralised section of seventeen and a half miles across Paris.

The problem really is that it's all very well for the professionals to do this on closed roads in the late morning, but I wasn't sure I fancied it at 5 or 6 a.m. with the Parisian traffic for company. What's more, the purpose of these neutralised sections is often to serve as a procession for the sake of the spectators; I somehow doubted that people would be out lining the streets just to cheer me on. On balance, I decided I would probably give these bits a miss, especially where they would cause unnecessary hassle, like the one in Paris.

Sometimes, mind you, I didn't think of anything during training. The bike is a wonderful excuse to clear your head. Unfortunately, I think it was during one of these extended periods of blankness that it slowly dawned on me that staying out on the bike on your own can actually become a bit of a chore. It can really be quite tedious.

I'd never really noticed this before, I suppose because whenever I got bored in the past (or probably before I even realised I was getting bored) I could just turn round and go home. On the rare occasions when that wasn't possible, the challenge of keeping going was enough to keep me occupied.

But now I had become increasingly aware of the boredom of having to cycle a certain number of miles. This was all the more alarming as Jon's training was compromised first by a flu-like virus and then by sore knees. Rest appeared to be the only cure, so I was left ploughing a lonely furrow until our planned trip to the Pyrenees at the beginning of June, where we intended to put in some practice in the mountains and judge our progress so far (a progress I hoped had been enhanced rather than compromised by a different form of 'stamina training' on a friend's recent stag weekend in Edinburgh).

Unfortunately, this didn't exactly go to plan. Instead of four consecutive days of 100 miles over lots of nice hills, I managed one and Jon none at all. Some of this was down to having misjudged the distance between Toulouse and the hills, which took up a day of our riding at either end. The rest, however, was down to my worrying lack of fitness and the even more worrying state of Jon's knees. In fact these previously robust joints continued to deteriorate until Jon had

21

to cancel any thoughts first of being able to ride the whole Tour with me and in the end of riding any of the Tour at all. The diagnosis was unclear – illio-tibial band syndrome, or post-viral infection of the soft tissue surrounding the patella, or . . . It all depended on whom Jon spoke to, but the outcome was in no doubt: no more cycling.

This was, of course, a massive blow, not least to Jon, who'd put in five months of training. More selfishly, it meant that I would now be riding on my own. The minor benefits in terms of perhaps keeping things a bit simpler would clearly be outweighed by not having somebody to keep me going, to share the hard work and simply enjoy the experience with. And what's more, I wouldn't have the company of a good friend for three weeks.

Once back home after my own struggles in the Pyrenees it was clear that I needed to make a big push over the last four weeks if I was to be anywhere near fit enough (I'd done maybe 2,700 miles out of a scheduled 5,200 at this point). So, while Lance Armstrong and his rivals were warming up with high-profile races such as the Midi-Libre, the Dauphiné Libéré and the Tour of Switzerland, I made do with the Tour of Sussex. Or rather, the Tours of Sussex, as I struggled to string together rides that I knew well enough not to have to think about the route. In the end I did laps of a circuit that I knew measured 50 miles. I managed three days of two laps each and then had to stop simply because I couldn't face riding on the same roads again – even going round the other way didn't make much difference.

I was sure this wasn't a problem that the professionals face, and nor could I imagine they have the same struggle as I had to find some serious hill training (or that they have to make their own sandwiches to keep them going during a ride). In an attempt to emulate the amount of time required for the longest climbs in the Tour I plumped for repetitions up Ditchling Beacon. Eleven successive ascents – about one and a half hours – was my record, leading to some very puzzled looks from the man in the ice-cream van at the top.

All in all I felt less like today's professionals and more like the *touriste-routiers* class of riders in the early tours who were invited to help spice up the race and to counter the influence of the trade teams. The only recompense they could derive from their participation was the money to be earned from the various spot prizes on route: a few hundred francs here, a few there, and just possibly the offer of a professional contract if they managed to impress their more illustrious colleagues. So lowly, however, was their ranking that they had to book their own accommodation and transport for the duration of the Tour – even though they were participating in the race.

And the touriste-routiers were not just required to act as their own backroom staff and organiser, the rest of their support network during the Tour was at best rudimentary as well. With no teammates they were more or less obliged to ride on their own. Nor did they have any team support at the end of the stage: no mechanics, no masseurs, no meals prepared for them by the team's dietician. I may not be entirely on my own, but not even my dad – recruited to provide transport and psychological support – would claim to have any talents as a mechanic or masseur (or even chef).

In spite of the hardships they faced, often as not these touriste-routiers managed to make it round, with some of them going on to fulfil the dream of becoming contracted professionals. I've had to admit that this is an unlikely outcome for me, but they certainly provided a degree of inspiration.

I assumed that all this training would have had at least some beneficial impact on my racing ability. As a result, the last piece in my preparation jigsaw was to ride in one of the V.C. Etoile teams in the enduringly popular team time trial organised by the Clarencourt Cycling Club. I was confident I could pull my weight in a team that might do reasonably well.

Of course, I should have known better than to make such assumptions – after scarcely six miles out of thirty-seven my pedal came off. I hadn't screwed it in tight enough. The whole of the past six months flashed through my head as I careered all over the road and came perilously close to writing off any chances I had of riding the Tour as well as my brand-new bike, loaned especially for the ride by Giant. In the end the only damage, other than to the team's performance, was to my ego, even if I did avoid auto-castration by only the narrowest of margins. The first castrato to ride the Tour de France? Not for me, thanks.

Apart from the disappointment and discomfort this engendered it had one benefit – the friendly service the bike received at Baker Street Bikes in Brighton, which I decided was essential in order to avoid similar embarrassments during the Tour. They succeeded in putting my mind at rest about the pedals now being firmly attached and I spent the last week finalising preparations for the trip.

The last thing I did before leaving was to inadvertently provide some sport for the rest of V.C. Etoile. Conscious to show me the extent of their support, they decided to organise a sweepstake based on how many stages I would complete before I dropped out. In spite of the somewhat alarming enthusiasm of my clubmates for choosing stages early on, they reassured me that this was designed to be an extra motivational tool, rather than as evidence of their lack of faith in my abilities. 'If you make it all the way round, you get to keep the kitty,' said Simon, the instigator. With these final words of encouragement, I was ready for the off.

## Prologue

## PARIS (4 MILES)

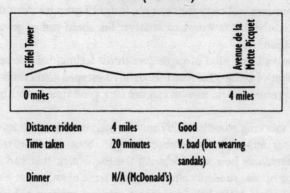

| | | |
|---|---|---|
| Distance ridden | 4 miles | Good |
| Time taken | 20 minutes | V. bad (but wearing sandals) |
| Dinner | N/A (McDonald's) | |

Dad's arrival on the Wednesday before we were due to leave on Friday was the signal that the time for preparation and prevarication had ended. Instead of just being aware at the back of my mind that I was going some time soon, I was suddenly conscious that I was off in less than two days. Everything became much more immediate, and all the potential flaws in my preparations came back to haunt me. Would all the hotels have records of my reservations? Was my first aid kit up to scratch? Was I fit enough? On this last question at least I was relatively sanguine as it was well beyond the point at which I could do anything about it. In fact it was quite a nice feeling to know that the last thing I ought to be doing was going out for a ride on my bike.

Thursday was spent packing and completing the 'things to do' list that I hoped was comprehensive. Then we went out for dinner as a kind of farewell treat. Whether it was a treat for us because we were going or a treat for Catherine and Molly because they were staying, I'm not sure – a bit of both, I suppose. Molly seemed to enjoy being taken to a restaurant, although she was less happy at us being provided with very obviously appetising meals while she was left with a Farley's rusk to chew on.

Although well fed and watered I slept only fitfully on Thursday night and woke up on Friday feeling a bit anxious. I think I always underestimate how taxing it can be to prepare for some kind of big venture and end up leaving things to the last minute, assuming a tide of enthusiasm will carry me through. Instead I get a bit worn down and need the first few days of whatever lies ahead just to get up to speed again.

I also had that kind of vague sore-throat feeling that is often an indication of being a bit low. I thought I'd escaped Catherine's cold of the previous week; now would not be a good time to feel below par.

The morning passed quickly until it was time for us to leave to catch our ferry. All I remember, though, about the short trip to Newhaven was how sad I felt. All the excitement that had been building up was suddenly replaced by the sense of sadness at leaving Catherine and Molly behind for three weeks. I suppose I shouldn't complain about feeling sad after having chosen to do something I've always wanted to do – nobody else was making me do it – but the feeling of loneliness that I was left with took me aback. The fact that the last thing Molly did as I walked out the door was to give me a great beaming smile that seemed to say 'see you in a few minutes' made me feel even worse. Even though I told myself not to indulge in self-pity, and that most of my discomfort was probably in fact guilt masquerading as some more noble emotion, I couldn't help but feel sad.

It also struck me that it's very easy to get carried away by the prospect of doing something exciting when it's a long way off. All the planning and aspirations tend to overshadow the practical consequences of what you're intending to do. Three weeks away – doesn't seem too bad a prospect when you're off to live a dream. Now we were actually en route, three weeks seemed like a very long time indeed. I told myself to remember this feeling once it had all finished and see whether or not it was outweighed by the anticipated euphoria. If it is then I guess I was just making a fuss.

My mood lightened a little by the time we were actually on the ferry as the sense of imminence began to grow. Catching a ferry is a very obvious sign of setting out on an adventure, and watching the whiteish cliffs of Newhaven disappear behind us helped excitement gain the upper hand over sorrow (and self-pity). I think the steak and mushroom pudding in a proper suet pastry helped as well.

The greyish cliffs of Dieppe soon welcomed us and the journey to Paris began well enough. Until we reached Rouen, that is, when we were alarmed to discover that the Armada had come to town. In spite of its warmongering reputation the good people of Rouen seemed keen to welcome this phalanx of tall ships. Well, those who were strolling amiably around the quayside were enjoying it anyway. Those of us – including most of Rouen's commuters – who were stuck in the same spot for an hour couldn't have been less impressed had a horde of bearded Spaniards with cutlasses and pirate flags come rampaging through the streets.

The one virtue we hoped would come out of this unplanned delay was that we would arrive on the *boulevard périphérique* (Paris's infamous ring road) after the Friday evening rush hour had ended. Unfortunately, we were wrong. Even at 8.30 p.m. it took us three quarters of an hour to do a quarter turn, a period enlivened only by the occasional presence of *voitures officielles* (the Tour's official cars). Given the importance and grandeur of the Tour and how significant it had become in my eyes, it was quite refreshing to see them stuck in the same traffic jam as us, subject to the same whims of Parisian drivers.

In the end we turned off a bit earlier than planned and took an alternative route to the suburb in which we were staying. For all the world it felt like we were driving down Streatham High Street. The further we went, however, the more grim our surroundings became, matched by the leaden skies in front that looked almost apocalyptic against the sunset. The prospects of finding the quaint old hotel I'd pictured us staying in seemed bleak, all the more so after we passed the inappropriately named 'Rev' Hotel' (Dream Hotel). A place more

RIDING HIGH

likely to induce nightmares I couldn't imagine; bed bugs and pimps were what sprang to mind.

After this it was quite a relief to find Hotel Balladins in Montgeron was no worse than an uninspiring modern concrete block in an out-of-town shopping centre. Even though it was the equivalent of staying in a hotel in a Tesco car park in Waddon, it had the distinct advantages of a warm welcome and clean rooms.

The only problem was that by the time we arrived the restaurant had closed and the Parisian traffic had sapped our enthusiasm for exploring the local area for something to eat. Instead we took the shameful decision to walk across the car park to the drive-through McDonald's – a more ignominious start to a trip to France I can't imagine. Here we were in the land of cordon bleu and haute cuisine, dining at the high altar of fast-food trash. I can't remember the last time I had to resort to such desperate measures.

What's more, this is a particularly emotive subject in France, where places like McDonald's are seen to symbolise not just *malbeuf* (bad food) but also the insidious undermining of French cultural values. So much so that French farmer José Bové has become something of a cult hero after wrecking his local McDonald's. Fed up with the buying power of fast-food chains and supermarkets, and constantly being hassled to reduce his prices and with it the quality of his produce, he took the law into his own hands. And there's nothing more likely to win over French public opinion than a doughty 'peasant' taking on the might of corporate America in the name of protecting the French way of life.

With this in mind I couldn't bring myself to have anything more than chips and orange juice, even though the steak and mushroom pudding on the ferry now seemed light years away. Dad had the very French-sounding 'Filet-O-Fish', although he said he wouldn't have known it was fish had it not advertised itself as such.

We returned to the hotel with our tails between our legs and were then confronted with the dilemma of whether or not to remove the bike rack from the car. It's not difficult to take off but it would have added maybe five minutes to the time needed to get ready in the morning, which held little appeal. The sight of the local disenfranchised youth using the supermarket car park as an obstacle

28

course/skid-pan in their souped-up cars suggested we should play safe and take it off, as did a warning from an Aussie fellow inmate (sorry, resident). Needless to say, five more minutes in bed and a bit less hassle in the morning won out.

Woke this morning after a reasonable night's sleep but I couldn't say I felt giddy with the enthusiasm. I spent what felt like several hours tossing and turning and bemoaning the fact that Dad had got up to have his shower *before* the alarm had gone off. It turns out that he was only ten minutes early, but it shows my concern to get enough sleep (it also shows how good I am at early mornings). Not able to face breakfast at McDonald's we set off into Paris itself so that I can ride the Prologue route (the bike rack having survived the night).

At a fraction over four miles I know it poses no difficulties from a riding point of view, but I'm nervous as we set off. It'll take us an hour or so to get into the city centre (the route starts almost directly beneath the Eiffel Tower) and then we have to find somewhere to park. I'm also worried that this could actually be one of the stages where roads will be completely closed a long time in advance of the actual event. This is partly out of contemplating the possible security concerns of the organisers, but more because I imagine the place will be heaving with wannabe Tour stage riders like myself. After all, riding such a high-profile route at the beginning of such a high-profile race seems to me very tempting. It's a bit like the chance to have a kick around on the pitch at Wembley on the day of the Cup final – surely everybody will want to have a go?

This anxiety is hardly eased by the fact that we inadvertently succumb to the vagaries of French motorway design and get sucked off the périphérique. Rather nonplussed, we find ourselves following signs for Bordeaux, which is quite clearly a long way from the Eiffel Tower. The Paris road map we have with us suggests a way to return towards the city centre, but not without first spending ten minutes travelling in the wrong direction. We then also have to negotiate an enormous commercial market where there is nothing as mundane as road signs, but finally we're back on track.

Almost inadvertently we end up close to the start, and even more fortuitously we find a parking spot right at the edge of the cordoned-off area. We take the bike off the rack and I decide to stick to my plan of riding 'incognito' – which is to say I don't put my cycling shorts and top on, instead just wearing normal shorts and a T-shirt – just in case they really are trying to discourage amateurs. Dad has spotted a café over the road where he can have coffee and croissants and we agree to meet there in half an hour or so. He bids me luck for my first Tour stage and I set off. To complete my attempts to remain inconspicuous I realise I've forgotten to put my cycling shoes on and will have to ride in my sandals.

It turns out, of course, that I needn't have worried about any adverse reaction from officials or police for trying to ride on the course. To make this abundantly clear, just as I arrive at the start and am heading straight for the bridge over the Seine before anybody tries to stop me, a vast bunch of cyclists hoves into view. All sporting proper cycling kit and revelling in their bright colours, about 50 or 60 of them sail past the start, waving at the gendarmes and looking every bit as though they own the road. The gendarmes merrily wave back – which is itself a pretty unusual sight in Paris – and even turn a blind eye as the group blocks the traffic at the next junction.

I latch onto the back of the group. It turns out – I might have guessed – to be made up of Australians and Americans, with a few Kiwis and Canadians thrown in for good measure (in the face of their brazen self-confidence I decide not to own up to having just conformed to the stereotype of the diffident Brit). They're all here on an organised trip that follows the Tour as far as l'Alpe d'Huez, combining watching with riding. The guides will stay longer and host a second trip from the Alps back to Paris. It sounds a good deal more relaxed than my venture.

I find all this out as we amble sedately around the course, even stopping at a few of the red lights we encounter on the way. The Parisian traffic gives us a surprisingly benign reception on the roads that are still open to cars. At the finish preparations are well under way, with the big *Arrivée* banner just being put in place and hundreds of heavy-metal roadie look-alikes trailing wires hither and thither. Nobody bats an eyelid at the number of cyclists getting underfoot.

I rejoin Dad at the café, where he's just finished his second round of croissants. Given the strength of this tacit recommendation I also order several to celebrate riding my first-ever Tour stage. It took me about 20 minutes (which Dad charitably says isn't bad for someone in sandals), but unfortunately I can't be more precise: I got so carried away with not wearing my cycling kit that I also forgot to take my brand-new bike computer. The same new bike computer bought specially for the trip and that I hoped would forever carry the total number of miles I rode when following the Tour de France route. Glad everything's running smoothly so far.

After successfully negotiating the périphérique on our return to Montgeron, we decide to try and find the famous Au Réveil Matin Café from which the original Tour started – and from which this year's Tour will start in earnest tomorrow. It turns out to be only about half a mile from our hotel, which is good as it means it will be easy to get to the start.

There are quite a few people milling around, several with bikes, all taking photos. There's also a Belgian TV crew looking for shots, and when I speak to them they become quite animated about the prospect of putting together a little piece about what I'm doing. I remain sceptical about their enthusiastic suggestions to meet me here at 6 a.m., but they insist on taking my mobile-phone number so they can arrange a rendezvous.

The café itself has metamorphosed from a traditional French brasserie into a Tex-Mex themed restaurant (perhaps the Texan part of the theme is a good omen for Armstrong), and has a very bright coat of paint suggesting that its current owners are aware of its prestigious role in the centenary Tour.

Or perhaps it's the 'municipality' who are keen to be seen in the best light, as there is quite an impressive roundabout just outside. Not only have they contrived to spell 'Montgeron' out of a sculpture of a bike and rider (in spite of their best efforts it remains almost illegible), they've also used the circumference of the roundabout to display tiles commemorating all the Tours to date.

Several of the tiles carry stickers, however, apologising for a 'technical error' that has prevented them from being complete in time – and this includes Lance Armstrong's name. By removing the sticker you find the 'technical error' is that they've misspelt

'Armstrong' as 'Amstrong'. Perhaps this doesn't bode so well for him after all. This whole thing adds up to a rather endearingly amateur attempt at civic pride – this part of the Tour at least hasn't become too commercialised. As the restaurant is actually a working entity we book a table for tonight. What better place to eat at before the Tour's first real stage?

Back at the hotel, I sleep through most of the Prologue, and turn on to discover David Millar's mechanical woes have cost Britain's only representative the yellow jersey. The TV commentary is rather downbeat about the performance of French riders, but at least it seems as though there may be some real rivalry to Armstrong this year. Most of the rest of the coverage talks about how glad the riders will be to have actually broken the ice, and how keen they will be to start tomorrow's first stage proper. I couldn't agree more – I now have an overwhelming desire to get going. I want to put all the logistical concerns about meeting points with Dad and what clothes to wear behind me and just get out on the bike. I feel that once I actually start riding everything else will fall into place, as it will be the riding that dictates the rhythm of our days – and this is why I've come, after all. All the planning and preparations are just a necessary evil.

Anyway, after making sure everything's ready for tomorrow, we go to the Réveil Matin and enjoy a much more pleasant meal than last night's farrago at McDonald's. Although I'm trying to emulate the achievements of finely honed athletes I can't resist a nice rare steak in a rocquefort sauce with a healthy portion of chips (and a glass of wine, of course). Dad makes me feel better by having pasta.

Preparing for bed I receive a message from Catherine and Molly wishing me luck and telling me I can do it. I certainly hope so as I'll feel as though this time apart will have been in vain otherwise. As it is I might miss Molly starting to crawl. She can already shuffle backwards, so it won't be long before she's fully mobile.

Then I'm surprised to get a call from the Belgian TV crew we met earlier – surprised because I didn't think they'd bother, but also surprised because I'm in the middle of cleaning my teeth. In spite of this handicap I understand that they will meet me at the Réveil Matin at 5.45 a.m. and film me beginning my ride. Excellent – I've always wanted to be a Belgian TV star.

The last thing I do before I go to sleep is scan through *Le Parisien* newspaper, and my eye settles on the horoscopes. Normally I don't think I'd even notice they were there, but as tomorrow's quite a big day I find the temptation to see into the future too hard to resist.

Under 'love life' I'm told that I should be less prosaic and should show more affection, which is probably fair enough (I'm sure Catherine would agree). Under 'success' I'm disappointed to be reminded that it's not always easy to resolve a problem at the first attempt, but I decide that this just means patience is a virtue.

More alarming still, however, is the 'health' section. With over 2,000 miles to ride in the next three weeks, it's a bit disconcerting to be warned against 'physical excess'. It strikes me as being a bit late in the day to tell me this – although I suppose if I were a regular horoscope reader I might have picked up this message sooner. I become belligerent (always a good thing to do if you're confronted with an unpleasant surprise) and manage to dismiss the whole notion of horoscopes as a load of twaddle and mumbo-jumbo. I wish I hadn't bothered to look though.

## Stage 1

# MONTGERON—MEAUX (105 MILES)

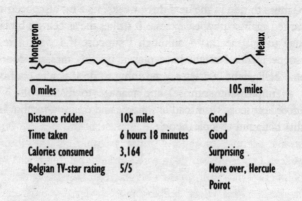

| | | |
|---|---|---|
| Distance ridden | 105 miles | Good |
| Time taken | 6 hours 18 minutes | Good |
| Calories consumed | 3,164 | Surprising |
| Belgian TV-star rating | 5/5 | Move over, Hercule Poirot |

Even though it's 5 a.m.– and only seven hours since I went to bed – the alarm ringing doesn't send me into a fit of apoplexy or depression, which I take as a good sign. In fact I feel quite refreshed. Hopefully this means that a few hours' sleep each afternoon will compensate for the reduced quantity at night.

The virtues of Dad's self-catering experience come to the fore at breakfast, when hot water from his flask provides a welcome cup of tea, followed by a bowl of cereals (Bran Flakes and Alpen – very French). I supplement this with a banana, and for once I stick to the coaching manual by drinking a pint of water ('drink 500 ml before effort' goes the mantra). It may not be the breakfast of choice for the pros, but at 5 a.m. in a pokey hotel room it's better than the alternative – which amounts to not very much at all, as far as we can work out.

On the short ride to the Réveil Matin I'm disconcerted to realise how dark it still is (I take this as vindication of my decision not to ride the neutralised section from the Stade de France to Montgeron). At 5.40 a.m. I can manage without lights, but at tomorrow's anticipated start time of an hour earlier it seems unlikely that I'll get by. I'm sure I worked out that it would be light here given the time the sun comes up at home, but I must have done something wrong somewhere.

In spite of last night's call I'm still slightly surprised to see the Belgian TV crew actually waiting for me when I arrive. I suppose in a country where cycling is a national sport, and where the Tour probably has saturation coverage, any new angle is gratefully received.

They set up some shots of me in front of the plaque that commemorates the starting point of the original Tour as well as this year's event, and then they say they want to interview me about what I'm intending to do. It might be something to do with the problems of understanding Belgian-accented French before 6 a.m., but the questions become more and more peculiar as the interview progresses. I try to answer them with a straight bat, but once I've had to accept that I may well appear a bit mad I find myself agreeing with the suggestion that I'll be keeping my powder dry until the race reaches the Alps, where I'm told I'll attack and keep the yellow jersey until the finish in Paris. And I thought I'd given up my aspirations for the real thing. They say they'll meet me again during the day to film me in action.

Dad arrives after wrestling with a couple of barriers that appeared overnight, blocking the road between our hotel and the start. Hopefully this won't be a sign of things to come or our plan to have frequent meeting points en route could come unstuck. Then the Belgians film us as Dad wishes me *bon voyage* and I'm off.

Almost immediately I feel bowled over by the sense of relief and freedom. The first seeds of desire for this adventure were sewn over a year ago and it's been slowly eating away at me ever since. I've been planning in earnest for more than nine months, and I've been training since Christmas. During that time I've given cycling priority over so many things – over decorating our new house, days out with

Molly and simply having a free weekend with no need to fit in several hours of riding. I may not have been monk-like in my strictness with a training regime, and I may not have been as single-minded as Lance Armstrong, but in the context of the life I'm used to this has been a significant commitment.

Now I've finally started, I feel as though it's the beginning of the holidays, with the world spread out in front of me and the peculiar impression that I'm on my way to see most of it. It is as though I've been suddenly released from a darkened room into a summer's day, creating a sensation both of bewilderment and incredible alertness. My senses are on overdrive and I am aware of everything, as though I am capable of hearing a pin drop in the next village. Even though I'm never still, I am involved with the places I pass through. Everything is so vibrant and intense: one moment it's the smell of a bakery preparing the first croissants of the day, the next it's a field of sunflowers, a child who stops to watch as I go past, an old man who mutters something friendly but incomprehensible.

In these few, serene moments I feel like I was born to ride a bike – a perfectly natural thing, the equivalent of drinking water when you're thirsty or lying down when you're tired. Some people go to work in offices, some in the fields – and what do I do, for now at least? I ride my bike.

With all this activity to occupy me, all worries and concerns just disappear. The conscious part of my mind is taken up solely with the immediate concerns of moving forwards on my bike – watch that pot hole, keep a nice rhythm up this slight hill, enjoy the descent on the other side. The rest of it is just enjoying the view (or the sounds or smells . . .). Nor does the unlikely prospect of riding more than 2,000 miles in the next three weeks bring a furrow to my brow. Even the constraint of having the route set out for me in advance is a form of freedom. It simply means there'll be no dilemmas deciding which way to go.

I wonder to what degree the professionals will have this sense of release. Perhaps not the seasoned pros, but what about the gaggle of young French riders that have so enthused the local media? I can't emulate in any way the fact that for them it's a job, and that there is a constant competitive imperative – the need to win, or be at the front, or do as well as possible to ensure a contract for next year. Nor can I emulate the fact that riding the Tour for them is not a self-indulgence but the means by which they earn their living and make their reputations.

Just to emphasise the point I pass through the first intermediate sprint of the day where the yellow jersey will come under threat from other riders intent on picking up the bonus seconds necessary to take over the race lead. It's unlikely to be as sedate as when I pass through with nobody for company except my shadow – we cross the line together, having agreed to avoid an unseemly tussle for first place.

But maybe the need to concentrate on the racing will bring the same kind of relief as I've found through focusing simply on the riding. After all, they can't help but be caught up to some degree with the anticipation and media circus that accompanies the build-up to the Tour. You'd hope that finally setting off and being allowed to get on with their jobs would bring a similar sense of freedom. And for some of the riders, if not most of them, it's perhaps more of a vocation than a job. Lance Armstrong says it's riding the Tour – and winning it – that makes him get up in the morning, so he at least must be pleased to be started.

All this excitement and reflection, added to which is the illicit thrill of cycling on the actual Tour route, means that I get a bit carried away and ride more quickly than I intended. In fact I'm soon well out of Paris and pass through a village that proudly proclaims its participation in the 'best-decorated village on the route' competition. After a few half-hearted floral arrangements and one old bike propped up against a shop window I realise that's all it has to offer. Either the inhabitants of Boutigny-sur-Essonne are a miserable lot or the competition is not a very prestigious one.

If this dampens the excitement slightly, the recurring presence of the Belgian TV crew, who are determined to help me inflate my already growing ego, livens things up again. At first they keep driving past me and then stopping to film as I ride in front of some pleasant view (the countryside has become surprisingly attractive as I've left the suburbs behind and it's a beautiful sunny morning on quiet roads, which makes it easy for all of us). Then they decide to film me from the car as I'm actually riding, making me feel for all the world like a lone breakaway seeking his moment of glory. All this attention is bad for me, and I start to be seduced by delusions of grandeur – it's a piece of cake, this Tour de France lark, that sort of thing.

The net result is that I arrive at Milly-la-Forêt, the first rendezvous with Dad, having covered 33 miles in 1 hour 50 minutes – an average of 17.3 mph. This may not break any records, but I've plenty of time and I really ought to take it a bit easier as it's only the first day. Nevertheless, I can't deny that I'm pleased to be going so well, and I've already been over two 'fourth-category' climbs without really noticing either, which is encouraging. Both of these were already being lined with supporters come to set up their picnic spots some seven hours before the race is likely to arrive – I'm not the only lunatic after all.

I also feel quite relaxed about the challenge ahead, which is a good sign as long as it doesn't indicate complacency on my part. In fact I'm more confident than I probably have a right to be, given the extent of my preparation. In an ideal world I'd have wanted to double the 3,500 miles I've ridden since Christmas.

Yet I'm confident because I know I'm fit and because none of my preparation took me anywhere near to full effort. I was tired after some of the rides, but never desperate. The knowledge that I have an unquantifiable amount of energy in reserve is more encouraging to me than knowing I'd prepared more assiduously but had put myself in the red to do so. As long as these first few days don't wear me out too much (and I'm on such a high at the moment I feel like I want to ride them all in one go), then I'm assuming I'll be even fitter when we hit the Alps – at which point I'll find out what these reserves are made of.

Dad has had some trouble working out a route away from the official Tour route, but as the Belgians have managed to follow me all the way so far without hindrance he decides to try and do the same over the next bit, which will make his life a lot easier.

I replenish my water bottles, fill my pockets and set off again.

Shortly afterwards I catch up with a French cyclist who's following the route as far as Fontainebleau which, as he points out, should be pronounced 'Fontaine-blow', not the anglicised 'Fontaine-bleurgh'.

This sounds peculiar and for a surreal moment I'm tempted to succumb to Englishman-abroad syndrome and tell him – a resident of the town – that this can't be right, but fortunately the moment passes before I make a fool of myself.

Apart from improving my French the presence of my new companion compels me to slow down a touch, for which I am grateful. At Fontainebleau, after a brief glimpse of the impressive chateau, our ways part, and I'm immediately confronted by arrows pointing me the wrong way up a one-way street. Just one more logistical hurdle that the Tour riders won't have to overcome.

I then catch a group of club riders just before the third climb of the day and have the satisfaction of leading them up the climb and winning the inevitable sprint for the top. I feel very pleased with myself, and leave the others seeming even more nonplussed when the Belgians arrive and start to film again. In fact the crew sit just in front of me, filming out of the boot of the car, sending my ego into the stratosphere – until they ask me to sing to myself for encouragement. I know my limits (even if I can con myself into thinking I'm a good cyclist) and in spite of several requests I decline – not even Catherine or my nan would be able to defend my singing ability, and I don't want to inflict it on a TV audience, even one in Belgium. Mind you, if they promise to drive in front of me everyday at about 20 mph I'll consider anything.

Dad has had an easy journey along the route to our second meeting point, where I begin to feel as though I've been out for over four hours. It's not so much that I'm tired, more that I realise I've still got a good couple of hours to go (it's amazing how quickly I've progressed from this morning's elation to a growing sense of tedium). Also, the countryside has taken a distinct turn for the worse, becoming much more open and undulating. Well, it's kind of flat – in that the horizon is a long way off – but up and down a bit all the time, and the roads are long and straight, with nothing other than wheat fields for company. The official Tour literature makes quite a thing about this being a big cheese-making area (I ride through Rozay-en-Brie and Coulommiers), yet there is a distinct lack of cows.

Not that this stops the fans from lining the roads, and the crowds are beginning to build up in surprising numbers. They also take to encouraging me as I ride past, which makes the last few miles into Meaux quite agreeable.

I manage to ride along the closed-off roads, underneath the red kite that signifies one kilometre remaining, right up to within 250 metres of the finish line where, surprise surprise, I find the Belgian TV crew waiting for me. The finish area is still under construction but in spite of the apparent chaos they reckon they can manage to stage a shot of me sprinting for the line to round off the day's footage.

Feeling slightly self-conscious I nevertheless oblige and at the second attempt I manage to give a convincing impression of a victorious lone breakaway – I even manage to raise both arms aloft in a victory salute, which they like very much, although the gathering spectators look less convinced. Then there's a final interview, by which time I've cottoned on to the idea of self-parody (at least I hope this is how it comes across) and I recount in detail how I managed to drop everyone on the run-in because I didn't fancy taking on the sprinters on such a fast finish. For good measure I add that I now feel confident of keeping the yellow jersey all the way until Paris.

After this it's just a short drive down the Marne valley to our hotel in La Ferté-sous-Jouarre, where tomorrow's stage starts. The accommodation is fine, except for having to negotiate a spiral staircase with the bike. When I ask for some ice in a plastic bag to put on my knees, which are a bit sore (the only discomfort after the ride), the hotelier asks how far I'm cycling. Once I've explained, far from looking at me like I'm some pitiful fool (the standard response) he simply says he had a guest last night who was doing the same thing but a day earlier than the actual race. They're obviously used to cycling round here, and I find it reassuring there are other riders who think it's feasible.

To save time wandering around town we have dinner in the hotel from the special Tour de France menu. This turns out to mean that any variety has been ruthlessly removed and we are faced with a choice between *moules-frites* (mussels and chips) and *moules-frites* – with a mixed salad as a starter. Having already given up any prospects of a sensible 'athletes' diet I enjoy the mussels with a clear conscience.

In fact, I decide that I'm quite happy to be on the 'Anquetil' diet – so called in deference to infamous *bon-viveur* Jacques Anquetil, the first rider to win the Tour de France five times. He once reputedly ate a whole lobster in white wine before participating in (and winning) a big race, and preferred foie-gras to grated carrot, whisky to mineral water. He also declared: 'I've crossed the word "diet" out of my vocabulary. I want to live life as I know it should be lived.' If it's good enough for him, it's good enough for me.

## Stage 2

# LA FERTÉ-SOUS-JOUARRE—SEDAN (128 MILES)

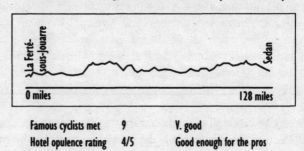

| | | |
|---|---|---|
| Famous cyclists met | 9 | V. good |
| Hotel opulence rating | 4/5 | Good enough for the pros |
| Anquetil diet rating | 1/5 | Pasta |

The good news about the hotel we're staying at today in Charleville-Mézières is that it's a very grand, old, town-centre hotel, with spacious, airy rooms that remain cool on hot days like today. The even better news, from the point of view of a cycling fan, is that it is also the hotel where the fdjeux.com team are staying. And it gets better still.

A few days ago the prospect of staying with the fdjeux.com team would have been appealing – seeing some professional riders during the Tour is quite an insight – but it would not have ranked on the same scale as staying with Lance Armstrong's US Postal team, for example. Its list of star names is not great, and its riders have only won two stages in the Tour since the team's first participation in 1997.

That all changed after the Prologue, however, in which Bradley McGee (of fdjeux.com) beat David Millar by 0.08 seconds (both riding it roughly three times as fast as I did, although neither of them were wearing sandals). In doing so he also won the right to wear the yellow jersey and more importantly, from my point of view, he managed to successfully defend his slender lead yesterday, and has just succeeded in doing so again today. This all means that we're staying in the same hotel as the yellow jersey. The *yellow jersey*.

This is as evocative an item of clothing as Pelé's number 10 Brazil shirt, or Marilyn Monroe's white dress worn when she danced over the air vent (although for different reasons, obviously). And here it is, in the hotel I'm staying in.

And not just that. The team is also celebrating the presence of the Tour's most romantic jersey, the red-and-white polka-dot one for best climber in the King of the Mountains competition. We may hardly have been over any hills yet but there have been enough points on offer for the team's Christophe Mengin to snaffle the jersey and probably have the privilege of wearing it until the real hills start on Stage 7.

Finally, to cap it all off, today's stage was won by Baden Cooke – of fdjeux.com, no less. Not only did he win the stage, he also picked up enough bonus seconds to wear the white jersey for best young rider. Which means this unassuming team in an unassuming hotel in an unassuming town now holds three of the Tour's four jerseys. Only the green jersey for the best sprinter escapes them at the moment.

The result is that you could say that the hotel is in a state of celebration. In fact, apart from the bikes and the lean young men with tan lines you'd be hard pressed to realise you were in the middle of a bike race, rather than at the end of one.

This impression is added to by the typically Australian celebrations of Cooke and McGee – who enjoy a glass of cold beer upon their arrival at the hotel. It's a great picture of satisfaction after a good day at the office – Cooke and McGee in the white and yellow jerseys sitting together drinking beer. I can't resist the temptation to ask for my picture to be taken with both of them, although the yellow T-shirt I'm wearing doesn't go that well with the real yellow jersey. Still, it's as close as I'll get to wearing the real thing.

What's more, in another apparent break with the austerities of the past there are a considerable number of friends and relatives about. McGee's wife and daughter are visiting, as are his brother and sister-in-law. I think Cooke's parents are here as well. They're only staying as far as Lyon (after Stage 6) but it must be nice to have them around. McGee junior is only about 18 months old and I envy the fact that Daddy can see her for a few more days at least.

Because of all this success the hotel is surrounded by admirers hoping to catch a glance of the riders, or of the jerseys, or both. Some are bold enough to come into the hotel bar for a drink, others hang around in the hotel lobby looking for a chance for an autograph and a picture. The team bus draws a lot of admiring glances, and the effect of having the mechanics do their daily maintenance and bike cleaning in the open in front of the hotel is a real PR coup.

There is also a coterie of journalists, looking for a story or an interview, although there is a distinct pecking order: pride of place very obviously goes to the elegant Celine from the nightly French sports-show-cum-Tour-round-up programme. This much is clear from the fact that she enjoys the privilege of sitting at the table of the team directors and sharing in their celebratory round of drinks, while the other journalists try and catch the eye of one of the backroom staff.

Every now and then she pops off to oversee the setting up of a temporary studio for the purpose of the planned interview. This results in lots of moving of chairs and settees to one side of the bar, and then lots of moving them back again until a suitable layout is agreed upon. Then comes the tricky bit of setting up the camera and all the lighting and paraphernalia associated with an outside broadcast. Dozens of cables are brought in from the TV van and then draped across the bar and restaurant from sockets that look about as sound as the plumbing in your average French hotel. It would be a shame if one of the success stories of the Tour so far were to see their hotel go up in flames as a result of making it onto the telly; I'd find it a bit of a pain as well.

This circus goes on while Dad and I have dinner – about 12 feet away – which just goes to show the peculiar relationship the Tour has with the places and people it comes into contact with. For a day at least it's little exaggeration to say that fdjeux.com and McGee, Cooke, Mengin and the others are the focus of the world's sporting attention. In addition to the hundreds of thousands who line the route each day, hundreds of millions follow the Tour in its every detail on television and in the papers. Yet here they are, the current star players in this three-week-long drama, drinking beer and champagne in a hotel that's just trying to go about its everyday business.

The locals continue to nod sagely to each other at the bar in the corner, and there are still other guests at the hotel to attend to, including Dad and me. In spite of all the fuss round and about we receive very attentive service and I enjoy a healthy tagliatelle bolognaise, which seems all the more virtuous for the amount of beer consumed by the team mechanics, whom I couldn't persuade to give my bike the once over, unfortunately.

The only concession to the presence of these 'stars' is that drinks from the bar are free to those associated with the team. I know this because when I ask for a glass of beer myself (when in Rome . . .) the barman scrutinises me and asks if I am doing the Tour. For a second I think he's mistaken me for a professional rider; then it crosses my mind he could think I'm a mechanic. The hesitation is enough for him to realise that I'm just a normal punter and he asks for my money. I'm tempted to explain that I am riding the Tour after a fashion to see if he thinks this also merits a free drink, but the prospect of doing so when there are real Tour riders here (and the *yellow jersey*) makes me think again. Besides, he's already back discussing next season's football with his mate, a clear indication that I'm not as interesting as the genuine article.

All this time the TV crew has been fine-tuning its preparations and once we've finished dinner we notice the crowd gathering to witness the live interview in action. On the agenda today are stage-winner Cooke and teammate Jimmy Casper, who in spite of his name is French, not Australian.

His particular claim to fame at the moment is that he fell very heavily in a crash just before the finish yesterday and had to be taken to hospital on a stretcher. Fortunately this turned out to be just a precaution, although his neck was jarred sufficiently for him to have to ride today's stage in a brace. He's still wearing it as he settles gingerly into his chair and, even though he's putting on a brave face, he really doesn't look very comfortable – it must have been very unpleasant to ride with, especially on a warm day like today.

Everybody stands around a bit longer (or sits if you're famous enough to be interviewed) until Celine says they'll be coming live to Le Relais du Square in Charleville-Mézières in a couple of minutes (even the hotel proprietor shows some excitement at this point). And then we get less than two minutes of 'action' – just enough time to ask one question to each of them – before it's back to the studio where they've obviously got something more important to talk about.

The hotel staff immediately go back to their jobs having regained their air of 'we've still got a hotel to run tomorrow when you lot have moved on' indifference. All the spectators linger a bit, a touch disappointed, and then disperse. Celine apologises for the coverage being so brief, but the team management don't seem to mind as they're getting ready to stage a group photo.

Under orders from the boss the whole team – mechanics, riders, sponsors – gathers in front of the team bus with the three jersey-wearers in the front row. Then they all start singing the French equivalent of 'We've got all the shirts'.

After the celebrations outside the evening ends with the team's *directeur sportif* proposing a toast (with champagne, of course) to their ongoing success. He then tells them not to get carried away and that they should go to bed as they have to race tomorrow – I suppose it doesn't hurt to remind them. It's a sentiment I know I should share, as it's gone 10 p.m. and I hardly slept this afternoon – partly because I kept waking up wondering if the team had arrived yet.

The other part was because I just couldn't seem to relax after today's ride. I suppose to some degree that must be accepted as it was in fact the longest distance I've ever ridden in a day. Only by about 2 miles (128 miles compared to 126 miles previously), but still, a new record is a new record.

The first hour this morning wasn't particularly pleasant as it did indeed turn out to be dark. Not too dark for me to be able to see the road ahead, but dark enough for me to worry about being seen. All I've got with me is a back light, so I put that on and just hoped that nobody coming towards me would be cutting any corners.

The only other problem this morning was that I couldn't work out whether I felt hungry or sick. I plumped for sick to start with (I was beginning to think that last night's moules weren't such a good idea after all) and didn't eat anything for maybe the first hour and a half, but when the feeling didn't change I decided that I might be hungry instead. This was confirmed at the first meeting with Dad, where I had tea and malt loaf and immediately felt much better.

Once the sun came up (another glorious day) I had a very pleasant couple of hours cycling along the Marne valley, riding through vineyards destined to produce champagne. Unfortunately this attractive landscape was soon replaced by the vast open wheat fields that surround Reims – even though this is the self-proclaimed capital of the champagne region, the vineyards mysteriously disappeared.

It soon got to the point where I was looking for something, anything, to enliven proceedings when I saw a cyclist on the road ahead of me. The thrill of the chase soon kicked in and I was pleased to find I was catching him at some speed on the hills. This self-satisfaction wore off somewhat when I was close enough to see that he had panniers (albeit only small) on both the front and the back of his bike and was wearing enough clothes to keep me warm on a winter's day – making my achievements a bit less laudable.

I finally drew level with him at the top of a brow, which gave us the chance to try and work out each other's nationality as we cruised down the other side. After several mumbled greetings in what purported to be French but was in fact international code for 'I'm not French, what about you?', it became clear my companion was also English.

I discovered he was called Jeremy and was then taken aback to find that he knew me, or at least knew of me, as well as what I was doing (all thanks to an article I'd written for *Cycling Plus* in which I outlined my venture). I'd not met anybody other than my family who'd read my articles before, so this was quite a thrill.

It turned out Jeremy was also trying to cycle an abbreviated version of the Tour route on his own – hence the luggage. Having set off the previous day from Paris he'd spent last night in his bivvy bag in a field somewhere just after La Ferté. This explained the extra layers, as he was still trying to warm up from what turned out to be a chilly night.

I expressed admiration at his fortitude and asked what kind of training he'd been doing for such an undertaking. He said he'd got himself quite fit in order to run in the 'Man versus Horse' running race in Wales and that he'd beaten 17 horses and even been on telly . . . and that was about it really. This was enough to make my preparations look distinctly professional, and we agreed that over-training was the real danger.

When Jeremy stopped to shed his extra layers I carried on alone across the endless plains. Only the village of Courcy provided any light relief, which was doing its best to compensate for the poor showing of Boutigny-sur-Essonne yesterday in the best-decorated village contest. Almost every house and shop front was adorned with crêpe-paper sunflowers, and on every corner there were old bikes all dressed up for the occasion. Some of these were being ridden by mannequins (or perhaps scarecrows would be a more accurate description), and there were flags and banners welcoming the Tour and its most popular riders everywhere. It may not have been to everyone's taste, but at least they'd made an effort.

Even more impressive was the way they'd created a big arch across the road at the entrance to the village and contrived to make a pun out of Courcy and cycle racing: '*Courcycliste*' was what they'd written on the banner, which when spoken sounds the same as *course cycliste*, meaning cycle race. I bet the judges will be impressed by that.

Soon afterwards, just as I was congratulating myself on maintaining 20 mph, a cyclist came sweeping past me on a long downhill bend. Although I was fully aware that the sensible thing to do with about 50 miles still to go was to just swallow my pride and let him continue on his merry way, that horrible subconscious competitive streak that afflicts all cyclists came to the surface and I raced after him. Thereafter it was all I could do for the next five or six miles to follow in his slipstream.

I vowed to let him go when we reached the next intermediate sprint in a couple of miles, but then with less than one mile to go he beckoned me through. In the international language of cycling this meant two things: that he was fed up with me enjoying the easier ride while he did all the work and that he wanted me to be at the front as we approached the sprint (for which inevitably we would compete, and for which he would be better placed if he were behind me).

By this point I was feeling a distinct pain across the kneecap of my right knee, but in spite of this alarming development – and the fact that I knew I was setting myself up to be outdone in the sprint – the sense of guilt I felt at having enjoyed the free ride for so long meant that I took over at the front. I kept the pace high and then jumped with about 400 metres still to go, reckoning my only chance was to deceive him into thinking I'd gone too early and then to try and make a second acceleration (if only I could think this clearly when I was in a real race; actually, if only I could get into this kind of situation in a real race). Unfortunately, it all descended into a shambles as the line on the road for the actual sprint hadn't been painted yet so we had no idea when we had finished or who had won.

As the pace dipped after our efforts we started talking and my companion was revealed to be an American over here on the same organised trip I had met in Paris when riding the Prologue. He said he'd left his companions behind as they weren't riding quickly enough for his liking. Little did he know, but this sealed the fate of our developing friendship, as I realised that if I slowed down and let him go I'd soon be caught by this group of around 50 riders and would have a comfortable trip to the finish in their slipstream as a result – so I waved him goodbye and waited for the group.

This was not as easy as planned, however, as I was having a pee stop (or seeing to my personal needs, as they say on the French commentary) when the group came past, so I had to work hard again for a couple of miles to be able to latch on. This made my knee hurt even more, and I struggled to keep up once I'd caught them while trying to eat a couple of chocolate bars to replace the energy I'd just expended.

I spent most of the rest of the ride sitting anonymously on the back of the bunch, chatting to Jeremy when either of us had enough energy to be able to talk (he, too, wasn't going to look a gift horse in the mouth). Only when the route began to cross the first slopes of the Ardennes did the group break up a bit, and at this point I managed to speak to some of those on the organised trip.

This included, to initiate the day's Antipodean theme, Australian former professional Neil Stephens, who was the sort of guide deluxe for the group. Apparently the purpose of the trip is not just to follow the Tour in order to watch it, but also to ride some or all of some of the stages. With a bit of luck I'll be able to take advantage of their inadvertent hospitality again.

I left them on the final run in to Sedan (no jokes about needing a Sedan chair to carry me off in, please) when they stopped at a bar to meet their companions, and I found Dad just before the finish. We were just about to set off for the hotel when I discovered I had a fan: a middle-aged fella standing just next to Dad asked me if I were the English journalist who was trying to ride the whole Tour route. My fame appears to be spreading as a result of yesterday's efforts by the Belgian TV crew and my new fan saw me on telly last night. Yes, I said, slightly taken aback, and he asked if he could have his picture taken with me. This moment in the spotlight was put into perspective when we arrived at the hotel and the fdjeux.com media circus sprung into action.

## Stage 3

# CHARLEVILLE-MÉZIÈRES—ST-DIZIER (104.5 MILES)

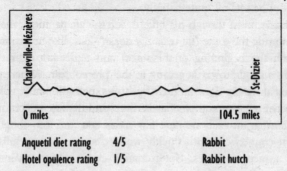

| | | | |
|---|---|---|---|
| Anquetil diet rating | 4/5 | | Rabbit |
| Hotel opulence rating | 1/5 | | Rabbit hutch |

The effects of yesterday's over-indulgence, both on and off the bike, are becoming clear today.

First of all I set off feeling very tired. This may not be surprising given that I didn't sleep for more than about half an hour yesterday afternoon and didn't get to sleep before 11 p.m. last night, but it is still disappointing. Nor is it a good sign for things to come as my assumption that I can successfully tackle the Alps is based on arriving at them still feeling fresh. Your legs and lungs might be fine, but if you're tired then there's a limit to how effectively you can use them; your mind starts playing games with you and your motivation can disappear in an instant (that's how it affects me, anyway).

I then find that after 20 minutes on the bike I've only just arrived at the official start for today's stage, having inadvertently cycled the neutralised section. Five miles for free – how careless.

Just as I reach the zero-mile mark I'm hailed by another cyclist

51

heading into town. We struggle to understand each other to start with as he doesn't seem to speak either French or English. In fact, he sounds like he's speaking Flemish so I persist in French, thinking that if he is Belgian he must have a smattering of French. When this is to no avail I try again in English to find out how I can help him.

This brings some success and I manage to detect through what now appears to be a thick Afrikaans accent that he's asking me where the start is. I gesture that we're right at the start, but he says no – he means the 'proper' start in town. I point him back over the bridge into Charleville – or is it Mézières? – and tell him it's a good five miles, but he sets off quite happily.

I assume, even though his bike is laden with panniers, that he's trying to ride the route (he certainly doesn't look like he's come just to watch the beginning of the stage) and reluctantly admire his stickler's attitude towards getting to the 'proper' start. Whereas I'm moaning at having done an extra five miles, he's voluntarily going to do another ten – on top of whatever he's already done to get this far.

I set off again and the next few miles take me into some very pleasant countryside with thickly wooded slopes, rolling hills and sleepy, attractive villages. Unfortunately, even the attractiveness of my surroundings and the refreshing coolness of the morning can't distract me from the insistent pain in my right knee. I could well come to regret my burst of speed yesterday to keep up with the American.

I'm not exaggerating a lot to say it feels like I'm being hit with a hammer every time I push down with my right leg. It may not be a full swing of the hammer, but it still leads to a very sharp pain. The only relief is if I stand out of the saddle, at which point it resembles more a toffee hammer – something that doesn't really hurt but would annoy you if it were to carry on all day.

What's even more of a concern is that this is after I iced my knee and had a cold bath last night to try and stop yesterday's symptoms from developing into something serious – although my attempts to wangle myself a massage from the fdjeux.com team came to nought. An offer was made once one of the team management had cottoned on to what I was doing, but this was not until after all the masseurs were in their 'I've stopped work for the night and am enjoying my dinner' mode, and the prospect of a massage from a burly Frenchman deprived of his dinner didn't appeal that much, for some reason. At least it's not yet the same pain as when I hurt the same knee last year after running the London Marathon. That kept me off the bike for three months afterwards, and it's been my constant fear whilst preparing for this trip that it would recur at some point and cause me to stop.

As I carry on I become slightly obsessed with analysing the pain and decide every 15 seconds that it is now a recurrence of last year's injury. Then I decide that I'm starting to ache somewhere else as well, probably as a result of compensating for what's happening to my right knee – in fact it's the back of my left knee that's now hurting.

Fortunately the symptoms, both real and imaginary, build up to such a crescendo that I begin to lose track of them all and it slowly dawns on me that I'm managing to keep pedalling and it's not that bad really once you get used to it. Then there's the day's first hill, giving me the chance to get out of the saddle a bit, which means I've now only the toffee hammer to contend with.

The countryside continues to be very agreeable and my humour slowly begins to reflect the peaceful environment through which I'm riding. The smell of woodsmoke from the odd farm I pass adds to the mountain feel of the place, even though the hills aren't particularly high. I make a mental note to put the Ardennes onto the 'future holiday destinations' list; perhaps this could coincide with the Liège–Bastogne–Liège one-day race . . .

Even though the sun's up now it's still nice and cool in the woods, and there's very little traffic. In fact it's so quiet I surprise a pine marten (or what at least looks like a pine marten, although I'm no expert) at the side of the road. It's just standing there on its hind legs, looking intently into the wood, and it's a good five seconds before it notices a free-wheeling cyclist whirring towards it, at which point it rather nonchalantly leaps into the undergrowth and vanishes.

As I start to leave the hills and woods behind I recognise the road from yesterday, and realise I'm arriving in Le Chesne, which has the privilege of seeing the Tour pass through it twice this year. It's also where Jeremy said he was going to stop last night, so maybe I'll have some company between here and St-Dizier.

Once in the town itself, there's a distinct feeling of 'the morning after the night before'. Yesterday the town hosted the *relais de l'étape*, which appears simply to be an excuse for a town on the Tour's route each day to have a bit of a civic shindig. I guess it's just another way for the Tour's organisers to make money out of the race.

When I stopped yesterday for a breather and a drink the reception was already in full swing several hours before the race was due to arrive. A big marquee had been erected in the town square, and a lot of red-faced people in suits and jackets were enjoying a barbecue and a well-stocked bar (even my press pass wouldn't allow me into this carefully patrolled party area). I say enjoying, but it depends I suppose whether you like putting on a collar and tie in hot weather and listening to minor dignitaries congratulate each other and give interminable speeches all afternoon – each to their own. There was also a large-screen television showing the race unfold, but it wasn't drawing an awful lot of attention. Anyway, it looks like the local bigwigs made a good job of celebrating the Tour yesterday, with the result that it might have a more understated reception today, second time around.

I arrive at the day's first rendezvous with Dad and enjoy the big innovation – a combination of hot water in the flask for tea and fresh croissants from the local bakery. Cover these croissants in myrtle jam and, hey presto, a second breakfast fit for a very hungry cyclist. The croissants are in fact so good that they even relegate malt loaf into second place, which doesn't often happen.

Nevertheless, I make sure I stock up on malt loaf before the next leg as it's just the right stuff when you start feeling hungry. Chocolate, energy bars and bananas are all very well when you just need to keep your energy levels up, but sometimes you need something to fill the hole that develops on long, slow rides like these. It also takes so long to chew and swallow that it can provide a useful distraction when external stimuli are noticeable only by their absence.

This turns out to be a particularly good decision. Once I leave Vouziers I realise that I'm back in the open, wheat field-dominated landscape that I rode through for part of yesterday. The roads are long and straight and there's very little to break the horizon. It strikes me that it's going to be a long, hot ride as there's absolutely no shelter from the sun, which has been getting more and more powerful day by day. Mind you, I shouldn't complain as one of my biggest worries prior to starting was that I'd be caught on this kind of stage in the driving wind and rain that can afflict the north of France just as easily as it can England, even in midsummer (especially in midsummer, you might say). The prospect of cycling on my own for more than a hundred miles into a headwind in the pouring rain on dull, flat stages like this was more intimidating than the thought of all the Alpine and Pyrenean climbs put together.

As I keep going the variety in the landscape continues to reduce (which is quite a feat), going from almost featureless to completely featureless in a few short miles. This is doing nothing to counteract my fatigue, once again more noticeable after I'd woken up a bit on the cool roads earlier.

I'm sure everywhere has its charms, and people can't choose where they're born or can't always choose where they work and what they do, but this kind of place holds no appeal for me. It's the kind of countryside you drive through en route for somewhere else and then forget about. It's also the kind of place that makes you realise that *la belle France* isn't all beautiful.

I feel particularly sorry for the gendarmes sent to enforce the road closures as the Tour approaches. This task is performed very diligently, which today means there are literally hundreds of them 'guarding' the most obscure farm tracks often, given the absence of trees, having no option but to stand in the blazing sun. At least I'm moving and will eventually ride into some shade. I hope they get paid plenty of overtime.

The only things to break the horizon – apart from an occasional copse that you temporarily think you might have the pleasure of cycling through but which is then by-passed by the road (for fear of making things too exciting, no doubt) – are the vast grain silos that appear every five miles or so. These are massive things, hundreds of feet high – well, probably. No doubt they need to be this big to house all the wheat and barley and whatever else it is they grow in these vast prairies. I must remember to find a route that avoids the Midwest if I ever try and cycle across the USA – I don't think I could cope with endless days of this.

There is a flicker of light relief as I ride past one of these monsters – bicycles are suspended from the whole length of one of the wire stanchions that keep the silos fastened to the ground. There must be at least 50 of them; evidence that the locals are aware that the Tour exists after all.

The other source of 'excitement' comes from the number and variety of tractors on the road towing trailers taking grain to or from the silos (it's remarkable what becomes interesting in extreme circumstances). In fact there are long periods when the only other evidence of human life is the tractors that are just ahead of me or just behind me – or, for real variety, travelling in the other direction.

Just how important these tractors are to the local community is confirmed by the repeated road-side adverts for competitions and spectacles involving *le tractor pulling* (even the entertainment is provided by tractors). I don't actually know what le tractor pulling involves, but I'm beginning to think that it requires an unsuspecting cyclist to be attached by an invisible thread to all the local tractors and then to tow them unwittingly along the road.

Even if I'm not caught up in some big tractor-pulling practical joke, the fact that I travel at the same speed as most of them adds to the feeling of being on some sort of vast treadmill – the tractor behind doesn't catch me, I don't catch the tractor in front, and the countryside repeats itself like it does in children's cartoons on the telly.

Where's Jeremy when I need someone to distract me? It seems particularly galling that both of us may be slogging along on our own but only a few miles apart. At least my knee is feeling a bit better.

Another variation on the theme comes when a tractor joins us from a side-road, just in front of me. This gives me the chance to slipstream for a while until the heat and dust and smell of diesel compel me to drop back or overtake – depending on my mood. Then there are the slight ups and downs, which can also lead to a change in the running order – tractors with empty trailers go faster than me on the inclines, whereas tractors with full ones can't keep up. I tend to catch them all on the downhills.

After a while I also become aware of the occasional tractor that is much more shiny and new and powerful than most of them (I mostly notice these when there's a crescendo of noise behind me and I'm then suffocated by the hot fumes and dust as they rumble past). This strikes me as a bit odd, given how proudly all the silos proclaim themselves to be part of an agricultural co-operative. Obviously some farmers are doing better out of the communal endeavours than others.

Only after my second meeting with Dad do things take a turn for the better. The countryside is still very flat, but I am now in a quite densely forested area – La Fôret de L'Argonne, according to the map – which is distinctly more attractive. The road also decides to wind a bit, and there are now a few spectators beginning to ready themselves for the real thing. I even get the odd cheer – always heartening.

Unfortunately, I've learnt over the past few days that the presence of spectators invariably also means the presence of a group of profiteers who try to exploit everybody's enthusiasm for the race. I first noticed them on Stage 1, when I was prepared to give them the benefit of the doubt, but seeing them now for the third day in a row is really beginning to get a bit trying, especially after Dad discovered the nature of their racket.

He was approached by them to take a French flag – apparently the free inducement – but was then required to pay more than £5 for the accompanying bar of nougat. When he said no and gave the flag back, thinking this was a bit steep – even though he's a big nougat fan – he was roundly insulted for being mean and unpatriotic. Well, he is English after all.

Nevertheless, my objection to them is more practical than moral. They seem to think that they own the road. This means they drive at breakneck speed between the clusters of supporters, trying to nab as many as they can before their rivals turn up. It also means screeching to a halt regardless of any cyclists who may be in the vicinity, opening car doors without looking, running about with complete disregard for anyone else who may be there (i.e. me trying to cycle past) and generally making a real nuisance of themselves. After five and a bit hours in the saddle under the hot sun through the countryside I've just described and after a bad night's sleep, I am no longer inclined to be tolerant towards them.

Eventually, after what I hoped was going to be a relatively easy day but which has turned out to be quite a trial, I arrive in St-Dizier. The finish area seems to be in the middle of some roadworks in a housing estate on the edge of town – not very charming. What's also worrying is that Dad's not there, and there's precious little shade for me to shelter under. I send Dad a text message but get no response so I try to call him. Again no answer. After about half an hour we bump into each other. Dad is late because of difficulties in finding a parking space – and, he reveals, he left his mobile in the car.

There is little relief at the hotel, where the baking-hot room is tiny and we only have a double bed to share between us. I have a shower and sleep fitfully for a couple of hours before I get too hot and uncomfortable and have to have another shower to cool down. I wash my clothes for the first time, as much in an attempt to cling on to a degree of civilisation as to reduce their growing pungency.

Just as I'm descending into a thoroughly foul mood we have dinner in the hotel (rabbit stew this time), which is pretty good, and the sight of everyone else in St-Dizier in festive spirit – there are band stands in the main square and fairground rides all over the place, fortunately not too near to our hotel – helps me cheer up a bit before I call Catherine at home. Molly's still not crawling, although she is in the process of cutting her second tooth, which is making her a bit grumpy and is causing her to wake up at night. I empathise with the lack of sleep, and manage to sound reasonably upbeat. At least tomorrow is a relatively easy day and we won't have to get up too early.

I ice my knee again (in fact both knees, as the back of my left knee is definitely a bit sore) and then decide it's better for all of us if I leave the good citizens of St-Dizier to enjoy themselves without me – as long as they do it quietly.

## Stage 4

# JOINVILLE–ST-DIZIER (43 MILES)

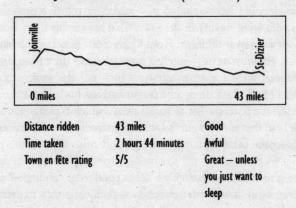

| | | |
|---|---|---|
| Distance ridden | 43 miles | Good |
| Time taken | 2 hours 44 minutes | Awful |
| Town en fête rating | 5/5 | Great – unless you just want to sleep |

I suppose I should have known that the night in St-Dizier would turn out to be a bit rum once the owner of Hotel Agriculture had phoned to tell me that she had a problem with my reservation – the only one of twenty hotels to do so.

If there was any room for doubt, this should have been dispelled immediately by the fact that although she did manage to find us a room it ended up being the size of a postage stamp. This was definitely a bad omen.

Not only was it stiflingly hot but Dad and I had to share the double bed. We also had to endure the fact that the visit of the Tour de France is probably the biggest thing ever to happen in the history of St-Dizier, and the inhabitants weren't going to let it pass them by without a party.

Unfortunately for me and anyone else wanting a decent night's sleep (like, for example, all those professional cyclists who also tend to be involved in the Tour de France) this meant an enormous din. Relatively speaking we were lucky in that our hotel was away from the main focus of all this enthusiastic partying – by about 11.30 p.m., maybe only two to two-and-a-half hours after going to bed, we'd got used to the noise and managed to drop off to sleep.

This good fortune was indeed relative, however, as we weren't far enough away to be able to avoid the massive firework display at midnight – that lasted for half an hour. In fact no one within about ten miles could have avoided it – including the five professional teams who were staying in the town. Dad says in his diary that 'the firework display at midnight would have been better appreciated in different circumstances' – surely a masterpiece of understatement.

I wonder what Lance Armstrong – just over the road – thought about it? Maybe he'll do us all a favour and use his influence to have St-Dizier struck off the list of stage towns – at least until it has a new mayor – so that nobody else has to suffer this horrendous assault on their sleeping patterns.

Suffice it to say that although we didn't need to get up until 7 a.m. I feel even more tired – and crotchety – than yesterday. I'm soothed somewhat by the now standard breakfast of tea and cereals and by the quite pleasant drive to Joinville where today's stage starts.

However, this late start almost backfires, even though the race is not due to begin until 2 p.m. Only reluctantly do the gendarmes at the entrance to Joinville let us go into the town, and then even with my press pass they don't seem too keen to let me set off on my bike, in spite of us making it clear that Dad and the car are going no farther on the actual route.

Still, they do eventually let me ride across the start line and soon I'm beginning the climb out of the town, which is quite a pull. Soon, also – much sooner than I would have liked – my knee starts hurting again. We're back to the full-size hammer now even though I'm out of the saddle going up the hill in an effort to alleviate the pain. I get to the top and realise that the combination of fatigue and my sore knee means that today could be rather testing.

I start bracing myself for a tough ride, but this is difficult as I'd been pretty much picturing today as a rest day – as it's the team time trial it's nice and short at only 43 and a bit miles. My theory was that this was therefore my chance to have a breather while all the pros are racing flat out to try and establish some sort of pecking order before the Alps. After all, there's nothing to gain by me trying to do it quickly. Grinding along at about 15 mph, wincing with every turn of the pedals and feeling like I've been up all night are not how I pictured my rest day, however. If it weren't such a short stage I think I'd be tempted to stop – which is ridiculous.

An added problem is that I thought I would be flying by now. I expected day two to be the hardest, when the exertions of the first day would still be felt and before the daily routine had been settled into. When this passed off smoothly I imagined myself clear of setbacks until we reached the mountains. Unfortunately, the result of this misconception is that it's hard now to maintain motivation on a stage that hadn't even registered on the list of potential problems.

Anyway, as with yesterday my knee seems to get a bit better after about an hour, by which time I suppose it's probably warmed up (the good thing about this self-pity lark is that it takes up quite a bit of time). I even manage to up the pace slightly now the route is a bit flatter, which is a relief as there are vast numbers of spectators on the roadside, by far the most to date.

I assume this is because the spectacle of the team time trial is really quite impressive – well-drilled teams of 9 cyclists working together to maintain speeds of more than 30 mph must be quite a sight. You also get the chance to make out individuals, which is something that's often difficult in a big group, and of course you get more than just a few seconds of action – the first team is off at 2 p.m., the last not until 3.45 p.m. and each comes past in turn.

This might help to explain why I feel so much like a fraud as I cycle along. The cheers are as enthusiastic and well intentioned as ever (any hints of irony are surely only present in my slightly deranged psyche), but it doesn't stop me from feeling as though I'm an interloper – a gatecrasher at a party.

I heard on the radio before I left that art critic Brian Sewell felt increasingly like a fraud as he drew nearer to completing his voyage along the pilgrimage route to Santiago de Compostela. His reasoning was that the purpose of his journey was simply to look at the architecture and art of the churches on the route, whereas the real pilgrims were inspired by their religion. This difference in their purposes grew more profound as the journey went on, leading him to feel like he was trespassing.

I know what he means. I feel that if I were a real rider then I'd be in the Tour de France, not just doing some pale imitation of it; or that if I were a real fan then I'd be at the side of the road, soaking up the atmosphere and waiting for the real riders to come past, not just trying to bask in the reflected glory of riding some or all of the route. What's worse is that I know these sentiments to be more or less ludicrous – if nothing else nobody on the roadside gives two hoots about what I'm doing there. But even though my logical self is telling me this in no uncertain terms, my emotional self still insists that I shouldn't be here. And I'm always susceptible to my emotions when I'm feeling tired.

My physical self (especially my right knee and the sleep deprivation alarm in my brain) is also doing its best to tell me I shouldn't be here either. And the trend for ever-hotter days seems to be continuing – even though it's still morning it looks to be heading for a scorcher.

Not that the route itself is particularly demanding. After the initial climb and the few undulations that followed it's been pretty easy going. The countryside is also fairly attractive – the fields are on a more human scale and there are luxuriant woods which the more enlightened spectators are taking advantage of to provide some welcome shade.

This benign environment is reflected by the number of other cyclists who are out enjoying a spin on the Tour route. Most seem to be travelling the other way, but after a while I catch up with a retired Dutchman who's nevertheless keeping up a very reasonable pace. We talk for a while (his English is, of course, impeccable, which is just as well, as my Dutch is pretty ropey) and I discover he's been coming to follow the whole Tour every year since he retired.

Apparently his wife, who still works, now positively encourages him to make his yearly visit to the Tour as he's too frustrated to be worthwhile company around the house if he's restricted to watching it on the TV. Last year he managed to persuade his daughter to join him for some of it (his son is more interested in fast cars, he tells me), but this year she pleaded lack of fitness. Her fitness is relevant because he always rides a fair bit of the route as well, but only the bits he finds appealing – how sensible this sounds.

I then meet four Englishmen wearing identical tops, all extolling the virtues of JD Cycles. I get quite excited and assume they must be from Ilkley, where I went to school and home to the JD Cycles I make Catherine accompany me to every time we're back there visiting my family. But they're not. At first I don't believe them, but it turns out there are *two* JD Cycles – one in Essex – and it is from here that my new companions originate. I am finally convinced when I realise they all have accents that owe much more to their proximity to London than to any Yorkshire heritage.

They stop for ice creams, which momentarily tempts me to call the whole ride off and join them, but I'm quite close to the finish now and manage to resist. Besides, the longer the ride takes me, the longer it will be before we're in the hotel in Troyes and I can try to catch up on my sleep.

Towards the end of the stage I ride past signs for Lac-du-Der-Chantecoq, where I remember staying for a night in the family caravan on the way to or from a holiday somewhere farther south. I then finally make it back into St-Dizier with the last couple of miles no more appealing than yesterday, but at least the finish is in the town centre this time.

Once I've arrived my impression that this has not been one of my best days is confirmed when I notice that my average speed for the 43 miles covered is only 15.7 mph – the slowest so far for the shortest stage so far. The early arrivals at the finish are then treated to my daily ablutions using what's left over in my water bottles. They may not be that keen on the spectacle, but then I'm not that keen on sitting in the car for a couple of hours covered in all my sweat and grime, so I carry on regardless.

Although the trip to Troyes goes quite smoothly it takes a bit longer than planned because the shortest route is now closed since it's also the route taken by the Tour. I am caught between falling asleep and knowing that we'll get there quicker if I help with the navigation seeing as we're not just following signs to Troyes at the moment. In the end I don't really do either, which is no good to anyone.

We find the hotel thanks to a combination of directions from the local drunkard in a petrol station and the more conventional ploy of visiting the tourist information. In spite of the preparations for the arrival of the Tour caravan later in the day – which means roads are closed and parking is restricted – we manage to park nice and close, which is just as well as I'm almost falling asleep as we carry in our bags and the bike. And then the proprietor says the room isn't ready yet and do I mind waiting an hour or so? Fortunately, I don't need to express my disappointment as I look so worn out that he takes pity on me and asks one of the waitresses to prepare the room straightaway.

The room is excellent, the exact opposite of last night. It could accommodate a family of four and is lovely and cool. I have a nice, cold bath, resist any temptation to watch the Tour on the telly and then, bliss of bliss, go straight to sleep.

I wake up four hours later feeling almost human again. Dad returns from the exile I impose on him every time we reach a new destination and says that he had no problem entertaining himself in Troyes for the afternoon, which turns out to be a very attractive medieval town (apparently this was helped by finding a very pleasant, cool *salon de thé* with wonderful iced tea). In spite of the town's olde worlde charms, Dad also found an Internet café, which allowed him the chance to send some more email reports on my progress and pick up some replies from his first missive.

He relays the messages of encouragement as we wait for dinner in the hotel, which are all gratefully received. A good sleep and some friendly banter from home make me feel better still. Nevertheless, I manage only a very poor attempt to follow the Anquetil diet today as I have to leave most of my chicken in cider with *gratin dauphinois* – I've just no appetite. It seems that I can either have enough to eat or have enough sleep but not necessarily both together. When eventually I do manage to combine them I assume my recovery from day to day will be much better.

Dinner also reveals the advances in Dad's French over the past few days. First of all he successfully (well almost successfully) orders a carafe of wine, which might sound simple but is rendered more difficult by the fact that 'carafe', although a French word, is not the word the French use to describe a vessel that holds wine. Instead they use *pichet*, for which Dad has developed the handy mnemonic of Pinochet.

This has obviously worked as Dad manages to avoid the trap of asking '*un carafe de vin*'. Unfortunately he takes the waiter rather by surprise by asking for a Pinochet of wine instead (presumably from Chile). Still, it's only one step from remembering the mnemonic to remembering the word it's supposed to remind you of.

The second advance comes with his investigations into the French word for racer – as in cycle racer. At first he isn't sure what the word is, but then he realises the TV commentators were saying '*coureur*' and '*les coureurs cyclistes*'. To check, he looks up the word in his French dictionary and sure enough it means racer. He also discovers, however, that the word means several other things – including man-eater and womaniser. Judging from my somewhat reduced physical state we both agree it would appear that these dual meanings (racer and man-eater and/or womaniser) are mutually exclusive – you can be one or the other, but not both. Maybe the professionals are better able to live up to this double billing.

After dinner I ice my knee again (I ignore the phantom symptoms of my left knee and concentrate my efforts on the real problem – my right knee) and then use some of Dad's ibuprofen gel. I've also got some ibuprofen tablets, but they don't seem to be any good for swelling and sometimes they make me feel a bit nauseous so I plump for the gel. At least it's quite nice to massage my knee with and hopefully this will pay dividends in the morning.

# Stage 5

## TROYES—NEVERS (123 MILES)

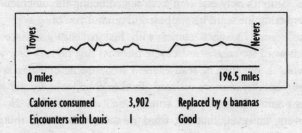

| Calories consumed | 3,902 | Replaced by 6 bananas |
|---|---|---|
| Encounters with Louis | 1 | Good |

Isn't it amazing what a good night's sleep can do? Nearly all the demons that had been building up for the past two days seem to have vanished this morning. Even our rather circuitous drive out of Troyes to find the official zero-mile mark on the Tour route doesn't send me into the 'I can't take it any more' histrionics I'd been fearing. In fact it's probably taken twice as long as it would have were I to have cycled it, but I suppose you can't have it both ways.

I say nearly all the demons because the demon – or gremlin perhaps – that is afflicting my right knee is still painfully obvious. In spite of another application of ibuprofen gel the first 20 minutes are agony. The only good thing is that my more robust state of mind means that I no longer feel as though this is the end of the world. In fact I manage to remember that the pattern from the past two days appears to be that the pain is at its worst as I set off and then dissipates a bit. Sure enough, this is what it does over the first hour, a situation that may have been helped by my decision to ride in an even lower gear today and concentrate on turning the pedals at a faster rhythm rather than trying to exert a lot of pressure. Not that I ride in a big gear anyway, but it strikes me that it can't help.

Anyway, it seems to be working. Now the concern is not so much the pain, which has been replaced by a dull ache, but whether I may be doing myself some form of longer-term damage. For the purposes of attempting to complete this trip successfully I'll assume not.

One other advantage over previous mornings is that Dad has managed to acquire a head torch so that I now have this as well as my backlight to illuminate me. It may not be the most powerful torch in the world but it does mean I feel considerably more likely to be seen by sleepy early morning commuters or late-night revellers on their way home. If nothing else I can shine my new light straight at them, which most people find difficult to ignore.

The overall effect of more sleep, a slightly less uncomfortable knee and a new head torch is that I feel much more confident about today's ride. Even an impromptu shower from an unavoidable irrigation sprinkler just before I meet Dad for the first time can't dampen my spirits (although obviously it dampens the rest of me).

Today's rendezvous point is the latest in a growing line of peculiarly named villages and towns we've passed through so far. It's called Tonnerre – thunder. The most apposite name we've come across is Avançon – in French a homophone of 'let's go' – where the Tour cyclists obeyed the imperative as it hosted an intermediate sprint on Stage 2. More enigmatically we've had Robert-Espagne (nowhere near Spain), Chaudefontaine (hot fountain) and St Loup en Champagne (Holy Wolf in Champagne), all on Stage 3. Unfortunately, I never managed to find out if 'Holy Wolf in Champagne' was an exclamation – like 'Holy Smoke, Batman!' – or an unlikely local delicacy (take one werewolf, freshly slayed with a silver bullet, and macerate in Dom Perignon '63 for several hours before roasting slowly over an open fire – I'm sure Jacques Anquetil, or even Delia, would be keen on trying this one).

When I arrive Dad pours me a cup of tea as normal (he knows his place) while I lather myrtle jam on some still-warm croissants. The tea, however, is a prize commodity this morning as for the first time since we left Paris Dad had his requests for hot water turned down – not once but three times. Up until now all the bars and cafés he has approached have been unfailingly friendly in their welcome – even if they haven't always understood what he wants or why he would want it. But today he was turned down by two barmen – who said it wasn't possible in spite of having exactly the same type of coffee machine that is de rigueur in French bars and has worked every morning so far – and one woman – who simply said a ferocious *non* when he pointed to the flask. I'm beginning to wonder if the challenges facing Dad aren't greater than those I'm having to confront.

I cycle off into the growing heat wondering if stopping in 'Thunder' has any meteorological significance. I wouldn't mind a break in this hot weather and a refreshing storm but there appears little chance of that at the moment – there's not a cloud in the sky. I'd rather it waits until I'm safe and dry in the hotel anyway.

My knee is worse again after the stop, but soon settles into being a tolerable ache, which I take as a good sign. After a few miles I catch a cyclist on the undulating road and discover it to be the South African who hailed me as I was leaving Charleville-Mézières. His name is Louis, and my supposition about him cycling the Tour de France route is substantiated when he tells me he's trying to follow it all – un-aided. This is the reason for the two panniers on the back of a bike that must weigh at least double mine in total. As if cycling with this amount of extra weight is not impressive enough, I find he's not sleeping in hotels like a softie, he's sleeping in his tent 'in the bush' instead.

What's more, he's not even come to France for the sake of the Tour. Instead he's here because he's qualified to ride Paris–Brest–Paris, an organised event of some 750 miles which you have to complete within a maximum time – 4 days if I remember correctly. As if to confirm my unspoken impression that this is probably equal to, if not harder than, trying to ride the Tour route, he says he decided to take advantage of being over here and ride the Tour as preparation.

We converse for a while and I become a bit more practiced at discerning what is being said through his thick Afrikaans accent, with a liberal smattering of 'farkit's thrown in for good measure (which sounds much more endearing and much less coarse than when pronounced in the Queen's English). Louis also tells me I'm not the only cyclist he's met trying to ride the whole route. He's also encountered an Australian rider by the name of Skippy doing the same kind of thing. Skippy's apparently quite a well-known character around the Tour as a result of having ridden the route on a regular basis for some years now. The prospect of there being quite a band of us – me, Jeremy, Louis, Skippy and probably some others as well – is quite appealing. Nevertheless, as Louis's pace is slower than mine – not surprising with the amount of stuff he's carrying – I take my leave after a few miles together, although I get the distinct impression that I'm bound to bump into him again.

One of the reasons for riding off is that I'm quite happy to be cycling on my own today, as the route lives up to its billing in the Tour preview as 'a really lovely stage through the Morvan region'. We're also passing near to Chablis, home to the famous white wine beloved of golf clubs and business executives everywhere, although there are no vineyards in sight. Maybe it's all a big PR exercise and there isn't actually any wine produced here – like Carlsberg Export being brewed in the UK, not in Denmark.

I put this scepticism to one side as I come to the part of the route described as 'quite hilly', which is actually a blessed relief after the long straight roads of the past couple of days. In fact there are two fourth-category climbs on today's stage, although these turn out to be no more or less significant than many of the other ups and downs we've already had.

The extent to which objective criteria are really used to judge the merits of various climbs for classification in the King of the Mountains competition is unclear. I suspect that it's more to do with making sure there are some points awarded before the real mountains arrive so that somebody can wear the polka-dot jersey, and so that the sprints that result add to the spectacle for the spectators.

Anyway, these 'lumps', categorised or not, just add to the picture of 'quite hilly' actually meaning rolling in a sort of Sussex weald kind of way, which is a fond reminder of home – although this parallel can only be taken so far. For a start there's only a fraction of the traffic there is at home, and those cars there are tend to be much more tolerant of cyclists. Then there are the supporters lining the road, which is something I don't normally get in the Ashdown Forest. If it stays like this, today's 123 miles don't seem such a bad prospect at all, in fact.

Apart from being a good day for me, so far, today is also a good day for José Bové – the latter-day French Robin Hood whose name is painted more frequently on the road than any cyclist's. 'LIBEREZ JOSE BOVE' is the normal motif – free José Bové. This specific appeal is necessary because, apart from smashing up a McDonald's (which brought him a great deal of sympathy and a suspended prison sentence), he subsequently damaged a crop of genetically modified plants, resulting in his imprisonment.

And this imprisonment doesn't seem to be particularly popular with the inhabitants of the rural Morvan, the more adventurous of whom have extended these slogans: 'BOVE A LA MAISON, CHIRAC EN PRISON!' (Bové at home, Chirac in prison) is the most blatant. Whatever the rights and wrongs of his actions it's clear where the sympathies of the locals lie.

The messages come so thick and fast I almost feel as though I'm being berated personally for my weakness at eating at the McDonald's in Paris (I'm sorry José, it was my one slip in over ten years). More likely is the realisation that the TV coverage given to the Tour offers a golden opportunity to have this message beamed into the living rooms – and dining rooms – of most of France, if not the world. I wonder if the sign-writers are aware of the irony of using such a powerful example of a global sporting brand to convey their messages of support for this unlikely hero of the anti-globalisation movement? Or are they deliberately trying to subvert the commercialism of the Tour itself?

Interestingly enough the previous two days saw much less support for Bové, even though the areas through which we passed were equally rural. The obvious difference is that today I'm riding through pastoral land rather than the rich arable fields of a couple of days ago. Maybe those large agricultural co-operatives are synonymous with the agri-business that Bové and his supporters dislike so passionately and are complicit in selling to supermarkets and using GM crops, whereas the smallholdings of today share his more 'anti-commercial' view of things.

I arrive at our second stop, on the edge of Vézelay, rejoicing in the opportunity that cycling offers to let your mind wonder on subjects like this. If you're feeling fresh – which I apparently am – then cycling demands just the right amount of mental effort to allow your mind free-reign to grapple with complex abstract ideas (or simple abstract ideas in my case). In this respect it's a bit like peeling potatoes, which I find has a very similar effect.

I suppose that Lance Armstrong and the other riders in the Tour will be too sidetracked by the demands of racing to take advantage of this opportunity. Maybe on training rides – or maybe not. In fact this could be why my training is never very effective – I find it too easy to let my mind wander instead of concentrating on the task in hand.

Dad's confidence in following the route and meeting me on time with the appropriate provisions is growing, and he says he's going to call into Vézelay to pay a visit to its famous church – La Sainte Madelaine – his first excursion off the route so far. We discuss vague memories of its importance as a cornerstone of romanesque architecture and the development of Gothic, and of the impressive bas-relief carvings above the original west door. As far as we can remember its renown was also in part established through being the starting point for one of the main pilgrimage routes to Santiago in Spain. Maybe Brian Sewell began his journey from here, before he started feeling like a fraud?

Apparently Lance Armstrong is a big fan of the churches and cathedrals of France and Europe as well. Not, as it turns out, because of any great piety or because they're beautiful but because of their age: 'In America we don't have any churches older than 500 years. When I saw those cathedrals in Europe, I believed then in the grandeur of mankind,' he said in an interview before the Tour.

For a moment I'm tempted to join Dad – on the bike, of course – but in spite of the church's proximity to the route I resist; I can't bring myself to justify any extra miles, no matter how culturally significant the attraction may be. What was it I was saying about having a pre-determined route to follow being its own kind of freedom? It's only Stage 5 and I'd already relish the opportunity to take off the leash – or at least just let it stretch a little. I'll have to be satisfied with sending Dad as my proxy.

71

I set off again, leaving Vézelay for another day, and instead have the pleasures of discovering very attractive countryside that in other circumstances I would probably have forsaken to see the town and the church. I ride along in good heart – even if my knee is still complaining – and it's only shortly before our third stop, Bazolles (visions of a screeching Sybil Fawlty pass before me, and I worry about the state of the next hotel), that Dad overtakes me.

When I catch him again he says the church itself was definitely worth the visit – if you like that sort of thing. He also says you'd have had no idea the Tour was in the vicinity. In stark contrast to most places so far that have been on or even just near the route, and which have gone to great lengths to take advantage of this connection, no matter how tenuous, Vézelay remained indifferent. Maybe its ecclesiastical heritage and subsequent guaranteed appeal to tourists means the ephemeral attraction of the Tour is surplus to requirements.

The final ride into Nevers, which brings the 2003 Tour vintage back onto the route of the original Tour, is equally pleasant, but the heat is now quite oppressive (I notice later that for the third day in a row Dad has written 'hottest afternoon so far' in his diary). It seems unlikely to get any cooler as we head further south; maybe the mountains will bring some respite.

The hotel is right in the middle of town and is pleasant, although it, like everywhere else, is fighting a losing battle to stay cool. I sleep for a bit, and then take advantage of the courtyard to change the tyres on the bike. I've been on lightweight racing tyres so far, and they've been excellent, but with the mountains ahead I decide to put on some heavier-duty alternatives. This may seem to defy conventional logic which suggests the less weight you carry in the mountains the better, but it's the prospect of punctures that alarms me the most. The last thing I want halfway up an Alpine climb is to have to stop to change an inner tube.

Dad has the car checked out at a local garage because of an occasional noise, which fortunately turns out to be no more than a loose hub cap. Then we go to a neighbouring pizzeria for dinner, as this is the option that opens soonest and will therefore allow me to go to bed soonest. Just as we're leaving, Bradley McGee's wife, daughter, brother and sister-in-law turn up. This is their penultimate night before returning to Australia, and presumably leaving Brad and the team to concentrate all their energies on the mountains. In fact Mrs McGee has a hint of concern in her voice when the subject of the Alps and Pyrenees is raised. I know the feeling.

## Stage 6

# NEVERS—LYON (143.75 MILES)

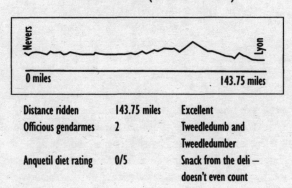

Nevers · Lyon

0 miles · 143.75 miles

| | | |
|---|---|---|
| Distance ridden | 143.75 miles | Excellent |
| Officious gendarmes | 2 | Tweedledumb and Tweedledumber |
| Anquetil diet rating | 0/5 | Snack from the deli — doesn't even count |

All being well, today is set to be my longest-ever ride on a bike. In a way it's a bit of a shame that this follows so swiftly on the heels of the ride on Stage 2 – which currently holds the record – as past experience suggests it could normally expect to hold the title of 'my longest ride' for several years at least. After all, I've been dining out for years on riding the 126 miles from Morecambe to Scarborough in a day, wearing trainers and riding a 1950s Claude Butler.

Anyway, today should knock both of those into a cocked hat – 143.75 miles compared to 128 miles on Stage 2. Not that I feel any particular trepidation about the length of today's stage. Having already managed to cycle as far as I have I'm sure I can make the extra distance – in fact I'm quite excited about the prospect. It's nice to know I'm taking on this kind of challenge when I'm fit and, without wishing to tempt fate, expecting to manage all right (although there is still a little frisson of nervousness as it does sound a long way).

My concerns are more about keeping up a high enough speed to ensure I reach Lyon before the roads are closed. The extra distance means the race itself is starting an hour earlier than yesterday, and given it will be travelling significantly faster than I will my leeway ahead of them is reduced accordingly. An extra 16.25 miles is about an extra hour, so judging by Stage 2 that should make about 8.5 hours riding. With a 5 a.m. start and maybe an hour of stops that'll be around 2.30 p.m. in Lyon – fingers crossed.

As it is, it's just after 5 a.m. when I start, having successfully negotiated the outskirts of Nevers in the car with Dad. I set off in the dark and ride along thinking about the fact that the first stage of the first Tour went straight from Paris to Lyon. It took the winner, Maurice Garin, just 17 hours and 45 minutes to cover 292 miles – a touch more than double the distance of today's stage in a touch more than double the time I'm planning. Remarkable.

Much less remarkable and much more commonplace is the tension I feel as I trudge my way along a main road – in these circumstances, with fairly frequent lorries in both directions, I'm really not that confident about my visibility in spite of the new head torch. The road itself is also quite demanding. The countryside is still the same as yesterday, which made for enjoyable cycling on small roads, but the main road treats the contours of the landscape with scant respect. Instead it ploughs a straight line uphill and down dale, leading to a succession of long, straight pulls followed immediately by long, straight descents (that lead all too quickly to the next incline). You wouldn't know that we were following the Loire, or that we were in a river valley at all.

I always find this combination a bit disheartening on a bike as it's very difficult to maintain any kind of rhythm. It's also very obvious that this kind of road is designed solely for motorised transport – rather than more traditional routes which originated in times when the horse and cart or walking were the most common means of travel. And the fact that we're all motorists now means that you end up grovelling up hills which you can't help but think are insignificant (you wouldn't even notice them in a car) – always bad for morale. At the same time lorries come hurtling past you, trying to maintain their momentum so that the hill doesn't become a chore for them as well and this is in danger of being bad for your health.

And my knee's hurting. Have I mentioned my knee yet? It's the one that some prankster has tied an invisible hammer to so that it bangs on it with every pedal stroke. Or maybe I was cruel to a woodpecker in a previous life and now it's come back to haunt me by pecking at me incessantly.

It's funny but it's almost the downhills that are worse. Why that should be I don't know, but as I start to turn my legs faster when I pass over the brow of a hill, so the discomfort grows. At least I can freewheel on these bits if necessary so progress isn't being particularly hampered at the moment.

Eventually, after nearly 20 miles, the main road turns off to the left and the route turns back onto local roads. Now the Loire is obvious on my right, and the broad-bottomed valley provides pleasant riding on the flat – or maybe slight uphill, but at least at a constant gradient. In fact the valley is so flat I'd have expected it to be covered in wheat and corn but it's actually all grazing and pastureland. I suppose it's the flood plain of the river and animals can be moved out of harm's way while crops can't. It seems strange that this isn't the route taken by the main road, but then maybe we're not going to the same place it is.

I meet Dad for the first stop in Lesme, having just cycled past a sign for the 'Village de Brain' – an interesting variation on the theme of village idiot. I arrive at 7.25 a.m., having covered 37.5 miles in two and a quarter hours, which I'm pleased about. Dad's had no trouble getting hold of hot water or croissants today, but petrol has been rather elusive. This is not because there aren't lots of petrol stations – there are. The problem is that most of them (at least most of those that are open at this time of the morning) are automatic, which is to say you pay by inserting your bank card into the pump which then takes the money before allowing you any petrol. There are, of course, no humans involved.

Unfortunately, not one of our combination of cards works in these machines, a fact which Dad confirmed this morning. This could have caused a significant problem, as petrol was low and service stations with staff thin on the ground. However, with great ingenuity Dad resolved the problem by asking a motorcyclist who was there at the same time if he could pay him cash and put our petrol on his card instead. The fella obliged, and one more logistical hurdle was overcome.

After I leave Dad the road continues to follow the Loire but begins to get busier again as the valley narrows. It's not until after Paray-le-Monial (home of another significant romanesque church and where I have an unofficial race over several sets of traffic lights against a girl on a scooter, who is not impressed that I overtake her every time) that I'm back on small roads.

This coincides almost immediately with an upsurge in the number of supporters on the roadside. The few main roads we've used so far have had sparse populations of fans, while as soon as we're back on country roads they're everywhere. And the more obscure the places we go through, the more popular the Tour is with the locals. You get the distinct impression that the passage of the Tour will provide something for the inhabitants to talk about for the next year.

This seems to indicate the depth of feeling there still is for the Tour in *la France Profonde* (deepest France), and how much the Tour needs to maintain its roots (and its routes) through this rural heartland. The past few days have suggested an uncomfortable relation with more motorised, urban areas. Not only are the roads, like this morning's, unpleasant to cycle along and awkward to close, they also offer little appeal to fans. Then there are the problems with modern 'street furniture' – traffic islands, speed humps, mini-roundabouts – which almost seem designed to inconvenience cyclists as much as possible, even lone ones.

Hence the Tour's efforts to maintain its links with the France you normally pass by en route for somewhere else. Such links have always been the lifeblood of French cycling, which has thrived by offering innumerable French farmers and labourers a way out of working on the land for the rest of their lives. But it's been a generation now since the last French Tour winner, and even if families still enjoy their picnics under the shade of a tree as the Tour rides past, the number of up and coming stars that results has diminished.

In fact the Tour route today goes through one of the last villages to produce a champion – Le Guidon (meaning 'handlebar', which must make it the most appropriately named village of all), birthplace of double Tour winner Bernard Thévenet. To add romance to the tale, Thévenet himself says it was seeing the Tour pass through the village when he was a boy that inspired him to become a professional cyclist: 'I saw the Tour pass my farm for the first time in 1961. I saw the peloton arrive on a false flat of 300 metres. For 40 seconds, I saw their toe-clips glittering in the sun. It made me think of horses and armour. It was like a fairy tale. I'll keep that image in my mind forever.'

With this talent for articulating his feelings and describing cycling it's perhaps no surprise he has now become a respected pundit for French TV, acting as a summariser – a sort of French Trevor Brooking sitting alongside the cycling equivalent of John Motson.

Maybe it's a job in TV rather than cycling that is the new career of choice for the children of rural France. After all, Laurent Jalabert, the last French cycling hero to come from a similar rural background, retired last year and has joined Thévenet on the screen. He's ferried around the course by motorbike and adds his expert opinion to the voices in the studio. You get a strong feeling that he's being groomed, Gary Lineker style, for a more prominent role in years to come. And as Jalabert freely admits, it's a lot less demanding than actually riding a bike.

When I arrive at Le Guidon the place resembles a scene from a *Keystone Cops* movie. There are cars everywhere, all being directed in contradictory fashion by a whole battalion of people in a wide variety of uniforms. All this is because of the arrangements for Monsieur *Le Maire* and various other cronies to pay tribute to the Tour – and Bernard Thévenet – in a suitably ostentatious fashion (and one that will be prominent on telly as the Tour passes by). I expect problems meeting Dad, but he's sitting quite happily amid the chaos, making notes in his diary right under the nose of a gendarme. The old tactic of going to the most unlikely spot and blithely ignoring the implication that you shouldn't be there seems to be working a treat.

It's 9.40 a.m. and it's only taken me 2 hours from the last stop. I've covered another 37 miles and I'm over halfway to Lyon now, which is nice to know. It's tempting to feel smug about this good pace, but with the extra heat of today and the fact the next section is much more up and down I prefer to consider this as insurance against slowing down on the second half of the ride rather than an indication of arriving early in Lyon.

My knee has lived up to expectations and has begun to settle down – although no doubt it will feel worse again once I set off. With this in mind, and the fact that Le Guidon has no shelter and the sun is really beginning to beat down now, I decide against an extended stop. I replenish my pockets and bottles and make a cheese and tomato sandwich to take with me, and then set off. Unfortunately, the terrain over the next few miles is not conducive to eating on the hoof and I almost end up stopping anyway. At least I provide some entertainment to the burgeoning crowds as I juggle with my baguette and trail bits of filling on the road behind me.

After I've finished my snack, but not before I've digested it, I hook up with a cyclist heading in the same direction – not Jeremy, nor Louis (who Dad's seen a few times today but who I've kept missing), nor even the legendary Skippy, but a Scotsman who's just been dropped off by his wife who will be waiting for him at the top of the Côte des Echarmeaux, the big climb of the day. I say big, but even though it takes the route to 700 metres above sea-level, it's only about 4 miles long and the gradient seems to be very gentle.

Not that I can express any great confidence about the prospect of tackling it at the moment for I have to struggle desperately to keep up with my new companion over some gentle ups and downs for a few miles. He's following the Tour for a couple of days until heading over to the Pyrenees to participate in the *Etape du Tour*. This is an event run every year in which amateurs can ride a complete stage of the Tour on closed roads – and this year it's Stage 16, the last day in the mountains.

The route goes from Pau over some relatively obscure climbs that don't look that challenging and then has a long, flattish finish to Bayonne. There was a slight feeling of disappointment from people I know who have entered it that it didn't take in some of the more prestigious mountain routes. However, I'm interested to hear the Scotsman confirm the impression that was growing before I left that this is in fact a very tough stage over some very demanding climbs – much steeper than your average climbs in the Alps or Pyrenees.

Just to bolster my confidence further he then rides away from me (or rather I fail to keep up with him – he doesn't even have to deliberately try and leave me behind). I struggle on for a few more miles until coming into the town at the foot of the climb. Not a moment too soon, either, as I've begun to notice the first signs of overheating, and I've all but finished my two water bottles.

The town is heaving with people doing the same as me – stocking up before the hill – and it's difficult to find a shop where I can keep an eye on my bike. When I do it's not only got Coke and cold water in abundance, it's also got air-conditioning. I spend ten minutes inside, cooling down, drinking two cans of Coke (which I normally can't stand, but is only rivalled by Irn-Bru in times of great heat and thirst) and chatting to the owner. He's not in the least perturbed by a scantily clad cyclist perspiring profusely in the doorway – another change from home.

Feeling a lot better I set off up the hill and immediately find a comfortable rhythm, as well as a reduction in the pain in my knee. Just as immediately the crowds become very dense, with every bit of roadside hidden under mobile homes, picnic tables, flags, loudspeaker systems – more than you could ever imagine is necessary to watch a bike race come past.

Here, more than anywhere else so far, it's abundantly clear that a large proportion of the support comes not from locals but from those in the never-ending line of mobile homes that seem to come not just from all over France but also Belgium, Holland, Germany, Italy . . .

In fact I've begun to recognise a fair number of such fans who are obviously here for the duration. Each day I cycle past as they're setting out their stall to support their favourite riders; the Belgians and Dutch have most support. Some are here to support whole teams – Lotto (Belgian), Rabobank (Dutch) – while others have eyes only for one rider – and often a fairly unassuming rider at that. The Belgian Marc Wauters does particularly well out of this, getting his name on the road every day as well as a massive home-made banner hung from some handy trees. Dutchman Servais Knaven has a support group of about four campervans which are fairly low key but which all sport several small posters of their hero. There's also a lot of generalised support for German riders and teams.

And, of course, there's tainted French hero Richard Virenque, the housewives' favourite. His popularity has endured in spite of him finally admitting to systematic doping, after having initially denied it, in the face of overwhelming evidence. With little appearance of contrition quite why this should be the case is beyond me, but each to their own.

Still, there's no doubting the depth of his fan-base – apart from the 'Official Richard Virenque Supporters' Club – Hyères', which is based in a mobile home that's seen better days, there are any number of 'unofficial' fans, who have a variety of ways of getting themselves noticed (polka-dot cars to mirror his success in the King of the Mountains competition are very popular).

Then there are other roadside dwellers whose reasoning is harder to guess at: the infamous Devil, who's been following the Tour in diabolical garb, waving a trident and towing a giant bike for as long as I can remember; the mobile home from Sedan which doesn't support anyone in particular but has a big banner saying simply 'Sedan'; the couple whose sole purpose seems to be to plot their exact position on a home-made map of France which they display everyday (this is quite useful, as they also say how far it is to the finish of each stage, and as they're normally towards the end it's quite reassuring to see them).

So far, none of them seem to have recognised me as the lone cyclist who passes by every day. I suppose I've often gone by the time they're looking at the road, their attention instead being focused on breakfast or setting up shop as I ride past. When I first saw them I thought I might be 'adopted' by them and receive special encouragement every day, but I don't seem to have appeared on their radar screens. It's probably because they are die-hard Tour fans, and my kind of escapade is of little relevance.

Today, however, because it's already late morning and because there are more people in place I get cheers nearly all the way up. I even hear 'good luck with the rest of the Tour' in a Scottish accent coming from somewhere on my right, although I can't make out the source or acknowledge the encouragement – I assume it was my riding partner from an hour ago.

I reach the top feeling comfortable again and then I have a long, fast descent to the next meeting point with Dad. It's rather a sombre valley, in spite of the sunshine, full of thick woodland and giving the impression of an abandoned industrial heritage. There are a lot of boarded-up buildings on the roadside, and the fans have all but dried up – they know where best to see the riders and where the best atmosphere is.

I meet Dad, who seems remarkably relieved to see me. I assume this is a reflection of his faith – or lack of it – in my ability to cope with the terrain, but in fact it turns out to be something entirely different. He missed me when I was taking refuge in the air-conditioned shop at the foot of the climb and since then he's been caught between thinking I must have been riding really quickly and he'd failed to catch me up, or that he'd just not seen me and that I was still to arrive.

My appearance resolves the dilemma and sets Dad's mind at rest. I learn my lesson from last time and take a good quarter of an hour to stretch and have a breather before setting off on the last leg. Dad heads straight for Lyon so as to avoid impending road closures.

Dividing the day into four, with three meeting points, seems to be working well as it makes each bit a manageable chunk. This is particularly the case today, as I've been considering each portion as a quarter of the whole but in fact I have less than that left to do – thanks to riding three long stints this morning of around 37.5 miles each I only have about 30 miles to go, which is a great relief.

Now that I've come down from the climb the heat is even greater, and the valley road seems to go on forever. The route is at last signed to the right and the last climb of the day begins. In itself it amounts to very little, but it's so open and exposed that it's quite uncomfortable. Even though I've built up quite a tan during my training and the past few days, I feel as though I've been in the sun too long.

As is always the way with climbs you don't enjoy there is no clearly defined top. Instead it's a succession of false summits before the long final descent into Lyon actually begins. The route is back on a main road now, completely closed to traffic and void of fans. The only people about are the gendarmes looking hot and frustrated at every junction and side street.

Rather than the sense of excitement that normally greets the impending arrival of the Tour, the air is heavy with tension – it's as if no one's allowed on or near this bit of the route even if they wanted to be on it (which I doubt). It feels like there's a presidential cavalcade on the way and there's been an assassination threat. Or maybe it's a Mafia boss on his way to court . . .

Perhaps even more sinister, it reminds me of the scene on the beach in *The Outsider* by Camus where the protagonist Mersault kills somebody for no reason other than that he can no longer take the heat. I hope it's not me that cracks.

My good run – I'm sure the gendarmes don't try and stop me solely because it's too much effort – comes to an end when I hit the city itself and a wall of officials. They're rather nonplussed when I show them my press pass, which they reluctantly agree should allow me to continue on the route. I cycle through the centre, which is by turns packed with supporters and completely empty (except for the gendarmes).

This last bit is becoming a real chore. I'm here now, and an extra five miles in town seems like rubbing salt into the wound. This doesn't stop me being really peeved, though, when a particularly officious gendarme finally calls a halt to my ride with scarcely a mile to go. As soon as I try to show him my press pass he starts showing me his police badge and trying to manhandle me off the road (I'm only saved this unpleasant fate by someone else trying to keep going – he nearly has to rugby tackle them to get them to stop).

I tell him I've just cycled all the way from Nevers, which he appears never to have heard of (he's obviously well travelled), and that I'm trying to ride all the stages of the Tour. He appears to ignore this and then plays his trump card: he realises I'm not French and asks where I come from. I say England and he tells me to piss off home and do the Tour of England instead, which throws him and his colleague into gales of mirth.

At this point the red mist almost descends but I remember *The Outsider* again and I realise I would rather spend the night in my hotel than in the local police cells. I content myself with an ostentatious display of gratitude and courtesy for being treated to

83

such a warm and typical Lyonnais welcome. They only begin to realise the implications of what I've said as I'm riding back into town, but by then it's too late.

I stop for directions to the hotel and arrive at the same time as Dad. It's big and cool and welcoming – and has 132 steps up to the bedroom on the 6th floor. Dad nobly carries all the bags, but I still have to cope with the bike. Finally I collapse onto the bed with a sense of relief and a great deal of satisfaction. It took exactly the eight and a half hours riding/nine and a half hours overall that I estimated, and I kept up an average of 16.9mph. And I feel all right. Well, I feel worn out and I'm not entirely sure I'm fit to run a full diagnostic of all my bodily functions, but there's nothing particularly untoward.

I have a shower and decide to cobble together dinner from what's available at the delicatessen over the road and then have an early night – rather than sleep, eat and then sleep again. As I'm eating my pasta salad, quiche, crisps and yoghurt I treat myself to watching the Tour on the TV in the room (I've hardly seen any so far as I've been asleep or on the move). I feel so sorry for Stuart O'Grady and Anthony Geslin, the day's breakaways who've managed over 100 miles together at the head of the race but whose bid for glory is overhauled by the bunch in the last quarter of a mile. If the interminable streets of Lyon felt like purgatory for me, how must they have felt for them?

I hang my clothes out to dry over a six-storey drop onto the roof of the hotel reception and hope the wind doesn't suddenly pick up overnight. Otherwise I may become the unwitting Jamie Oliver of the cycling world – the naked cyclist. Would this be the longest streak in the history of sport? I'm sure it would at least grab some attention, but possibly not for the right reasons. I go to bed at 6 p.m., with the alarm set for 3.30 a.m. After all, tomorrow it's the mountains.

## Stage 7

# LYON—MORZINE-AVORIAZ (144 MILES)

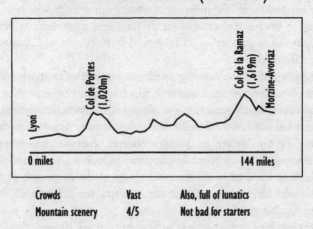

| Crowds | Vast | Also, full of lunatics |
|--------|------|------------------------|
| Mountain scenery | 4/5 | Not bad for starters |

A morning that was already bad enough simply because of the alarm going off at 3.30 a.m. – the earliest so far – has been made worse by a minor disaster outside. The bike rack has been stolen from the car.

Presumably it's been taken by a cyclist, or someone who wants a birthday present for a cyclist friend, as there are no other marks on the car – no signs of an attempted break-in or even of petty vandalism. Just the absence of a bike rack. It wasn't even a particularly good bike rack, no fancy, roof-rack-mounted affair, just a strap-on cheapy. It was no more than the one we already had when we were planning the trip and therefore the one we were using.

We hadn't even given a second thought to removing it, with the car parked just opposite the hotel in a pleasant, leafy square that gave no particular impression it was home to thieves and brigands. Not since our initial uncertainty in Paris had it crossed our minds that we might lose it.

But now it's gone. Initially this seems like a pretty insurmountable hurdle that will scupper plans to cycle the route for today at least, but then we realise a simple solution – put the bike in the car. It only takes a couple of minutes rearranging the bags for the bike to fit in quite comfortably, having removed the front wheel.

So the damage done is only about five minutes' added time this morning and a gnawing annoyance at not having seen the threat coming. And there's the prospect of wasting some more time later on trying to find a replacement, as at least one more bike is being brought out to join us – two bikes and three people will definitely not fit inside the car.

Slightly miffed but drawing on all our reserves of Dunkirk spirit, which don't amount to much at 4.30 a.m., we set off – in the car. Today's neutralised section is the longest since Paris, amounting to eight miles not counted in the route description, which is already either slightly longer or slightly shorter than yesterday's epic (depending on which route description you look at). On top of that I'd have to cycle at least two miles to get to the beginning of the neutralised bit, which would make an extra ten miles in all. Not today, thanks.

Our bad luck doesn't appear to have run out yet, however, and we spend five minutes driving around central Lyon before returning (inadvertently) to the square from which we'd just departed. When finally we do get out onto roads that can be identified on our town plan, things get little better. The bridge the Tour uses to cross the Rhône is closed to cars already, so we have to take an earlier one. This takes us off the signposted route and it takes another ten minutes to find it again.

Once back on it we can't stay on it for more than a quarter of a mile because it points us the wrong way down a one-way street – and not the kind you can sneak down without anybody noticing. So we end up spending a good 20 minutes faffing about, turning this way and that through backstreets and alleys trying simply to stay as close to the route as possible.

It's a farce. The map we have shows all the roads but neglects to include useful information like which are one way, or which have been converted into a tram route, or which are dead ends. More by luck than judgement we eventually land up back on the route, with the recognisable black arrows on a yellow background to follow. After that it's just another couple of miles until the Lyon suburb where the real race begins, but it's taken us nearly an hour from the hotel, and it's already after five. In fact, it's already later than yesterday's start time, and today's stage – whether actually longer or shorter – is considerably harder. If I didn't finish yesterday until 2.30 p.m., it's looking unlikely I'll be done any quicker today.

I finally set off at 5.20 a.m., sporting my usual combination of backlight and head torch. A minute later I'm back at the car for my water bottles, which in all the confusion I'd left behind. After all this excitement my start is further delayed by needing to pop into the bushes to see to a 'personal need'.

I'm then confronted with several miles of semi-main roads running through modern commuter towns, which look even sleepier and more nondescript than normal this early in the morning. It's all quite flat and there's no wind, but I can't seem to get going. I can't even really blame my knee for my slow progress as it's just uncomfortable at the moment rather than painful.

I find it hard to get above about 16mph, whereas this type of flat terrain has normally seen me bowling along near to 20mph. I tell myself that it's just my usual morning sluggishness, but I think I know that it's more than this, even at this early stage, although I'm loathe to admit it to myself yet. Either way I should really be taking advantage of the 25 flat miles in the Rhône valley to get a good start ahead of the day's main difficulties.

Dad comes by to collect the head torch and backlight as the sun finally comes up over the mountains that are silhouetted ahead, rising abruptly out of the plain. I'm looking forward to the mountains: the scenery, the freshness, even the cycling, but they do seem rather precipitous and impenetrable from here.

They're still quite a long way off, though. First I have the pleasure of cycling past the nuclear power plant at Bugey. Even by French standards, and they produce a much higher proportion of their electricity by nuclear power than we do, this seems recklessly close to a large centre of population – we're only about 20 miles from the centre of Lyon, where more than a million people live. And even if the prevailing wind might blow the other way (then again it might not), the river runs straight through the heart of the city.

I'd be more relaxed about the apparent confidence in the plant's ability to make sure things are working perfectly all of the time if the perimeter fence weren't decorated with murals painted by local schools. These are very nice and pretty, depicting the six continents, which is actually my first cause for concern – I always thought there were seven (Europe, Asia, Africa, Australasia, North America, South America and Antarctica – not bad while riding a bike).

It turns out that the Americas have been combined, which is acceptable, but then I come to the last panel. This portrays the mysterious, hitherto undiscovered continent of the Arctic. You might charitably think that this was a simple typo, and that they meant the Antarctic, which really is a continent, rather than the Arctic, which is just frozen sea.

But the contents of the mural suggest a rather more confused picture: the Arctic quite rightly contains Eskimos, igloos, polar bears and . . . this is where things start to go wrong – penguins. Why don't polar bears eat penguins? Because they live about 10,000 miles apart: polar bears in the Arctic, penguins in the Antarctic. I just hope the nuclear power station looks further afield than the local schools when recruiting its staff.

I cover a further ten miles, following the Rhône as it inscribes a nice loop round the first foothills of the Alps, and then that's it. The signposts take me off to the left and I start going upwards at the beginning of the Col de Portes. Although I've already ridden 25 miles I have to cross this before the first rendezvous with Dad today, as the terrain has dictated an uneven division of the stage.

This is the first serious climb in seven days of cycling; it's category two, only category one and *hors catégorie* (beyond classification) to go. The first one where I'll need to use my last few gears, where my lungs will begin to feel the strain. This is also the arena I've been looking forward to for the past seven days, the one which I've always enjoyed and the one where I perform best. In general I actually like cycling up hills – gone is the uncertainty of purpose of the flat. Where am I going? Is it far? What's coming next? In the hills these questions are easily answered: you're going to the top, it's bound to feel like a long way and it's a safe bet to assume it will all be uphill.

The question 'why?' may appear more difficult to resolve, but the answer to this is also simple – because it's there. Not everybody may want to accept the challenge of it being there, but at least people understand the concept. To my mind it's much harder to justify seven hours on the flat in this fashion. You can't say 'because it's there', or if you do not many will believe you. Even if the desire to explore, to see what's round the next corner, what the next town is like can explain a lot of it, this generates no real sense of purpose. This is a lovely thing to do, and so is aimless wondering, but neither provide a reason to keep going when you're feeling low. You can only motivate yourself to carry on for so long on the vague promise of coming across something round the next bend. Going up a hill you know you have to keep going until you get to the top – if you want to get to the top in the first place, that is.

And yet in spite of this general enthusiasm, in spite of my physiological predisposition to climb hills effectively (which is just a polite way of saying I'm as thin as a rake), in spite of having cycled six days on the flat just to get here, I go up this first climb like a recalcitrant donkey. It's an awful struggle. I'm reminded of Desgranges' comment in 1907 when the Tour came to the Alps for the first time: 'Watching the effort of these men on this abominable climb I was exposed to the most cruelly intense emotions of my sporting career.' Thanks a lot, Henri.

It's not a problem of motivation, just a simple one of having really heavy legs and burning lungs. I suppose I should have reappraised my assumption that I would thrive on the hills after all this cycling on the flat when I was going so slowly this morning. I think I didn't do this because my morale wouldn't have coped with two blows: feeling like I was cycling through treacle on the flat *and* realising this would mean equally slow progress on the hills.

Anyway, the nine-and-a-bit-mile climb takes an age and does little to compensate for my slowness earlier on. Even at 7 a.m. the crowds are thick on the lower slopes, although a lot of them are more intent on cooking their breakfast than watching me come past. Given the speed I'm going and the amount of grimacing, this is probably a good thing. The only other good thing is the almost instantaneous improvement in the state of my right knee. As soon as the gradient becomes properly steep, the pain in my knee eases almost to the point of disappearing. To my mind, even though I'm going badly, this improvement just confirms how much better for you it is to ride up hills than chug along on the flat in a big gear.

There are a surprising number of other cyclists about, although most of them seem to be on mountain bikes carrying vast numbers of panniers, so even at my reduced speed I pass them by. Perhaps they're hoping to get up the climb before the heat of the day. If so they must be a bit disappointed as it's hot work already – the sweat from my brow has begun splashing onto my handlebars and making my eyes sting.

In the periods when I can see again after wiping my eyes I realise it's a very pleasant climb in terms of the scenery – all woods and glades, with every now and then a splendid panorama across the Rhône and the way I've just come. I also get a chance to read the names painted all over the road – there's nothing like a hill to encourage people to participate in a bit of sporting graffiti.

For the first time I see Italian names added to the multi-national list of the fans' favourites. Gilberto Simoni is the most popular of these transalpine cyclists, followed by Stefano Garzelli, Paulo Bettini and Danilo Di Luca. This will be the first chance to see whether the likes of Simoni and Garzelli can live up to their pre-race talk and actually cause Armstrong some trouble in the mountains – they'll need to be feeling better than I am. Then I come across another flag for the increasingly popular Virenque – although this might well be another coup for the local schools as it's spelt 'Vrenque'.

Nearer the top the support starts to become vocal, perhaps out of pity more than anything else. Then, with half a mile to go, I'm joined by a car full of 'youths' who are full of exuberance and enthusiasm. So much so that the passenger assumes the roll of my *directeur sportif*. To start with this is simply shouted encouragement, but then he and his friends warm to the task: the ring-leader climbs part way out of the car and sits in the window, while the driver beats out a rhythm on the horn (those in the back just wave and shout madly).

The result is that I am accompanied for the final two or three minutes of the climb by my very own team car. I am exhorted to 'keep my rhythm' and 'ignore the pain' and reassured that I'm 'nearly there' and there's 'only 250 metres' to go. Needless to say this stimulates a degree of attention from the other fans on the roadside, a situation which is exacerbated as I succumb to the temptation to pick up speed. The summit approaches and there is a crescendo of noise. Nobody knows who I am or why I should be cheered, but it's like a snowball rolling downhill and once one person's started everybody else gets involved. Even the gendarme at the top, who looked like he was toying with the idea of stopping my support vehicle, yields in the end and gives me a celebratory peep of his whistle while still trying to look sternly at the miscreants in the car.

The temporary euphoria that this excitement induces lasts only as far as the next incline – by which time all this new set of fans sees is another anonymous cyclist struggling up a bump in the road. It's quite clear by now – to those at the roadside and to me – that I'm not having a particularly good day. The descent from the Col de Portes is punctuated by brief uphill sections, and after I labour to the top of each of these I feel too weary to do anything other than freewheel down the far side. I recover fairly swiftly each time, but can then only maintain a slower speed than normal for what seems to be more effort.

This all conspires to reduce my motivation. It's amazing how soon after something has become hard work that you start telling yourself it's not worth the effort. The problem is made worse here by the fact that the countryside is glorious and it really is much nicer to freewheel where possible and take in the views, the smells and the sounds.

I reach Dad in Pugieu after nearly forty-eight miles that have taken me three and a quarter hours. This works out at an average speed of only 14.8 mph – it's going to be touch and go whether I make it to the end before the roads start closing. Dad tries to boost my morale by telling me he's calculated that until the beginning of today I'd covered 650 miles at an average speed of 16.8 mph – I'm delighted, although this is only including the time I've been on the bike rather than total time taken. We reckon the average would be down to around 15 mph if stops were counted as well – significantly slower than Maurice Garin 100 years ago.

I don't stop for long and am soon off on the next leg, which is only about 32 miles, although it contains another second-category climb – the Côte du Mont des Princes. It's much shorter than the last one, but a bit steeper, according to the profile in the route book. In case it proves as demanding as the first I try and up the speed on the flattish section in between, but to no avail. The mind is willing but the body's not able. It's one of those hot, mountain valleys and once again the route is on busy roads – it all makes for quite a torrid time as the sun is getting hotter and hotter and the air is still. The only light relief comes in the form of a sign for a conker factory. On reflection it could be that *Usine de Châtaignes* is its name rather than a description of what it does – I hope so or all those schoolboy illusions of picking the best conker in the school will have been shattered. Instead of throwing sticks at trees I should have been buying them from a factory. No wonder I never won.

Finally I start to tackle the climb, and make as slow progress up this one as I did the last. This time I even struggle to overtake the mountain-bike riders, which tells me everything I need to know about my pace. As before, when my speed dips so does my motivation. There is also another concern which is distracting me – whether or not I can finish the stage before I get caught or the roads are closed. And if I can't, what should I do then?

My original plan had been to assume I could just stop at the side of the road, have a breather while the race came through and then carry on, but this doesn't seem like such a good idea any more. This is partly because of the practicalities of finding somewhere comfortable to stop, but more because of the practicalities of carrying on afterwards. The roads would probably be closed for three hours as first the publicity caravan and then the Tour itself pass by, and then there's the impact of all the fans trying to leave at the same time. This would be made worse if I were caught part way up a hill, as would be most likely: I would then have to negotiate the stream of traffic, cyclists and pedestrians coming the other way once the roads had reopened as I resumed my attempts to reach the end. By my reckoning all this would add up to a delay of maybe four hours – and that's four hours on top of the time at which I would be expecting to finish, which would mean arriving at the hotel four hours' later and missing out on four hours rest and recuperation.

In some ways I'm cross with myself for thinking these negative thoughts (all based on the assumption that I won't finish before the riders), but then I tell myself I have to recognise the importance of tomorrow as well. If I'm tired and going badly today, how will I be the next day without four hours of the already limited amount of sleep I was expecting? And at the back of my mind is the realisation that tomorrow's stage finishes at l'Alpe d'Huez and is probably the most prestigious of the race. The last thing I want to do is compromise that.

All of these thoughts are occupying my mind, and probably distracting me from the task in hand, as I meet Dad for our second rendezvous, having just cycled through the village of Chilly (which wasn't). I don't arrive until 11.10 a.m. and I can tell that he's concerned about my state – both mental and physical. Once I calculate that my average speed for the last section was below 14 mph, I realise I have to confront the likelihood of getting caught by road closures and not making it to the finish. It's taken me nearly six hours to do eighty miles and there's still sixty miles to go. At this rate I won't be there until virtually four o'clock – well after the time even cyclists with press passes will be allowed down the road.

I mull this over as I have a cold drink and a banana. I ask Dad what he thinks. He says he's quite happy to carry on and he's sure we'll arrange something if our plans for meeting are messed up by road closures and me being held up. But he says I shouldn't ignore having to keep going the next day either (and the day after that, and the day after that).

I decide to stop.

## Stage 8

# SALLANCHES—L'ALPE D'HUEZ (137 MILES)

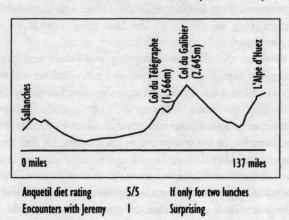

| Anquetil diet rating | 5/5 | If only for two lunches |
| Encounters with Jeremy | 1 | Surprising |

I suppose if I were feeling disappointed then it would be quite clear that I'd made the wrong decision to stop yesterday. As it is, far from feeling disappointed I feel delighted, so at the moment I'm assuming the decision taken was the right one.

And I certainly take the absence of disappointment this morning as a good sign for the rest of the trip. I could have spent yesterday afternoon moping around, feeling sorry for myself and regretting a precipitous decision. This was definitely something I was worried about as I was weighing the pros and cons of what to do. After all, deciding to stop effectively means that the trip is now a failure: whatever else happens, I won't have cycled the complete Tour de France route as I set out to.

Instead of feeling down, though, all I felt yesterday was an enormous sense of relief – apart from when I was feeling starving hungry or was about to fall asleep, that is. This was probably because, although my original aim was to do all of the Tour, if it turned out that I couldn't do all of it then my back-up plan was to do as much as possible. And, to be honest, a realistic appraisal of my chances when I set off would have suggested completing the entire course was at best possible and at worst improbable. As a result, if it came to this second option, I was aware there were two ways of looking at it.

The first possibility was to ride myself into the ground completely, until I could go no farther. In practice this would have meant continuing yesterday, because although I was running on empty I wasn't completely spent. The result, however, would probably have been getting caught by the road closures, losing out on several hours' recuperation and almost inevitably paying the price somewhere down the line. I say almost inevitably because you never know, I might have staged a miraculous recovery, but it's much more likely that the next day, or the one after that I'd have simply had enough, or been caught again, or both.

And if I'd really been pushing myself to the limits, once I'd finally gone over the edge I would probably not have recovered properly for the duration of the trip. After all, recovery has been a difficult enough task even when I've been feeling relatively good. Then, instead of resting and being able to take up where I left off, I would most likely have suffered a series of similar setbacks all the way to Paris, with a decreasing amount of success each time until eventually I could hardly ride at all.

There would definitely be something heroic about this kind of 'all or nothing, do or die' approach – any wholehearted attempt ending in spectacular failure is always a winner. If only for this heroic aspect, it has a lot going for it. It's also the only option available to the riders in the real Tour. They don't have the luxury of being able to stop if they're having a bad day and then start again tomorrow, and in some ways I regret not having this competitive imperative. For a start, it would have made my decision for me: I would have been compelled to find out how far I could have gone until I could do no more.

But to my mind this wasn't the best way to try and ride as much of the route as possible, even if it meant accepting that I could no longer ride all of it. And if I was prepared to accept this, then the second option seemed more appealing. And this second option was to push myself as far as I felt I could without compromising the next day's ride – and more importantly without compromising the days after that as well, and possibly the whole of the trip that remained. The likely outcome of this was that I would miss some of one stage, or perhaps more, but would end up able to rejoin the fray the next day – and be able to keep doing so all the way to Paris.

The attraction of this choice is based on more than just the fact it would allow me to stop when I was tired. It also acknowledges that each stage itself is an important achievement within the bigger picture of the whole Tour. By doing so it also provides a new source of motivation: instead of a slow and painful failure to do the whole thing, each day becomes a goal in itself and is part of the new challenge to do as much as possible.

All this is particularly resonant given that today's stage – the one I was thinking about yesterday – is the stage to l'Alpe d'Huez. *L'étape reine*, as the French would call it – the queen among stages. To do all the rest but not to finish this one would have been unbearable, in fact it would almost be better to complete this and no others.

It could also be said that taking the Tour stage by stage in this way resembles the approach taken by most professionals. With the exception of those competing seriously for overall victory, or victory in one of the other competitions – points, King of the Mountains, best young rider – most of those present will be aiming for victory in a stage. All their energies are focused on the stages they think they can win, and all the rest will be ridden to conserve as much energy as possible – although of course they do still have to finish every day.

So, faced with these two options, yesterday's key question was: did I think I could still ride the whole Tour route? And the answer, unfortunately, was no. Not so much because of how I felt at that very moment – although I was pretty close to the limit – but because of how I think I would have felt if I had continued. And in a nutshell that's why I stopped, and so far I'm glad I did.

I was especially glad once we'd arrived in Sallanches yesterday and

I'd resisted the temptation to go straight to bed. Even as I was having a shower in the hotel I still felt no hunger pangs in spite of having cycled 80 miles in the morning, but just as I was about to lie down they set in with a vengeance. Thus prompted, Dad and I decided to go into town and have lunch before the restaurants stopped serving as it was already nearly 2 p.m.

And, boy, was this a good decision, although it did make me wonder whether skipping a proper dinner in Lyon the day before was actually such a good idea. Following a good-size steak and chips of my own (and a salad on the side) I was so tempted by the look of Dad's sausages and chips (with salad) that I ordered one of those as well (eat your heart out Jacques Anquetil). And then I had three scoops of ice cream to finish off, and could probably have eaten more if there had been anything left on the menu that I fancied. The waitress knew when she was on to a good thing and asked if we would be coming for lunch again today – which would have been nice, if somewhat impracticable.

After that we went back to the hotel, where I digested my two lunches before calling home. Catherine consoled me for not finishing the stage and then recounted her struggles to remove all the unpacked boxes from the spare room, left over after we moved house several months ago, so that the woodworm in the floor boards could be treated. It reminded me that my travails are of my own making.

Once back at the hotel I confirmed arrangements for leaving early tomorrow, iced my knee, which definitely seems to be on the mend, and then watched a bit of the Tour – they were already past the scene of my capitulation. I watched a bit more before deciding to call it a day, assuming that lunch was sufficient to act as dinner as well. In order to leave nothing to chance for this morning the alarm was set for 3 a.m. and by 4.30 p.m. I was in bed.

I slept well, although the sound of the start village being installed in Sallanches' main square disturbed me on occasion, and I woke this morning feeling fresh. In fact I can't emphasise enough how refreshing it was to feel fresh. It even made breakfast seem appetising, and when you went to bed over 10 hours ago even 3 a.m. doesn't seem too bad.

No need to use the car this morning, as Sallanches is a small place, and I'm almost immediately out of the town climbing the Côte de Megève, the day's first obstacle, by 4 a.m. Although it's early and I'm taking it easy I go up this well enough for me to exorcise some ghosts from a previous visit.

In fact, three years ago on the climb of the neighbouring Côte de Domancy, which is just an alternative road up the first section of the same hill, I probably came the nearest I've been to wanting to cry on a bike. All I can really bring myself to remember about it was that it had been raining incessantly for the eighty miles I'd cycled to get this far, and tackling such a steep climb with maybe only five miles to go was the last straw. Even the relatively easy portion that shared the same road as I'm on now seemed like a cliff face.

It's reassuring, therefore, to be making smooth progress now. The gradient levels near the top and I even get some toots of support as I cycle through Megève – there's obviously more than one foolish cycling fan on the road at this time of the morning.

After a couple more brief uphills the road snakes down for nearly 20 miles into Albertville. Although the surface is good and the gradient even, it's tricky to descend as quickly as I would like because it's still dark. It's difficult to distinguish the grey of the road from the grey of the rocks and even the grey of the sky at times.

Still, it's fast enough for me to arrive at the day's first meeting point earlier than expected, having done nearly thirty-eight miles in only just over two hours. It's so early that Dad hasn't yet managed to find a bakers that's open, so it's a good job I still have some malt loaf left. There's also some hot water remaining in the flask from breakfast for the essential cup of tea – although by now tepid would be a better description than hot.

I set off again promptly as I'm anxious to get to the hills as early as possible in order to avoid the heat later on and to give myself as much time as I can ahead of the inevitable road closures. L'Alpe d'Huez is incredibly popular with fans so it will probably be difficult to enforce a strict closure until the publicity caravan is actually on it, but I don't want to take any chances. I reckon if I'm at the bottom by 1 p.m. I should have a chance of getting up and down again without getting trapped.

I'm also keen to reach the mountains simply because I'm feeling so much better than yesterday and am once again looking forward to them for their own sake. They also seem to have done the power of good for my knee, the discomfort in which is only a pale shadow of what it was even yesterday morning.

This enthusiasm sees me flying along the gentle incline of the Maurienne valley, which I must follow for some 30 miles before the hills start. Even though I'm going slightly uphill and realise I'll be following the same river valley up-stream all the way until I turn off, I can't get rid of the idea that it will start to descend gradually at some point. This misconception results from having cycled the last part of it before, and even though I know full well I must be remembering incorrectly, it still comes as a bit of a blow when I reach the bit I recognise and the road continues to rise. I finally reach St-Michel-de-Maurienne. It's 8.40 a.m. and I give myself until 9 a.m. before I have to set off.

There are still more than 60 miles to go, but this is the last meeting point with Dad today as the road over the Col du Télégraphe and the Col du Galibier is bound to be closed by now. Instead he'll drive over another Tour favourite, the Col de la Croix de Fer, and meet me at the hotel in the valley near Bourg d'Oisans. There's no point in him even trying to get anywhere near the climb to l'Alpe d'Huez itself.

I stuff my pockets, drink my first isotonic drink of the whole ride as a kind of good-luck charm and set off. Fortunately I've ridden the Télégraphe and Galibier before so at least I know what to expect. Last time I was here was with Jon, and we were lured into racing up the Télégraphe by some Italians in smart clothes on posh bikes. To be honest, we took them apart up the climb. Only one out of ten was able to keep with us, and we even dropped him with about a mile to go; we then waited ten minutes at the top and not one of the others made it in that time. Yet it turned out to be a pyrrhic victory. We absolutely crawled up the Galibier and it was only by bribing the shopkeeper-cum-café owner just over the top to give us some hot food after he'd already closed for the day that we made it back down the other side.

So this time I take it easy. There are still some cars on the Télégraphe, which is a bit annoying as they don't go too well with the number of spectators already installed, but apart from that it's a comfortable climb. I'm up by just before 10 a.m., which keeps me on course for reaching the top of the Galibier by noon. The descent into Valloire takes longer than I remember and I'm caught between pressing on or stopping to replenish my bottles while I know I can. I decide to keep going and am soon part of the throng of cyclists tackling the Galibier's first steep slopes.

I manage these with a fair bit in reserve (and two gears left unused), and then try to keep a good speed without using up too much energy on the next, easier section. Every now and then somebody comes rifling past, but in general I'm one of the fastest on the road, which is a good sign.

The next landmark is Plan Lachat, which to all the world looks like it's just a mile or so from the top. Instead the steep hairpins immediately above lead to a second tier of mountains invisible from below. When first-timers cross this 'heartbreak ridge' they suddenly see the four miles that remain – and it can be a demoralising sight.

Luckily, forewarned is forearmed and I've already braced myself for what lies ahead. Today, in fact, the hillside is covered with spectators, although they're not yet that dense at the roadside because the mountain is so big it can absorb them all comfortably until the race calls them to closer attendance.

I've only got one spare gear, but I know I'm going to make it comfortably when I see an unexpected hut offering water and cold drinks. With only a quarter of a bottle left and a long way still to go to the bottom of l'Alpe d'Huez I decide to call in. I suppose technically this means I still haven't ridden all the way up the Galibier without putting my feet down, but I've got more pressing things to think about at the moment.

A can of Coke and two refilled water bottles later, I'm off again and continue at a fairly sluggish pace now to the top, with some of the steepest slopes reserved for the very last bit. I arrive just before midday and reward myself with a hastily consumed sandwich (and although it's hot these are considerably better conditions than in 1996 when the route was abridged to avoid the Galibier because the snow and wind made it impassable). Just as I'm about to set off on the epic descent to the Col du Lauteret and thence Bourg d'Oisans I see Jeremy appear over the brow. I'd begun to think he'd been a figment of my imagination, a result of too much physical activity and not enough sleep.

We ride down together and the first thing I notice is his lack of luggage. He tells me he's hooked up with a set of Austrians who are doing the same thing as he is and who have a van, with an Australian driver, which can cope with all of their stuff. I congratulate him on his apparent good fortune but he says his new companions are sometimes a bit earnest for his liking.

For a start, he describes their obsession with riding through the night and their occasional reliance on a possibly illicit, white powdery substance to keep themselves going. Then he says they've already lost their original driver because he got fed up with it all. He finally convinces me they're genuine lunatics (as opposed to the part-timers like me and him, I suppose) when he says one of them is riding a 1947 Swiss Army bike with only one gear – they must save all their extras for their knives.

The route is all downhill but takes us over the top of the Col du Lauteret – which I'll be riding back over tomorrow – and I take my leave while Jeremy waits for the Austrians. I'm getting nervous about l'Alpe d'Huez being closed, and it's looking unlikely that I'll make my target time of 1 p.m. The result is that for the first time since Paris I actually go flat out for the whole of the downhill. Not that it is actually all downhill – there are several undulating sections and one climb of a mile or so – but the first bit is certainly a dream descent. And although I'm pushing myself as much as I can it's quite a release to be able to go as fast as possible and not have to worry about what's to come.

Well, I am a bit worried about climbing l'Alpe d'Huez, but there's no point in me being fresh if the road's already closed, so I race on. But the roads seem interminable; one false dawn follows another. It goes on for so long that I almost give up hope of the climb still being open. This would be a really bitter pill to swallow after yesterday and the fact that in effect I sacrificed finishing the stage to have a better chance today.

It's 1.15 p.m. when I arrive at the foot of the climb and I'm all prepared to foam at the mouth with indignation and to have a massive row with a gendarme before collapsing into tears at him not letting me through when I realise that he's not going to stop me. Almost immediately I become scared at the prospect of now having to do the climb, but I manage to keep going in case he changes his mind.

In fact the next two gendarmes do make a rather token effort to discourage cyclists, but by the simple expedient of getting off and then getting back on again once I'm past them they're easily negotiated.

And then that's it, I'm on the climb. The television pictures I've been brought up on are no exaggeration: there are people everywhere, and I'm still in the first couple of miles. I don't have time to notice the aches engendered by my madcap chase to get here because there are so many people around I can't help but be distracted.

There are people going much faster than me and people going so slowly you'd think they'd have to stop. There are people on top-of-the-range racing bikes and people riding tandems. There's even one couple on a tandem towing a trailer with twins in (fortunately I overtake them, rather than them overtaking me).

The farther I go, the more enthusiastic the crowds are until I come to one long line of mildly inebriated Dutch fans. By dint of their number alone they manage to concentrate all the cyclists into one cacophonous tunnel of orange and then cheer every pedal stroke for the 50 or so yards it takes to reach the other end. Even in my fatigued state it brings a surge of adrenalin and a change of pace, which receives an extra cheer. This is surely as close as I'll ever come to knowing what it must be like to do the real thing.

After this the rest of the climb is almost an anti-climax, but it's too hot and noisy to think about that sort of thing. In fact, it's only when I get off my bike as the gendarmes finally make a concerted effort to stop cyclists with only just over a mile to go that I notice just how hot it is. Immediately my face starts to burn and I feel parched. I think in all the excitement I forgot to drink enough as I've still got most of my water left.

I try to ride back down but to my consternation no one is allowed to cycle downhill now either. It's 2.30 p.m., so there should still be time but the gendarmes are having none of it. I toy with the idea of scrambling down the mountain side and climbing back over the barriers lower down, but I decide neither my bike nor my body are up to this. Instead I turn the other way and worm my way across town until I come to the other road which leads back downhill (a little forward planning can work wonders). Apart from the cars and coaches parked on every available space this is still open, and to my relief the main road is also still open when I rejoin it – or perhaps the gendarmes are just looking the wrong way.

After another mile or so I find the side road that is my cunning escape route, and within less than a hundred yards it's as if I'm in a different world. I have the road almost all to myself and am contentedly freewheeling towards the village at the bottom that houses our hotel when I'm rudely interrupted by some uphill. At first I groan, but it's actually so little compared to what I've just come over that I don't really mind. I carry on down, and the air just keeps getting hotter and hotter. Once in the valley the last mile to the hotel is nearly too much for me in the suffocating heat, but finally I arrive and the veranda is almost cool.

Dad sees me coming and looks relieved that I'm still able to walk and think for myself. After a couple of minutes and two cans of Coke (I could be an advert for Coke if I didn't find it so horrible the rest of the time) I realise that it's a relief to me as well. I'd got so caught up in the day that I don't really think I knew what state I was in by the time I'd finished the climb. But now I feel as though I'm all right. In fact, I feel euphoric.

If I felt the need to justify my decision to stop yesterday, this would be it. Simply sitting here having completed the stage to l'Alpe d'Huez. I'm tempted to say that if I don't complete another one I'll be happy to rest on the laurels of this achievement, but I'm aware of the danger in doing this. I may not be able to ride the whole Tour, but to get round everything else will do me. So I'd better not let myself get too smug.

## Stage 9

# BOURG D'OISANS—GAP (115.5 MILES)

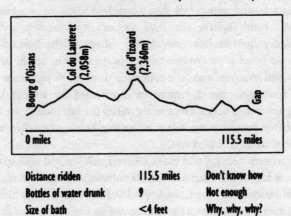

| Distance ridden | 115.5 miles | Don't know how |
| Bottles of water drunk | 9 | Not enough |
| Size of bath | <4 feet | Why, why, why? |

The rest of last night was a very pleasant conclusion to an epic day. I think I can call it that as it took me 11.5 hours from when I set off until I finally arrived at the hotel. After showering and washing my kit – this might seem extravagant, but it certainly needed it – the only place that looked likely to serve dinner before 7 p.m. was the campsite next door, so we headed there. This turned out to be a good choice as we had to wait less than half an hour before they started serving (not bad for a late Sunday afternoon), which gave us just enough time to watch the last 20 minutes of the climb to l'Alpe d'Huez on the television. I felt remarkably humble watching the way the riders flew up it.

We were back at the hotel by 7 p.m. and I was about to go to bed when I heard a voice I recognised next door. This was not quite the surprise it might seem, as I knew that my former news editor Justin and his dad were staying in the same hotel, but I'd come to the conclusion that I would miss them as they would probably not be back in time. Instead we shared a drink downstairs in the hotel bar, and Justin provided me with copies of *Plant Manager's Journal* and *Contract Journal* – the two papers I used to write for – to stuff down my jersey and keep the wind out on future descents.

Ironically enough, given that I've missed quite a bit of the Tour by being asleep when the race has actually been taking place, I updated them on how the last bit of the stage panned out. Between us, we created a fair picture of the run of events and were universally surprised and refreshed to see so many attacks on Armstrong. He's ended up in the yellow jersey and would probably say he was in control on the climb, but the race is better for being so open and he'll have earned his victory if he does hold on to the lead into Paris.

Justin's dad, a genuine cycling fanatic, then plied me with technical questions about my bike, which I struggled to answer. I could tell him it's a Giant TCR Composite, which means it's got a sloping rather than a horizontal crossbar, and is made from carbon, which means it's very light. Beyond that I had to rely on subjective criteria like 'It's very comfortable' and 'I like it a lot' – which would be OK had the questions not been more oriented to the number of spokes I have or the gear ratios (I know the gear ratios – 53x12 to 39x25, which are more or less the same as the professionals use and which get a favourable response as a result). Before I revealed my ignorance completely I went to bed, looking forward to a slightly easier day – a mere bagatelle, in fact, at 115.5 miles.

Perhaps this assumption that things would be easier today wasn't such a good idea. It means that I cycle up the Col du Lauteret in a constant state of denial – denying it can go on for so long or seem so steep. I only cycled down it yesterday, so I should know what I'm letting myself in for, but although it took an hour to come down I'm still not ready to accept how long it's taking me to cycle up.

It's also rather an uncomfortable ride as a result of the tunnels I have to negotiate – some of them are unlit and the almost continuous traffic means I'm constantly worried about not being seen. Most of this incessant flow seems to be made up of the campervans that lined the road up to l'Alpe d'Huez yesterday. I wonder whether they're heading home or looking for a place on today's route.

The answer is provided when I finally reach the top of the Lauteret, which has become an impromptu car park for thousands of white mobile homes. Why do they all look the same? There's an almost endless variety in even modern car designs compared to this homogenous lot. Maybe it's to ensure a kind of group identity so that you can easily be recognised as a member of the 'campervan-owning-cycle-fan' sect. It's all a bit sinister, if you ask me.

After this long slog my spirits are raised by Dad, who looks surprised to see me so soon. He buys me some fresh croissants from a stall placed strategically to take advantage of the crowds, while I admire the sunrise over the mountains. As I'm eating I see Louis, the South African. We recount our journeys since we last met and at first I'm relieved to hear that he also didn't finish the stage into Morzine. This relief turns into compassion, however, when he tells me this was because he got lost in the dark and ended up miles off route near Annecy, and only at this point did he call it a day. In spite of this 'failure' – much more heroic than mine – he's still here this morning at over 2,000 metres, with all his luggage (although I'm not sure he rode l'Alpe d'Huez yesterday). He's been sleeping for between two and three hours a night in fields, and yet he's still going. He also asks me if I've seen Skippy yet and, as I haven't, I wonder fleetingly if Louis has created him as an imaginary friend to keep him company on his lonely vigil.

I leave before Louis on the descent into Briançon, which is as pleasant and easy as the climb up was unappealing and laborious. After passing round, but not through, the town – which results in missing Dad when I was hoping to give him back my extra top – it's the turn of the Col d'Izoard to occupy my horizon. I've been up it before but from the other side, so I don't really know what's in store. The profile says it's not that steep, but it's definitely long.

The crowds aren't very thick for the first few miles, but once the real climb has started they appear again in their thousands (or tens, or maybe even hundreds of thousands – the year I watched the Tour go up Mont Ventoux the police said there was a crowd of 300,000). The heat is bearable, partly because the fans are not yet crowded along the roadside and partly because there are lots of trees.

Dad read me a report in the paper when we met on top of the Lauteret that said it was 35°C at the bottom of l'Alpe d'Huez yesterday and that this rose to more than 40°C in places, with the sun beating down on the road. The same report concluded that the performance of Armstrong and his main rivals was dictated in part by the need to conserve energy for today's stage. For good measure it then rather ominously added that the stage finished in Gap, 'one of the hottest places in France'.

It doesn't seem that it's breaking any records yet, but then it's only just after 10 a.m. and I am rapidly approaching 2,360 metres – nearly 8,000 feet. Well, progress isn't that rapid, but I'm going OK, especially considering yesterday's efforts. I'm also rewarded by scenery that is very grand and although it's benign at the moment (notwithstanding the risk of heat stroke) this must indeed seem a fearsome place in inclement weather. One of the great legends of the Tour is that Apo Lazaridès stopped when climbing the Izoard alone at the head of the race for fear of being attacked by bears.

I'm more worried about being inadvertently attacked by the spectators who seem to consider the cyclists among them a bit of a nuisance – although they're not as bad as the crowds on the second Tour in 1904, when an Italian rider was beaten so badly by fans of a rival that he couldn't carry on. He was spared a worse fate only when a race official shot his pistol into the air. I know we're not the real thing that they've come to see but surely they appreciate it takes a considerable effort to ride up these passes. Sometimes you'd think not, however, at least not if it means they have to control their urge to walk all over the road with little thought to anyone who might also be there. It's as if the sudden closure of the road to cars means they feel freed of all the normal considerations for other people.

Yet even this occasionally one-eyed bunch seem particularly appreciative of the efforts of the next cyclist I pass – who has obviously lost the use of his legs and is powering himself up the hill with his arms. I say cyclist – his machine resembles as much as anything a wheelchair like those used by disabled athletes and marathon runners, but in these circumstances I'd call it a trike.

He's within about a mile of the top, on the steepest slopes, and is completely involved in the effort required to keep going, but he looks like he's used to it. I wonder how easy it is to go downhill on three wheels, where you can't lean into corners like you can on a normal bike. I'd stop to ask him, but we're both a bit caught up in our endeavours so I carry on.

Just before the top, an Italian on a mountain bike goads me into a race for the finish. For reasons of his own – I think he's trying to impress his girlfriend – he won't let me past and then when he has to yield he launches a long final sprint. I satisfy myself with latching onto his wheel until the last bend and even though he tries to counter my attack I open a gap of more than 50 yards by the top. Almost immediately I regret our good-natured foolishness as I nearly cramp up in my left calf, but it soon passes.

Once I set off again I remember the descent from the Izoard takes longer than might be thought, but even though I'm prepared for it I still find it trying. The first section is super, apart from the frustrations of the crowd who are less irritating but potentially more dangerous on a descent. It also resonates with legendary Tour memories: I stop first to have my photo taken at the memorial to two of the Tour's greats – Fausto Coppi and Louison Bobet – and then carry on through the Casse Desserte, the great rocky amphitheatre in which they made their names.

Below the village of Arvieux, however, the valley is long and empty and hot. To make matters worse there is a considerable headwind, and it's not until I'm caught by a pair of cyclists working in tandem, whom I then join, that I have the impression of making real progress.

The heat now in this steep-sided valley must already be the equivalent of yesterday, but the effect of the wind is to make it seem even warmer. If yesterday was like riding in a conventional oven, today is like riding in a fan-assisted model. It's not really conducive to appreciating the charms of Guillestre, which we pass through, nor of the fine Alpine landscapes around us.

The benefits of riding in a three are so great that I'm tempted to keep going, but in the end I stop, as planned, to meet Dad at the junction with the main road because I'm virtually out of water and supplies. As soon as I get off the bike the heat is even more pronounced. Everything in the car is warm, so I drink warm Coke and eat warm bananas and melted chocolate biscuits. Then I make up an isotonic drink (warm) and gulp the whole lot before deciding to set off again.

I contemplate the main road and headwind before me and realise it's only taken about an hour to go from the satisfaction I felt at the top of the Izoard to a feeling almost of despair now. I warn Dad that even though it's only 39 miles to the finish I'm bracing myself for it taking three hours. The phrase 'I may be some time' passes worryingly through my head, although the circumstances, and the temperature, could hardly be any different. Besides, not even cycling has produced a hero on a par with Captain Oates and I've no intention of emulating him.

As I ride down the long, open road which is the principal route between Briançon and Gap, my one ray of hope is to catch, or more realistically be caught by, a group of cyclists with whom I can share the load. But the farther I go the more unlikely this becomes as there are simply fewer and fewer people about. Even the Dutch and Belgian fans who are normally content to sit in a dusty lay-by in full sunshine for hours on end have beaten a hasty retreat to the inside of their campervans.

I start to feel not just hot and tired but lonely and a bit fed-up as well and also rather foolish – cycling on nice roads in inappropriate weather is one thing, but riding on horrible roads in this heat is just masochism. Whether this state of mind is a cause or an effect I don't know, but I also start to feel physically weak. Even though I've just taken my fill of food and drink at the last stop, I feel as though I'm coming to the end of my resources.

The road may generally be tending downhill, but I labour over a succession of inclines before reaching Embrun. I spy a baker's that's open and although I don't really have an appetite I reckon I'm not going to be able to go on much longer without some more food, so I call in. Nothing takes my fancy but I choose a large, mixed-salad sandwich on the basis that it looks like it will do me good. I eat it without any pleasure, have another can of Coke and set off again.

There is no immediate improvement and I begin to think about avoiding the next two climbs on the run in to Gap. Both of these are detours from the main road and the realisation that the signs saying 'Gap 15 miles' are not for me is an added source of disappointment.

Nevertheless, and more out of momentum than anything else, I follow the signs towards the Côte de Saint-Apollinaire. I try and deceive myself into thinking that I'm going well, but I can only concentrate on one thing at the moment and that thing has to be keeping going. I've already drained both bottles that I filled up half an hour ago, and it's only thanks to the buggies that give free samples of the Tour's official water to spectators along the route that I can replenish my stocks.

Even so, I think the heat – or is it dehydration? – is beginning to get to me. Along with someone knocking on the inside of my head (presumably asking to be let out), my tongue is all leathery and my lips feel swollen as though I've been punched. Needless to say I'm in bottom gear and the looks from those at the roadside who can bring themselves to acknowledge me are of pity rather than encouragement.

The sweat and the latest application of sun cream washed off with it are making my eyes sting so much that I feel like crying. I even think at one point that it might be an improvement if I were crying, but a splash of water from my once again dwindling supplies revives me just enough to wipe my face and keep me going.

I'm not really aware of the last mile or so as the road has suddenly become genuinely steep and all I can think about is turning the pedals. It's the cycling equivalent of a spent boxer clinging onto his opponent to avoid falling to the canvas. By the time I reach the top I feel as though it could have taken five minutes or an hour – I've really no idea.

The descent passes all too quickly, and then there's another flat bit back on the main road into the headwind. The only way I find this tolerable is knowing that as long as I'm on it I'm not yet on the last climb of the day, which dutifully arrives and mercifully is not as steep as the last one. I also feel a flicker of strength returning – perhaps the salad sandwich is beginning to kick in – and this and the prospect of downhill for the last six or seven miles to the finish is enough to get me over the top. The initial downhill is not without its alarms – I never know how much to trust a melting road surface – but then it's three straight, gently descending miles to the finish, which is almost bliss.

I arrive in Gap at 2.50 p.m., over three hours since leaving the last meeting point. I'm not yet sure if I feel OK, but assume I must be. Nevertheless, I have to sit down for 20 minutes on the way to the car and send Dad on an errand for food – 'anything will do'. He very efficiently rustles up another sandwich and I eat a crêpe from a street stall before we set off again. I feel desperate to eat but still don't really have any appetite. I also drink more Coke and more water while we're on the way to the hotel, which Dad has fortunately already found.

The first thing I do when we arrive is have a cold bath. In most ways this is a good thing, given that I've had to make do with showers for several days in a row now. But why, oh why do French hotels insist on miniature baths that have no plug? My 'bath' is little more than a large bucket with a hole in it, although the ashtray (in the bathroom?) solves the problem of leaking water. However, the refreshment and relaxation are marred to some degree by the constant gymnastics required to avoid dislodging the ashtray and to keep as much of me submerged as possible.

Still, I feel better for it and watch the last few miles of the race on the telly, including Lance Armstrong's spectacular cross-country route to avoid falling over the unfortunate Joseba Beloki (I'm glad I was cautious on the melting tarmac), before dozing for an hour or two. When I wake up I try to take advantage of the fact that Dad has foreseen the difficulties of eating conveniently in Gap on Bastille Day and has arranged provisions for eating in the room. The selection of salad, couscous, quiche, crisps and yoghurt looks appealing, but my appetite has disappeared again.

I can't decide between accepting that I'm not hungry and therefore not eating anything or forcing myself to replace the vast amount of energy and resources I must have used up today. I plump for the latter and wade my way through as much as I can manage of everything that's on offer. Eventually I stop, more out of boredom than anything else, as my stomach is offering no indication of whether I've eaten enough or too much.

I join Dad at the bar downstairs, but almost immediately I start to feel a bit peculiar. I assume the night air will do me good (it does in Victorian novels), but after five minutes I need to lie down. I go back upstairs, and by the time I'm in bed I feel distinctly unwell.

## Stage 10

# GAP–MARSEILLE (137 MILES)

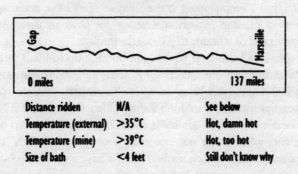

| Distance ridden | N/A | See below |
| --- | --- | --- |
| Temperature (external) | >35°C | Hot, damn hot |
| Temperature (mine) | >39°C | Hot, too hot |
| Size of bath | <4 feet | Still don't know why |

Unfortunately I don't improve overnight. In fact, I take a rather disturbing turn for the worse.

Within ten minutes of lying down I feel like I've contracted a virulent form of flu. I ache all over and feel both hot and cold at the same time. I ache in my forearms, in my elbows, in my hips – right in the bones, it seems. My right knee, which had cleared up miraculously over the past three days, feels like somebody's smashed it with an iron bar and my left knee's come out in sympathy in spite of not previously having shown any signs of frailty. In fact I feel like I've been beaten up – although I've never actually been beaten up, and I certainly don't want to be if this is how it would feel; I'd hate to have to blame somebody else for this kind of discomfort.

It's impossible to find a position that I'm happy to stay in for more than five minutes. I normally sleep sprawled out flat on my front, but this is no good – somebody is very thoughtlessly jumping up and down on the small of my back. Lying face-up is no better as my hips don't like the impression of being pulled from the rest of my body by a team of horses. I'd sit up but my head weighs several tonnes and my neck doesn't have the strength to keep it upright.

The place I keep coming back to is the open window where there's just a hint of a cool breeze. Hunched, leaning on the window sill can't look very comfortable but I can at least manage this for about ten minutes at a time before I need a change. I spend most of the time drinking. I can't consume too much too quickly as my stomach feels bloated in spite of my throat feeling parched and my tongue swollen, but I keep sipping at the isotonic drinks I've made up. In this way I manage to consume about six pints in three hours, although most of it seems to go straight through.

In spite of all this cold liquid I am burning up inside. I feel like the lyrics from an old Queen song, something along the lines of being 200 degrees and being called Mr Fahrenheit, were written for me – except that these are from a song called 'Don't Stop Me Now'. (The next track on the album is called 'Save Me', which is much more appropriate; and no, not even 'Fat Bottomed Girls' could induce me to want to ride my bicycle.) I'd have a cold bath, but the prospect holds no appeal. Besides, after ten minutes at the window I feel all shivery and need to pull the sheet over me, even though I still feel hot inside, so a bath doesn't seem like a good idea.

I want my mummy, but in her absence Daddy does a good job of looking after me. When I'm still pacing, wraith-like, around the room at 1 a.m. and showing no signs of improvement we take stock of my symptoms: thirst that drinking doesn't seem to quench; general aching; feeling both hot (without sweating) and chilly at the same time. Dad asks what I think about calling a doctor.

I've been thinking about plucking up the courage to say this myself, but as soon as Dad mentions it I suddenly find a comfortable position for the first time all night. The ability to relax is a partial cure in itself and seems to take the urgency out of the situation. I may not feel well but I can cope like this now, so we decide to leave it for a while and see what happens.

In the end I pass what's left of the night in this state of tolerable discomfort, dozing fitfully until the morning. We've already written off the prospect of me cycling any of today's stage. I can't even bear to think about getting on a bike.

In fact it takes a considerable effort to walk downstairs when I wake up. I don't want anything to eat or drink but decide a glass of fresh orange would probably be a good idea. The hotel owner brings it over and begins to ask me what time I'm starting today – we'd talked about what I was doing when we arrived at the hotel yesterday. When he sees me he changes his question to 'What happened to you?' He's a friendly kind of chap who was enthusiastic about my ride and his concern is genuine. He offers to make me a paracetamol drink, which he swears by for flu-type symptoms, and I accept. After half an hour or so I begin to feel a bit more with it and Dad and I decide the best thing to do with the day is simply to head straight to Cavaillon, where we were planning to spend tonight anyway. There's nothing to be gained in following the Tour and going via Marseille.

Even in the car the route along the Durance valley seems long and hot. It's a most peculiar valley to anyone like me brought up in the verdant landscapes of the Yorkshire Dales. In weather like this the river itself is almost imperceptible in the vast, wide, dry river bed. The stone and sand that is exposed exacerbates the feeling of heat and the scrub vegetation and stripling trees that grow up in between the periodic floods create an impression of constant upheaval.

Yet, were it not for the motorway and the main road that run parallel to each other and all the soulless concrete industrial buildings dotted in between, the valley would have a kind of dusty charm. On foot or by bike on the old roads you'd probably spend most of your time in the lee of poplars or in the shadow of the fruit groves and orchards that occupy the more fertile ground out of reach of the flood waters. Even the Spartan river bed has the merits of appearing like a habitat undisturbed by man, which is in itself a rarity to be admired.

Not that any of this makes me want to leave the relative comfort of the car and get back on the bike. Even a gentle exploration for a couple of hours has no appeal. Instead we whizz past at speeds that seem all the more artificial for having been on the bike for the past nine days. We make good progress until Apt, when there is an unexplained traffic jam backing up several miles outside the town. After five minutes of inertia we decide to put to the test my claims to be able to find an alternative route – I've lived and cycled round here for nearly two years in the past and trust that my memory is up to the job.

The decision is a success, and after the stifling heat of the main road we have a very pleasant last few miles driving through the villages of the Luberon made famous by Peter Mayle's *A Year in Provence*. Mayle lived in Ménerbes, but my favourites are the diametrically opposed villages of Lacoste and Bonnieux. Bonnieux appears like a fairy-tale citadel. It sits on top of a hill, with its buildings rising pyramid-like through a series of terraces to an ostentatious church at the top. Its aspect means that it seems to glisten in the sunshine. Lacoste, on the other hand, frowns down over the valley in between. It seems dark against the hillside and instead of a church it is dominated by the former chateau of the infamous Marquis de Sade. Lacoste gets my vote any day.

All these familiar sights help speed up my process of recovery. Even the painful memories induced by driving through the village that hosted the only bike race I'm convinced I should have won (but of course didn't) don't induce a relapse. Nevertheless, a combination of the heat and tiredness from such a disturbed night means I reach Cavaillon intent only on going straight to bed. Dad points out I've not eaten anything all day, but I've still no appetite. Besides, it strikes me as though last night's problems were at least in part the result of having forced myself to eat when I wasn't hungry. I reckon the blood that should have been used at the surface of my skin to cool me down was in fact stolen by my stomach for digestion, with the result that I overheated. Whatever the medical or physiological merits of this analysis – quite possibly none at all – it's reassuring to have settled on an explanation.

The hotel is lovely, as I knew it to be, but we've got rooms on the top floor, which is effectively the attic. This means that they are stifling, which is not what the doctor ordered. I think about asking for another room – any other room – but I fall asleep before my resolve hardens sufficiently.

I sleep for maybe three hours and wake up dripping in sweat. This is not pleasant, but I'm reassured by the fact that I'm now sweating freely again – I must at least be rehydrated. I decide that I now have the energy to face up to another miniature bath, and this time fashion a plug out of the glass with which people rinse out their mouths after cleaning their teeth (not as good as an ashtray, which has a lower profile). After five minutes of contortionist agony I refine my technique and discover a way of submerging my complete torso, which is the desired outcome given that I'm trying to cool down.

The way to achieve this is to first place your feet behind the taps and then gradually inch them up the wall until your legs are vertical – parallel to the wall. This allows everything from your hips to your neck to be under water, and would even be quite comfortable were it not for the step in the bath which digs into the back. Still, by sacrificing one of the towels to absorb this pressure I manage to stay there for a good 20 minutes, feeling better all the time.

Once dry I realise that I still feel weak but am no longer cowering in the heat. Nevertheless, I retire to the hotel lounge, which is the coolest part of the building, and watch the Tour riders do what I should have done. It looks mighty hot, especially when the main group is held up by protesters supporting José Bové – obviously names on the road don't attract enough attention in this neck of the woods.

Watching the last few miles into Marseille I feel neither disappointment nor relief at not having done today's stage. I'm simply aware that I couldn't have done it, so I didn't, although I confess to a slight sense of frustration as it was the last stage before the rest day, when I would have had a chance to recover from the mountains anyway. I am, however, full of admiration for the professionals who continue to take all that is thrown at them in their stride, even if the favourites for the race overall are happy to lose more than 20 minutes to a breakaway.

Even more worthy of admiration, perhaps, are the participants on the first-ever Tour, for whom the second stage finished in Marseille after having come straight from Lyon. Notwithstanding a couple of rest days after the epic first stage from Paris, it's a remarkable achievement to ride the 233.75 miles between Lyon and Marseille in under 14.5 hours – which is what the winner, Hyppolyte

Aucouturier, managed to do. And I should remember not to complain again about having to start early – they started from Lyon at 2.30 a.m.

I go out to phone Catherine and hope that having to tell her about my failures doesn't become any more of a habit than it already has. On the way to the phone box I walk past our old apartment and have a brief stroll around the town. It's strange to be back, especially for such a fleeting visit.

I return to the hotel in time to meet Paul, who's come to join us for the rest of the Tour. It was with Paul that I rode from Morecambe to Scarborough to establish my record for miles ridden in one day that had not been surpassed until this tour started. His arrival helps lift my spirits further, and then Dad, Paul and I all go for dinner with Lino Lazzerini, a friend from when I first came here.

Lino, in fact, is not an ordinary friend. It was he who converted me from occasional cyclist to wannabe racer and now foolish amateur Tour follower, although I don't blame him for knowing in advance the can of worms he was about to open. Nor is he an ordinary cyclist. His passion is such that he has amassed a personal museum – and to call it a museum is no exaggeration – of over a hundred bikes, with at least the same number again ready to be returned to their former glories (which means they are currently sitting, and have been for at least ten years, under a ragbag of tarpaulins in his garden).

The extent of this passion can be judged by the size of the museum, which occupies much of the large utility room to the side of the house and includes a special extension on the garage with both a shower and a bar – essential tools in the recuperation of many a visiting cyclist. We all get the tour, and pride of place in the collection at the moment is a bike of the same make and year as that ridden by Maurice Garin when he won the Tour in 1903, complete with wooden wheel rims. Lino tells us about using this as a prop when dressing up in period cycling costume for the pre-Tour celebrations of the local TV company, and he then happily dons his 1903 outfit for our benefit. He's so wiry and tanned and leathery-skinned that he could quite easily pass for the genuine article, especially with his turn-of-the-century moustache (turn of the nineteenth century, that is).

He then turns his beady eye to my bike, which I've intentionally brought to show him. When I lived here my bike at the time was a source of constant disappointment and amusement to him – in my ignorance I thought all bikes with drop handlebars were suitable for racing, but not in Lino's eyes.

Now, however, he's impressed by my new carbon-fibre mount, even though he has a bit of difficulty pronouncing Giant as an English word rather than its French equivalent. Fortunately, and unlike with Justin's dad, this time I manage to avoid a conversation about the technical bits I don't understand because he can see the answers for himself. Beside, he knows better than to ask me.

Apart from the bikes, the best thing about a visit to Lino's is the quality of the food. He is insistent on everything being fresh and anything prefabricated (or just not to his liking) is dismissed with a curt 'C'est pas bon, ça' (That's no good). The result is that he plies us with glorious melons fresh from his brother's smallholding and cured ham from his friends in the mountains. The real cooking, however, is undertaken by his long-suffering wife Collette, as for Lino to do this would mean taking up too much time that could be spent working on bikes – or more likely riding or talking about them.

Just before dinner we are joined by Guy and Danielle – or Monsieur and Madame le President as they are known, not necessarily because either of them have any official position but because of the French predilection for titles, both real and imagined, and because of their prominence in the local cycling club.

I'm disappointed to find that they were on the roadside for today's stage and had been looking out for me most of the day with their grandchildren. My first genuine supporters and I missed them. They're all sympathetic about my illness, though, and are universal in their assertion that this is the hottest summer for years, although I'm sure they also said that when we lived here in 2000. Pragmatic Lino suggests that I don't need to tell anyone about not doing the route.

Dinner of baked aubergines stuffed with mozzarella is enough for even my feeble appetite to be whetted, although I don't eat enough for Lino or Guy: 'You must eat more to rebuild your strength' etc. I protest that until now I've been eating enough for two, but they're not impressed, especially when I mention chips, which upsets their traditionalist approach to diet – 'C'est pas bon, ça'.

Lino is particularly appalled by my breakfast arrangements, insisting that I should have fresh pasta at least two hours before I set off each day. Even the explanation that cheap hotels tend not to run to this at 2 a.m. does little to mollify him. We return to the hotel and I go to bed with their admonishments ringing in my ears, already dreaming of the proper rest day tomorrow – and maybe even a proper breakfast.

# FIRST REST DAY

| Distance ridden | N/A | Hooray! |
|---|---|---|
| Duration of lie-in (after 7 a.m.) | 3 hours | Not bad |
| Anquetil diet rating | 4/5 | For the breakfast alone |

Maybe it was the prospect of a large, leisurely breakfast, or maybe it was just the stifling heat which even the fan could do little to alleviate, but either way I didn't sleep that well. The quantity was great, but the quality left a little to be desired. Fitful would be the best description.

Nevertheless, I permit myself the enormous luxury of rolling over and going back to sleep when Dad gets up at 7 a.m., and this alone compensates for any amount of nocturnal disturbance. Even better, when I finally decide to surface, some time around 10 a.m., I'm not faced with the usual parsimonious breakfast rations that so distressed Lino. Instead I can look forward to the banquet that I imagine is waiting for me downstairs.

I decide to delay the pleasure a little longer and have another cool, miniature bath. This allows me to practise once more my skills as a contortionist, and I even manage to get out quite easily this time.

By the time I arrive downstairs Paul is already installed enjoying the feast. Dad, however, has not yet returned from his morning run, which he's been trying to fit in every day. Unfortunately I think the demands placed on him by being the Passepartout to my Phileas Fogg have stopped him from being able to do this on a few occasions, but he's managing to get out most days. He also knows the lie of the land in Cavaillon, having visited Catherine and me when we lived here, so hopefully he's taking advantage of a day off as well.

Paul says he didn't sleep that well either, as a result of the heat, which at least means it's not just me feeling sorry for myself or still suffering the after effects of yesterday. Breakfast manages to console us, however, as it lives up to and perhaps even exceeds expectations (in a continental breakfast kind of way – no fry-ups here).

With a bit of luck the vast array of delicacies will restore a little zest and energy – or even *joie de vivre* seeing as we're in France – to give me confidence for the rest of the ride. Don't get me wrong, I feel OK today – especially compared to yesterday. It's just that I'd like to feel a bit better than just OK by tomorrow morning, the start of the second half of the Tour.

Both cereals and tea are still on the menu, but for some reason I decide to vary the normal routine and add a little local flavour with some fresh croissants and pain au chocolat. Add a couple of bowls full of milky coffee, with some fresh orange juice and some creamy yoghurt for good measure, and I'm feeling considerably more vibrant, even if continuing to sit at the breakfast table is the height of my ambitions for the time being.

The sin of gluttony is only just avoided, probably as a result of having two newspapers to divert our attention from eating. *The Times*, even a couple of days old, allows me the chance to catch up on things back home, and in particular the continuing pantomime that is Leeds United at the moment. How can we let Harry Kewell go for £5 million, even in this buyers' market? How is it that we only receive £3 million of this fee, with the rest going to Kewell and his agent? More pertinently, perhaps, how did such an unusual contract come into being in the first place and how do we account for the survival of a board that let this fiasco develop, allowing us to drop like a stone from high-rollers to paupers? They may have had all the right reasons for risking so much, but surely they've been shown once and for all to be of questionable competence. Even more importantly, will we have any players left for the new season?

Paul calms my growing sense of annoyance by reading from *L'Equipe* about Lance Armstrong's comments on the weather for the

Tour thus far: 'It's definitely the hottest Tour de France I've done – we've always had hot days but never like this,' he said after the stage yesterday. This is both unnerving, in that it confirms the extreme nature of the weather, and reassuring: I'm not making a fuss about nothing. Paul also reads out Armstrong's plans for the rest day, which sound quite appealing in the main: 'We'll do some training and I'll take a big nap in the afternoon. Going to see the family, the kids and take it easy. With the big time trial coming up that's the best thing to do.'

Apart from the prospect of the training ride I'd quite happily follow this regime, especially if it meant seeing Catherine and Molly. In the run up to the Tour we had made tentative plans for them both to fly out to Marseille yesterday and then stay with us as far as Toulouse, but in the end the logistics of it all proved insurmountable, at least given that spending all day in the car with a nine-month-old baby wasn't a desirable option. Still, I'm virtually halfway home now.

The need for rest and recuperation is reiterated by Laurent Jalabert in his newspaper column. His advice is for those who are suffering from some form of ailment to simply stay in bed all day if necessary, while those who are coping OK should go for a short spin simply because their bodies will be expecting it. I class myself in the former category and hope that a few hours in the car will be a reasonable substitute for staying in bed.

However, we first need to repack the car to accommodate Paul, St Christopher's law that a traveller's luggage will expand to fill the available space having been once again proven over the past ten or so days. We also need to acquire a bike-rack, otherwise Paul may have to sit on his bike in the car if we want to fit everything in. Even if he doesn't mind this the arrival of Jon in two days' time, possibly with a bike as well, makes finding a rack the day's most important task.

Fortunately, Cavaillon is just big enough to merit a Decathlon sports superstore which, while lacking the personal touch of your local bike shop, more than compensates for this at the moment by having very cheap bike-racks. They are also considerably better and simpler than the original bike-rack that was stolen in Lyon, which begs the question why the thief didn't just go and spend £20 in his local Decathlon instead.

Although the racks and the prices may be good, the store has a very strange policy on letting you try their products: we're not allowed to test the rack on the car to see if it fits because this would mean breaking the seal on the box, but if we buy it and it doesn't fit then we can get a full refund, even though we have of course broken the seal on the box . . . A scheme developed by and only justifiable to accountants, I'll wager.

Anyway, the rack fits and after a brief lunch we set off for Narbonne, the start of tomorrow's stage. The drive is longer than anticipated and involves two and a half hours of monotonous motorways in the heat of the day across the plains of the Languedoc. There is also a strong wind from the west today, the first since the Tour began, and I hope that it doesn't persist tomorrow or it would be a head wind all the way to Toulouse. I may have had the heat to contend with, but I almost fear a headwind more as it's so debilitating and disheartening to a lone rider.

The wind is also having the unfortunate effect of fanning the forest fires that have sprouted up across the south of France during this dry spell, and we see several thick plumes of smoke rising into the sky on the horizon. At least they seem a long way from where we're staying.

We arrive in the outskirts of Narbonne and almost immediately come across the Hotel B&B; in fact we can see it from the motorway junction, which is not usually a good sign. It also conforms exactly to the stereotype of cheap, modern chain hotel, being a prefabricated concrete structure with as much grace as a breeze block. Worse than its aesthetic limitations are our concerns that it will be the hotel equivalent of a storage heater, absorbing the sun's rays all day on the outside and then slowly cooking those who are on the inside.

Our joy knows no bounds, however, when we round the corner and see the sign in big letters proclaiming '*Hôtel Climatisé*' (air-conditioned hotel), and I make no apology for this euphoria. Even though I am fully aware of the environmental damage perpetrated by air conditioning units the world over, if only in the amount of fossil fuel they consume; even though I am appalled by the laziness and mean-spirited short-term thinking that chooses to build such an unsightly hotel out of materials that make air-conditioning necessary in order for it to be habitable; even though I am an avowed advocate of the kind of old-fashioned hotel with thick walls and airy rooms that doesn't need air-conditioning and that is an attractive addition to the architecture of a town; in spite of all this I will sleep here tonight without the shadow of guilt on my conscience, with not even the slightest hint of moral unease to disturb my slumbers. Right now all I'm concerned about is a good night's sleep.

Isn't it amazing how quickly principles can be discarded when your physical comfort is compromised (or perhaps just how quickly I discard my principles)? I suppose that it's this sort of attitude that sets you on the slippery slope towards justifying drug use in sport. An air-conditioned hotel room might not quite be the same thing as doping, but performance enhancement, through keeping cool and sleeping well, is definitely the motivating factor.

Anyway, we arrive at the hotel and find there is no one there to greet us. Not that we were expecting a civic reception, but somebody to tell us which room was ours would be a good start. Instead we are confronted with a sign telling us that we can use the automatic check-in machine or otherwise wait until 5 p.m. when the reception opens. It's now 3.45 p.m.

After a bit of head scratching we manage to fathom out how to use the machine but are confronted by the need for a reservation number, which we don't appear to have. Just as we're planning all sorts of malevolent retributions against such an inhuman system Dad finds the reservation number – on Catherine's mercifully comprehensive list of hotel contact details – and we manage to satisfy the requirements of the electronic receptionist.

I wonder rather uncharitably whether this is just the logical extension of the kind of traditionally obstructive, seemingly inhuman French hotel receptionist with whom generations of Tour riders and tourists have had to struggle in the past. Especially the poor touriste-routiers who had to book their own accommodation and from whom I have inherited a lot of logistical challenges – early starts, own back-up etc. Would they have preferred the surly, uninterested Frenchman of legend or this new automated version?

To add extra spice to this diverting saga, once inside the building we discover the hotel staff are in fact present, apparently in a meeting no doubt being held to congratulate themselves on the quality of their customer service. We are not impressed.

All this excitement means that I don't quite manage the couple of hours of sleep I'd been promising myself, instead succeeding only in washing some clothes, having a quick shower and dozing until I begin to feel hungry. We ask at the reception, which is now home to real people, where it might be possible to eat at 6 p.m., given the normal French fastidiousness about restaurant opening hours. To our surprise, and not least because the hotel gives the distinct impression of being in a car park at the side of the motorway, we are told there are several likely candidates, all within five minutes' walk.

They are of course all chain restaurants, and for want of any other distinguishing feature we plump, somewhat tongue in cheek, for the one called *Courte Paille* (short straw) – memo to the international marketing department: consider a name change before expansion into the UK. Unfortunately the name is an accurate warning for those unlucky enough to have made the same decision as us, and we eat an altogether disheartening meal of fatty meat and overcooked vegetables. It may be convenient – and our options at this time are severely limited – but it couldn't be described as pleasant.

We also suffer the ignominy of letting ourselves get excited about receiving the free *salade de bienvenue* (welcome salad), which turns out to be no more than lettuce in a bowl – and nothing else. I'm not sure this is the kind of welcome I'd be flaunting if I were a restaurateur.

Nevertheless it's nice to be able to take our time over eating, and Paul's enthusiasm for the rest of the trip is infectious. He's brought both his bike and his camera equipment, and is keen to do as much riding and photography as he can, although he claims to be out of shape for cycling and intends to ride no more than perhaps a leg of each stage with me

I am, of course, wary of these assertions, having had plenty of experience of the enthusiasm and vigour he brings to any physical endeavour, which normally result in me toiling laboriously in his wake. His inherent fitness never takes long to surface, and I also know how quickly the bug will take hold once he's on the bike. I reckon the only limits on the amount he rides with me will be those placed by his desire to take pictures, rather than any physical shortcomings. We'll see.

After this feast we return to the hotel for an early night and that is about the sum of our experiences of Narbonne. We're not even really sure it is Narbonne, it could just as well be Nottingham or Nuremburg for all we know. We've seen absolutely nothing of the town – apparently it has a charming old centre and was the first Roman city to be established in France, or Gaul as it then was – and know nothing more about it as a result.

We walk back past a couple of other hotel chains in this 'hotel village' and notice the coaches of several cycling teams, including the Quickstep team of Richard Virenque and David Millar's Cofidis outfit. I wonder what they think about this kind of anonymous existence. Is it simply the same reaction of relief as we had when we saw that we had air-conditioning? Or is it disappointment at another roadhouse that could be anywhere?

Perhaps they don't care, their minds simply focused on the cycling to come, but surely the emotional side of the body needs as much tending to as the physical in such a demanding three weeks as this? A nice view out of the window, a friendly chat with the receptionist, a *fin-de-siècle* restaurant to eat in . . . I'd have thought these little extras would have made all the difference between effective relaxation and the impression you're on a chain gang.

I also remember reading some comments by last year's Tour de France green-jersey winner Robbie McEwen during the Paris–Nice race saying that he for one enjoyed staying in traditional hotels in French provincial towns that he wouldn't otherwise get to visit. And this is coming from a notoriously hard-nosed competitor, one who you wouldn't have associated with unnecessary niceties. He said it gave him a chance to get a feel for a place; that's certainly not something you can do here.

Back at the ranch it's not quite 8 p.m. and with plans set for a 6 a.m. start tomorrow (up at 5 a.m.), there should be plenty of time for a good night's sleep. I'm trying hard not let the prospect of this and tomorrow's 'easy stage' lull me into a false sense of security; I think it was a degree of complacency on the stage from Bourg d'Oisans to

Gap that contributed to my problems that evening. If I'd started earlier and ridden harder to start with – I took it quite easy up both the Lauteret and Izoard – I'd have avoided some of the heat later on and would have had more time to recover. Oh, the wisdom of hindsight.

Anyway, although tomorrow may be the second-shortest road-race stage (after the final stage into Paris), it will still require considerable effort – it's only just under 100 miles long, it will take a good six hours of riding, and it includes a category-three hill which climbs to over 600 metres – 2,000 feet in old money. Until two weeks ago I'd have gone to bed apprehensive at the prospect of taking on such a ride; now I'm in danger of thinking it's too easy.

## Stage 11

# NARBONNE—TOULOUSE (96 MILES)

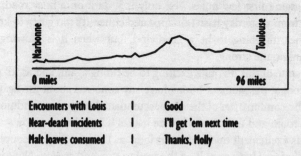

| Encounters with Louis | 1 | Good |
| Near-death incidents | 1 | I'll get 'em next time |
| Malt loaves consumed | 1 | Thanks, Molly |

The alarm goes off at 5 a.m. and it's back to the old routine of cereals and tea from the flask for breakfast. At least the cereals have changed since Bourg d'Oisans as we've finished the muesli and Bran Flakes and are now onto Special K.

To our surprise we're not the only ones up and about as we leave our rooms and put the rack and the bikes on the car (no chance of us leaving the rack outside anymore). Even more surprising is that it's some journalists from *L'Equipe* who are preparing to make an early start. They must be a different breed over here.

We have no alternative but to put the bikes on the car this morning and drive to the start even though it's less than two miles away, as the only way to get there is down the motorway. Even when we turn off the motorway onto the Tour route it's clear that it's not going to be a pleasant country lane that I'll be riding on, to start with at least.

It's also still surprisingly dark at 6 a.m., which I suppose can be explained by the fact that we're further south and further west than we have been. I realise now that my original miscalculation over the time it would be light stemmed from thinking France was an hour behind us rather than an hour ahead. This reminds me of *The Day of the Jackal* where an attempt to assassinate General de Gaulle backfired because they used last year's calendar to work out when the sun would rise, or something along those lines – not that the consequences of my miscalculation have turned out to be quite so profound.

We take off my bike again – I imagine we'll become quite practised at this by the time we reach Paris – and I brace myself for a challenging first few miles. Not only is it dark on a busy road, the wind from yesterday hasn't disappeared either. It's too gusty to know whether it's going to be a headwind, but when it is blowing it's certainly quite strong.

In spite of this it's quite exciting to be riding again, and as it's nice and cool at the moment I don't have any concerns about the heat. In fact the combination of the chill accumulated in the air-conditioned hotel room and now in the breeze makes it feel almost nippy.

This excitement doesn't last for long, as I only manage a couple of miles before I have to pull off the road to stop and stretch. Not to put too fine a point on it, my buttocks – or more scientifically my *gluteus maximi* – are very stiff. The result is that I have to lie down at the side of the road in order adopt the ungainly position required to stretch them and relieve the tightness.

Of course this is just the moment at which Dad and Paul drive past in the car, and they come screeching to a halt in the lay-by ahead, thinking something infinitely more serious has caused me to be lying on the ground in apparent agony at the side of the road. Oblivious to their concerns I get up and start leaning against a sign-post to stretch my calves and it's only when Paul arrives to ask how I am that I can reassure them it's only a touch of tightness and cramp after being off the bike for a couple of days.

Mutually relieved we all carry on, and although the wind is against me when it blows it's inconsistent enough for me to make reasonable progress. After about seven miles I turn off the main road and the combination of a quieter road and the gradual arrival of daylight makes for a distinct improvement.

After a short while cycling on my own, during which time I'm pleasantly surprised to find how well I'm going, I see two more cyclists at the side of the road. As I ride past I realise there are actually at least three of them, with possibly another in a van parked nearby. They don't notice me, as they're in the midst of making their preparations to set off, but I think I recognise them as the Austrians I saw in the distance the last time I met Jeremy, on the top of the Galibier on Stage 8.

I wonder if Jeremy's still with them and assume I'll find out when they catch me, which they should do if there are three or perhaps four of them. If we all ride together it could be a quick and pleasant ride – and I'm in the mood for some company.

Before I'm caught, however, I catch a cyclist ahead of me who turns out to be none other than Louis. There is a growing feeling of inevitability about these unplanned rendezvous – Louis seems to be the kind of chap who, once he's decided to do something, will just keep going and going. He's certainly doing nothing to dispel the Afrikaans' reputation for resilience. This is further enhanced by the fact that he looks particularly weary and uncomfortable today, and with good reason – he says he only slept a couple of hours at best last night because of being disturbed by rats and because it was cold (he left his bedding mat in Paris as it was too bulky). He also has a dodgy tummy this morning.

We talk for a while and even in his current state he finds it within him to commiserate with me for not doing the stage from Gap to Marseille. He says he didn't make it to the finish either, instead accepting an offer of accommodation from a Frenchman with whom he'd been cycling for an hour or so and who lived nearby.

Louis makes this seem the most natural thing in the world, which is all the more remarkable for his complete lack of French. He then says his new friend's hospitality also extended to a shower and a bed (for the first time since Paris), as well as being provided with a breakfast to put to shame even the one I consumed yesterday morning. Thus fortified, he caught the train to Narbonne before finding an apparently inhospitable field to sleep in last night, which has undone most of this good work. I decide not to mention my air-conditioned hotel room.

Even though I'd be on my knees in his state, and probably not on the bike, he manages to follow my wheel and we continue to ride together. It crosses my mind that if Jeremy and the Austrians catch us (with one of them on a 1947 Swiss Army bike) as well as the apparently mythical Skippy, we would make a very motley crew indeed. I wonder if we qualify as an unlikely postscript to the Beat Generation. I suppose following the Tour is a road-story after a fashion – we're all suspending the normal constraints of life to make a journey. It's not quite the free-wheeling lifestyle of Kerouac or Ginsberg, and we may not be following our whims and desires, but you could say we're all united by a common purpose, and one that most people don't understand, or even admire. Surely all that's missing are the girls and the drugs – although the Austrians may in fact have both of these.

My musings are cut short by the appearance of Dad and Paul on the road ahead. Dad's generous shopping trips mean there are plenty of supplies with which Louis can replenish his dwindling stocks. It's a very agreeable stop on the edge of town with the sun just peering above the cornfields. The Austrians – I assume – ride past while we're taking tea and croissants (no scones or cucumber sandwiches available this morning, apparently) then we too set off again.

The route is now gently undulating and makes a beeline, through fields of corn, for Carcassonne. Louis claims to be feeling much better now, and we soon pass the Austrians (who've stopped in their turn) at a reasonable pace. The Black Mountain beyond is living up to its name, shrouded as it is in cloud, and for the first time I wonder if this means we're going to have some rain – even though the sun is now fully up and doing its best to suggest a hot day is in the offing.

As we ride into Carcassonne I ask Louis if he's been before and he reveals that this is in fact his first trip to France. Not only that, this is also his first trip outside South Africa. He is astounded by the sight of the mediaeval city, even if he is less impressed by the number of more contemporary traffic lights in the newer bit of town. He vows to come back and bring his family next time.

The road out of Carcassonne is quite hairy as it's a dual-carriageway with lots of junctions, and neither cars turning onto nor off it seem to pay too much attention to cyclists. It doesn't last long, however, and we're soon onto a switchback road heading straight for the hills ahead. We enter what is obviously the last village before the day's only serious climb starts and Louis bids me farewell. Even feeling restored, his luggage is too much of a hindrance for him to maintain the same pace as me up the hills, and the cycling lore dictating that everybody rides up hills at their own pace comes into force.

The climb is not steep but has some long, straight sections which are disconcerting as it takes a while before I feel like I'm making any progress. I arrive in the very attractive village of Saissac which, in theory, marks the top of the climb and is indeed the point at which the points are awarded for the King of the Mountains. In practice, however, the village is merely part way up. The road itself, unaware of the needs of the Tour route designers, continues rising at the same gradient for another three or four miles.

Fortunately my fears of complacency last night led me to study the route profile in some detail and I am aware of this potentially dispiriting development. In fact this bit of the climb is more pleasant, as it runs partly through trees, partly through open heathland, and is more winding. For the first time today there are also fans lining the route in significant numbers and I'm reminded of the morale boost that can be provided by their cheers.

I also feel as though I'm recognising bits of the route. The only time I've been anywhere near here before was during the 1998 football World Cup when four of us drove around France in my VW Campervan (which is obviously very different to those horrible white monstrosities). We drove to Toulouse for when England were playing there and stopped somewhere after Carcassonne. It struck me at the time that it would be unlikely that I would happen this way again as it seemed extremely remote – and the campsite we ended up staying at was in fact called *Camping au Bout du Monde* (World's End Campsite). And then, lo and behold, I see a sign for the very same campsite off to my left.

If I didn't remember that it was at least another ten miles down tracks of ever-decreasing width I'd be tempted to call in since it was a remarkable place. Even though it was July when we were there we

133

were the only visitors, yet it was vast, with glorious views across the surrounding hills.

Most striking of all was the barn which passed as the dining area and the enormous rustic paintings it contained that purported to be from the end of the 1800s. These paintings were very stylised and conveyed a very romanticised view of rural life, full of scantily clad buxom maids. It gave the distinct impression of being a former artist's colony where sexually liberal Parisian painters could come and appreciate (in all senses of the word) the pure, innocent and, no doubt, earthy locals. I suppose if I were real Beat Generation material I'd go and shack up there for a few months just to see if it lived up to expectations, but as it is I decide to carry on following the Tour route to Toulouse. On the bike rather than *On the Road* for me.

It's all downhill into Revel, the next meeting point, and I make good time except for when a Frenchwoman in a car tries to run me off the road. Actually I make very good time for the next few hundred yards as I'm in hot pursuit, but of course it's to no avail and I slow back down to a sensible speed again.

In Revel Paul is all ready, kitted up in his cycling outfit and keen as mustard to join me for the last 30 or so miles to the finish. He says he's concerned about keeping up with me, but I suspect that it'll be more a case of the other way round.

After I have my daily cheese and tomato baguette and Dad has remembered to tell me that they saw Jeremy come through the previous stop a few minutes behind me (I'm glad to hear he's still going as well), we set off, and sure enough I'm soon hanging onto Paul's wheel. In part this is because he has nobly volunteered to ride in front all the way to Toulouse in order to give me a bit of a breather; mostly, though, it is down to not being used to going quite so quickly after a break. The hastily consumed baguette is in danger of making an equally hasty reappearance.

I have to ask Paul to slow down while my stomach catches up with the rest of me, but once my digestive system is up to speed I have a very enjoyable ride, now comfortably able to follow Paul and not having to do any of the work. Paul too is enjoying himself, this being his first direct exposure to the Tour and his first ride for a while. The fans at the roadside cheer us both along, and in no time at all we're approaching the finish in Toulouse. Once again it's only the profiteers and their erratic driving that threaten to undermine things, but there are enough fans to sidetrack them and we make good our escape.

We're nice and early – it's not yet 1 p.m. – so we ride without obstruction right up to 200 metres from the finish line. Paul's obvious delight at having actually ridden this close to the finish rekindles the enthusiasm and thrill I felt on the first couple of days but which I'd taken for granted a bit recently. We reminisce about the ride and note that we've arrived two and a half hours earlier than Hyppolyte Aucouturier who won the third stage of the original Tour into Toulouse. This makes us feel quite pleased with ourselves until we remember he'd come from Marseille and had actually set off at 10.30 p.m. the previous day to cover the 271.75 miles.

We then follow some rather garbled instructions towards the city centre and in spite of these make it to the hotel by 1.30 p.m. Dad's already booked us in so I go straight to the room and, after a quick shower, sleep for an hour and a half. When I wake up hot I notice the room has air-conditioning and once again put all ecological qualms to one side and switch it on, which results in a doze for another hour.

I wake up feeling as I hoped I would after such a relatively short stage as today. There is no all-pervading sense of fatigue, just an acceptable level of tiredness, and my right knee shows no signs of a relapse after its remarkable cure in the Alps. The back of my left knee, however, was sore towards the end of the ride, so it is this that receives the ice treatment.

The afternoon continues on this happy trend as Dad returns bearing a package addressed to me that he'd been given by the receptionist. It turns out to be from Molly, although I suspect Catherine had a hand in it too, and it contains not only a photo, some Tunnocks Caramel Wafers and some cereal bars, but also two malt loaves. Even better, these are the very hard-to-come-by Sunmalt brand, rather than the ubiquitous Soreen – a real coup.

I can't resist consuming a whole one immediately with a cup of tea and this adds immeasurably to the experience of watching Arnold Schwarzenegger on *Vélo Club*, the post-Tour round-up programme.

Big Arnie is obviously in training for his tilt at the governorship of California as he responds to every single question with the same answer (which basically amounts to saying how cyclists are 'remarkable athletes' in a variety of ways), just like an experienced politician.

Just before it's time to go in search of dinner Jon, the final member of what's rapidly becoming 'Team Howard', arrives. Up until a few weeks ago he was still hoping to try and ride the whole route with me, but his knees have shown no real signs of recovery so he's now not even brought his bike with him. I'm delighted that he's still come, I just hope that only being able to encourage from the sidelines doesn't turn out to be too galling given that he's also trained since Christmas for the ride. On reflection my recent performances suggest that this is more likely to induce great relief rather than frustration.

At 7 p.m. we mosey on down into Toulouse to find somewhere for dinner, stopping at a phone box on the way to call my sister, Caroline, and wish her a happy birthday. In contrast to Narbonne, we're right in the heart of the city today and are spoilt for choice. However, there are now four of us to satisfy which is initially a bit tricky until we plump for the almost invariable default option in such circumstances – an Italian restaurant. With the words of Lino and Mr President still ringing in my ears I am tempted by one of the pasta dishes – in fact I'm not tempted as such but feel I ought to be tempted – but end up being unable to resist the appeal of a four-cheese pizza.

It's a balmy evening and there is plenty of activity in the surrounding streets to provide us with free entertainment. Not that we don't converse with each other, and Jon makes Dad and me feel less inclined to bemoan the problems at Leeds by recounting the trials and tribulations that Luton Town have been facing. I think he's quite glad to get away from it all for a while.

Even though it's only a time trial stage tomorrow, which effectively means a short, easy day for me, we go back to the hotel early. Tomorrow's schedule for the pros means that I'll have to set off riding at 6 a.m., and as the start is the best part of an hour's drive outside Toulouse this necessitates a 4 a.m. alarm call. In spite of this Paul says he thinks he'll ride the route with me if I don't mind – I'm delighted – as it will be too early for much photography. Jon says he thinks he'll stay in bed if I don't mind as it is the first day of his holiday.

## Stage 12

# GAILLAC–CAP' DÉCOUVERTE (29.5 MILES)

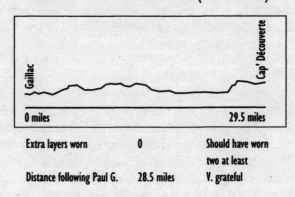

| Extra layers worn | 0 | Should have worn two at least |
| Distance following Paul G. | 28.5 miles | V. grateful |

No sooner have I closed my eyes than it's 4 a.m. and the alarm goes off. By 4.50 a.m. we're putting the bikes on the car, much to the astonishment and amusement of those just returning from a night out, who seem to be the only other people about. Whether it's simply because Paul and I are already in our cycling outfits, or more specifically because my cycling shorts are deteriorating rapidly towards a state of indecency, we draw a volley of lewd comments.

Thus inspired, or chastened, we set off for Gaillac – which appears to be a simple matter of about 30 miles away straight down a motorway. For once our assumptions are correct, and even more remarkably we manage to negotiate getting from the centre of Toulouse to the beginning of the motorway with scarce a hitch, in spite of the chaos caused by the extension of the city's underground network.

It dawns on us that this was why yesterday's stage finish was quite a way out of town at a disused aerodrome – we thought it was a strange place to choose for the race to finish. Normally the arrival of the Tour prompts an unashamed flowering of civic pride, with the most prestigious locations given over to welcoming the race, whereas yesterday there was a distinct feeling of indifference, as if the event had been shunted into a siding. The most obvious manifestation of this was, ironically enough, the absence of spectators, both at the time Paul and I arrived and then later on when we watched the stage finish on TV. Up to now the last mile or two of each stage has been packed three, four, even ten deep. Yesterday there were gaps in the crowds along the barriers up to the 500 metres-to-go marker – a very disappointing turn-out in comparison.

The journey to Gaillac is smooth and we manage to drive right into the heart of the town. The preparations for the start area are underway and we seem to have caught everyone by surprise with our presence. It also seems to provoke the gendarmes into a flurry of activity, blocking off roads hither and thither. In fact their speed and diligence leaves us momentarily concerned that Dad might be trapped as the roads are closed behind him, but then we realise they're unlikely to let him stay here if he's in the way.

Paul asks me if I've been wearing any extra layers at this time of the morning, to which the answer is no, even though it does feel slightly chillier than normal today. The only extra I have today is the picture of Molly that was in the package yesterday, which is now in my jersey pocket for luck. He seems unconvinced but I persuade him that he certainly doesn't need any more than the arm-warmers he's already put on.

Within a couple of miles of the start I feel justified in my flippant disregard for Paul feeling cold as we're flogging ourselves up a considerable incline which carries on for a couple of miles. Paul has his arm-warmers rolled down to his wrists and we both have perspiration on our brow.

Most of the road is already thickly lined with spectators, far more than at the finish yesterday. Perhaps more surprisingly, a lot of them are already up and about and alert to our presence – in fact this is probably the busiest non-mountain day of the Tour so far in terms of spectators. It's certainly on a par with the team time trial on Stage 4. The chance to see riders individually obviously holds a lot of appeal.

Maybe these are the real cycling fans, come to see the riders and the race, rather than the occasional fans who visit more for the spectacle than the sporting event. Even if this is the case they've certainly picked a nice spot for their troubles, with a backdrop of very attractive countryside. The climate's got a lot going for it as well if this nice, healthy coolness after the scorching day yesterday is anything to go by. Having said this, the descent puts a different complexion on things, and although the undulating miles that follow require us to work hard enough to keep ourselves warm I find myself longing for the first time in a long while for the sun to be fully risen. The pleasant coolness has become a distinct chill.

We skirt past the attractive village of Cordes-sur-Ciel, and then have several miles in a narrow river valley where the distinct chill is replaced in turn by genuine cold. I apologise to Paul for misleading him about the appropriate attire, which he takes well, and then he seems to decide that the only way to keep warm is to make an extra effort to ride quickly.

Whilst I'm once more hanging onto his wheel I consider the merits of this approach, as opposed to cycling slower so that the relative windspeed that does so much to influence how warm or cold you feel is reduced. It's a question I've never managed to answer satisfactorily, a bit like wondering what to do when it starts raining. Do you ride quickly, which always makes you feel as though the rain is heavier but at least gets you home sooner, or just carry on at a normal pace, which exposes you to the rain for longer?

Normally I plump for the 'fast' option in both these circumstances, although for no convincing reason, and here Paul has made my decision for me. The net result is that we shoot along and generate some enthusiastic encouragement from the fans. Then we come to the hill that signifies five miles to go, and for only the second time since Paris I decide to ignore all thoughts about tomorrow's ride and give myself free reign to ride as fast as I like – which in reality means as fast as possible. In fact it's almost not a conscious decision to do this, simply a reaction to today's more relaxed circumstances, and I seize the opportunity.

It's a wonderful feeling, and even though the hill's not more than maybe two miles long it provides a real chance to blow away some cobwebs. I feel like I'm eating up the ground, and once I reach the top my appetite is not sated. Fortunately, Paul too has got the bug and we race through the village of Blayes-les-Mines just before the finish, sprinting like maniacs up the final rise. Satisfied at last we ride gently past Dad, who's obviously found the finish all right, and cross the line before returning to the car.

It's a peculiar stage finish, a converted coal mine that now serves as an outdoor-activity centre. You can 'discover' all manner of activities here, hence Cap' Découverte (Cape Discovery); I originally thought it was something to do with explorers. The surrounding area was once a big mining area (as Blayes-les-Mines and a host of similar names might suggest), yet it's all very rural now. It's quite a shock to see run-down pit villages in what's otherwise typical rural French countryside.

It's only 7.50 a.m. and, as Paul remarks, we've already ridden a complete Tour stage. We are happy to feel smug, but to put this in perspective it's taken us an hour and three-quarters for 30 miles, which the pros will probably do later on in an hour or thereabouts.

Just as they were at the start, so the gendarmes are now trying to close the roads in the finish area with some urgency, and upsetting a number of locals frustrated by the limits placed on their movement as a result. The urgency is a consequence of the very early start for the stage today. The publicity caravan is off at 8.30 a.m. (maybe this is why most of the supporters were up and about, already jockeying for position to receive the most freebies) and with the first rider off at 10.20 a.m. this is probably the closest I'll have been to riding the route at the same time as them.

Bearing all this in mind, it's turned out to be a good idea that my mum and David, my step-dad, decided not to come and see today's stage, or at least meet me afterwards. They're currently enjoying their annual caravan pilgrimage to France and are not that far away – maybe 50 miles off. Initially we thought I'd be doing this stage at a reasonable time in the morning and we could maybe meet for lunch afterwards, but after such an early start the last thing I fancy is hanging around until lunchtime. Fortunately, we'd already decided that I'd probably be in need of a quiet afternoon even more than their encouragement, so the plans were quietly shelved. Given that there are now no meetings planned we decide to make a swift exit and return to Toulouse via Albi.

I've always wanted to visit Albi as this otherwise obscure town was one of the strongholds of the Cathars, a Christian sect that was deemed heretical by the Pope in the twelfth and thirteenth centuries, resulting in a crusade against them. Although Albi wasn't necessarily the Cathars' principal power base it became known as the Albigensian Crusade, and as is the way with these things resulted in horribly brutal acts of repression and murder. What kind of place is Albi to have been associated with such misfortune? I'll have to wait until next time to find out as we drive past on the ring road – the priority being to return to the hotel for a relaxing day and hopefully some sleep rather than enjoying an interesting but somewhat superfluous history lesson.

By 9.30 a.m. we're back at the hotel and are amused to find Jon still in bed, not least because he has a reputation for being an early riser compared to the lethargy in the morning for which Paul and I are renowned. Before going to bed myself I remember to check my phone and discover that not only is Molly capable of sending me packages she can also send text messages – a skill which I've found rather difficult to master. I suppose this goes to show what a child of her times she is: texting before she can walk, as it were.

'Njoy short stage 2day & ride like the wind 2morrow. Hope ur pair of knees r OK in Pyrenees. XOXOX Molly'. Once translated into English the advice seems to be to take advantage of today's short stage before the return of the mountains tomorrow when I will thrive, as long as my knees withstand the terrain, followed by hugs and kisses. Not bad for a nine month old.

I sleep fitfully – there seems to be no other sort at the moment – until about midday. This time it's worrying about trying to make the most of the time available to me to sleep that keeps me on edge. I suggest lunch, but Dad's tummy is feeling a bit delicate and he says he'll just eat when he feels up to it rather than come along now for his big meal of the day. I hadn't really given any thought to the trip being put on ice as a result of someone other than me being unwell

– which shows how self-centred I've become – but it's a distinct possibility. Still, Dad says it's nothing serious, just a case of having to use the loos in Toulouse rather more frequently than he might wish to.

Jon, Paul (no Ringo unfortunately) and I stroll into the centre and Paul and I immediately notice how hot it's become since this morning. It seems remarkable after how genuinely cold it was when we rode the route that it's now surely as hot as it's been. We resist the temptation to sit outside and find a very elegant restaurant with a very cheap menu that overcomes its reservations about our slightly scruffy appearance and lets us sit in the cool, shady interior – although we are quite noticeably ushered towards the back, out of sight of the elegantly attired Toulouse inhabitants who are the preferred clientele.

I tell Jon about the bike rack having been stolen in Lyon and he comes up with what would have been an excellent solution: 'Why didn't you just take one of the roof-racks from one of the team cars, like US Postal? They've got so many spare you could have taken the bikes as well, I'm sure they wouldn't have noticed.' If only we'd thought of it at the time.

After a very pleasant lunch of salad and pasta that Anquetil would have frowned on for being far too healthy (though maybe the local rosé wine would have brought a smile to his face) Jon and Paul head off for a bit of sightseeing but it's back to the hotel for me for an afternoon out of the heat in the air-conditioned room.

I write a postcard to Molly – so much simpler than a text message – to thank her for her gratefully received gifts, and then enjoy the second malt loaf as I once again permit myself the luxury of watching the Tour on TV. All the commentary is focused on how hot it is now, and sure enough the favourites for the stage all fail to better the current fastest time set much earlier in the day in more clement conditions. I also read in *L'Equipe* of how Armstrong is not the only one to take the view that relaxation is the best preparation for this type of stage: his eternal rival Jan Ullrich said that he wasn't going to do anything special last night, instead he would simply go out for a big meal.

I watch until Armstrong, the last man, has begun but then I switch off as I feel sleepy. Even though it's only 4.30 p.m. the prospect of the first long day in the Pyrenees is now looming large and I still feel as though I've not caught up on the sleep lost when I was unwell. I'm also concerned that watching the stage on TV might all get too exciting and stop me from sleeping soundly.

## Stage 13

# TOULOUSE—AX-3 DOMAINES (123.5 MILES)

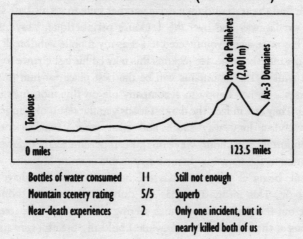

| Bottles of water consumed | 11 | Still not enough |
| Mountain scenery rating | 5/5 | Superb |
| Near-death experiences | 2 | Only one incident, but it nearly killed both of us |

I can't imagine that today's stage is going to be that difficult compared to those in the Alps. There are only two climbs, although both are late in the day, and the distance isn't that great – 123.5 miles. I suppose I shouldn't think like this as in reality it's the equivalent of an average flat stage with two big climbs added, but it just doesn't strike me as being that bad a prospect.

In spite of this relaxed attitude we're up at 3 a.m., partly so that I'll have plenty of time for the ride and partly to give us enough time to find our way from the hotel to the Cité de l'Espace where the stage begins. This turns out not to be too tricky, although it's fairly long-winded, and once again we are hailed by the slightly inebriated nocturnal inhabitants of Toulouse en route.

One lady decides to engage us in conversation while we're at a red traffic light and delights in repeating how much admiration she has for cyclists, especially those from England. This is very flattering, although I suspect her real reason for coming to speak to us is to be able to prop herself up on the car as she's none too stable on her feet. It's a nerve-wracking moment for her when the light goes green and we have to interrupt her sincere compliments but, she manages to stay on her feet and then totters off to find some more-permanent support.

We find the start and then drive another mile to get us past some dual carriageway and over the Toulouse périphérique. I say 'us' as Paul has once again volunteered to act as my mobile windbreak and ease me into the stage. He reckons this may be his last chance to ride for a while – the mountains will be the best place for him to take pictures – so he's happy to accompany me on this morning's dark roads. They are, in fact, the darkest roads yet, the result of being both early and a long way south and west, and it makes for an uncomfortable first hour. We're on quite important roads and even at this time in the morning there's a reasonable amount of traffic.

Paul, being at the front, has the head torch while I have the backlight. This means Paul has the dubious pleasure of trying to make out the road ahead without veering off into the plane trees or ditches at the side of the road, while I hold my breath every time I hear a car or lorry approaching from behind, hoping that the combination of light and reflectors on my shoes is enough to alert them to our presence. Most people – even the French equivalent of white van man – seem remarkably considerate, passing us at a respectable speed and apparently not intent on clipping us with their wing mirrors, but every now and then there's some joker who tries to put the wind up us. The worst incident, however, is when a lorry coming the other way is suddenly overtaken by a car, with the inevitable result that it strays onto our side of the road in a wide arc. Working on the assumption that he hasn't seen us we come to a halt, which is just as well as his trajectory doesn't alter and would have brought an untimely end to our endeavours.

After what seems like an eternity of frazzled nerves we arrive on quieter roads and a suspicion of daylight allows us to relax a bit. I tell Paul that until now I've quite enjoyed these early morning starts, by and large having the roads to myself and being able to appreciate the dawn in all its glory, but I can see he'll need a bit more persuading.

This relaxed and relieved state of mind is probably the reason we miss a turning. There's nothing specific to suggest we've gone off route, but I check the directions and have a nagging feeling we've been on the same road for too long. There is, of course, no way to be sure but we decide the most sensible thing to do is to return to the last point at which we knew for certain we were in the right place.

This is a real blow as it's been about five miles since the last town, but within maybe two miles we notice the junction that we had missed and manage to get back en route. There were no signs at the turn-off itself, but the straw bales at the roadside were a bit of a giveaway, and 100 yards down the road there was a tell-tale black arrow on a yellow background.

The most likely explanation for the absence of signs is the apparently irresistible temptation they afford to Tour fans to acquire a free souvenir. Most of these end up pointing anywhere but in the right direction on the dashboards or back windows of the plague of white campervans that line the route. If you're being charitable, as I have so far, you can assume that these arrows aren't taken until the Tour has passed through and the fans are actually helping to tidy up afterwards. After our little diversion this morning, however, I'm feeling less charitably inclined.

Paul continues to tow me at a good pace to the first rendezvous with Dad and Jon, yet it's still two and a half hours since we set off when we arrive. This is slow going – less than 15 mph for the 36.5 miles so far – and it appears the dark roads to start with and our impromptu detour have taken their toll. It turns out that Dad also missed the same turn-off as we did and has not been here that long as a result. I set off on the next leg alone, a bit down. It seems like a lot of this morning's effort – getting up early, Paul towing me along – has been wasted. It's after 7 a.m. and there's still a lot of the day left to do. I also feel tired. Not sleepy as such, just weary, or lacking in enthusiasm. I may be over halfway to Paris now but I'm aware how much effort has been required to keep going this far and the prospect of having to do almost the same again is quite daunting.

The arrival of the 'team car' with Paul leaning out of the window intent on taking photos of me as I cycle past endless fields of sunflowers helps to raise my spirits (as do the endless fields of sunflowers themselves, which never fail to bring a smile to my face). Paul seems satisfied with his shots, and all the attention reminds me of the Belgian TV crew, who, incidentally, have conspicuously failed to re-establish contact as they said they would. My dreams of a career on Belgian TV will have to be put on hold.

After several more miles of verdant, arable landscapes the road dips into a river valley and winds its way through a succession of attractive villages, most of which boast of their locally made *foie gras* and similar delicacies. We're in a land with a rich gastronomic heritage.

Every now and then I catch a glimpse of the Pyrenees outlined on the horizon, which should serve as inspiration but instead generates a sense of trepidation, not least because of the growing heat. The sun is fully up now and the mountains are scarcely visible through the haze.

At one point a pair of portly, middle-aged cyclists join the route from a side road just as I'm passing the same junction and to my considerable alarm manage to stay with me for several miles. In spite of their improbable shapes and ageing bikes they also manage to engage me in conversation and profess admiration for my steed. I'm aware that good cyclists can come in all shapes and sizes, and that a new bike is no guarantee of being any good – just look at me – but it strikes me as though I ought to be riding a bit faster than this unlikely pair. Eventually they tire and to my relief I begin to put some distance between me and them. Their company wasn't at all unpleasant, but it suggests to me that I'm not riding quickly enough or making sufficient effort to reach the stage finish in time, so I resolve to raise the tempo.

The apparent head of the valley turns out not to be the head of the valley at all but instead the beginning of a long, gentle climb before the road drops down to Quillan, the day's next stop. My self-chastisement has had the desired effect and I ride well up here. I stop for a pee near the top, and just as I'm about to set off again two more cyclists ride past at a good pace. In fact, I figure they're maintaining the kind of pace I should be looking for so I race after them and catch them after half a mile or so.

Once I've caught my breath and we've exchanged greetings, to my great surprise one of them says, 'You're Paul, right?' I confess that I am, and it turns out that my new companions are doing more or less the same as me and have also met Louis as a result – hence knowing my identity. However, we only stay together for a short while as at the bottom of the sweeping descent into Quillan I stop to replenish my supplies at the car while they decide to press on.

Again I wonder about sticking with them – judging by my deterioration after spurning company on the ride into Gap perhaps I should – but again I decide against it. I don't think being flexible once I've set my mind on something is one of my strong points. For the past couple of hours I've been focusing on reaching Quillan, and a last-minute change to that plan doesn't really register as a possibility until the opportunity that makes it possible has passed.

So I stop and refill my pockets, which I suppose is the practical justification for not carrying on. There are still nearly 50 miles to go and I don't want to be caught short. Chocolate bars are proving a bit of a liability in this weather, although I still take some as there's little better for instant energy, and even the bananas are taking a bit of a battering – they're fine as long as you don't mind them mashed. In fact most of my preferred foods are suffering in this heat: the supply of boiled sweets I make sure I always have in my pockets is almost back in its pre-boiled state, the malt loaf is also in danger of disassociating into its constituent ingredients and today's novelty – BabyBel cheeses, the small, red mini-Edams – is now curds and whey. It's a good job Catherine – sorry, Molly – sent me some cereal bars or there'd be nothing I actually recognise by the time I come to eat it.

After a bottle of isotonic drink I take to the road and it's immediately apparent that it's going to be a hot ride. What's more, the farther I progress along the valley the more the heat is exaggerated by the steep walls that stifle all breezes. It's quite an impressive gorge, in fact, with a fast-flowing river in the bottom and precipitous sides that rise for more than a hundred feet before tapering gradually out of view.

It will probably look even more impressive on the television when filmed from the helicopter above, or from the motorbikes brushing against the rock faces with the riders in the background, but it's not great for riding while the road's still open to traffic. The road has two lanes but is narrow and winding and the opportunities for overtaking even slow-moving cyclists like myself are few and far between. This engenders a good degree of frustration from drivers, who then make reckless moves to get past. The quality of the driving and consideration of the drivers have definitely deteriorated since early this morning, and as is always the case the most likely victim of such rash behaviour is the cyclist, but I continue to escape unscathed.

The gradient is also a challenge, being just enough to require a constant effort without ever being quite enough to make me think I ought to be pedalling as hard as I am. The difficulty with this kind of terrain is the temptation to think it's not that difficult when in reality it can be very demanding.

Even though I looked closely at the stage profile last night and saw the gradual ascent, I think subconsciously at least I'd told myself there were no difficulties until the climb proper began in earnest. A result of this underestimation is that I find I'm drinking a lot of water and realise I've already drunk one bottle in not much more than 20 miles. By the time I reach the foot of the climb, which I greet if not with excitement than at least with relief as it means an end to all the psychological games involved in riding at a gradient that appears easy but isn't, I'm well onto my second bottle. I'll definitely need to refill them again on the way up.

I realise too that the climb is going to be a tough one. I'm out of my saddle immediately and trying desperately to avoid having to use my bottom gear – a psychologically damaging development at such an early stage (I know the logical approach to riding uphill would be to let the terrain dictate which gear you need, and if that happens to be the lowest gear then so be it, but at times of great effort like this logic is an infrequent companion). Nevertheless, resistance proves useless and I'm soon in bottom gear thinking I'll be in trouble if the gradient doesn't relent.

It doesn't ease much, but I arrive in a village which I assume will be the last chance to obtain water so I at least enjoy a breather while I fill up from the local fountain. The water is gloriously fresh, and I hope this will act as an elixir – I certainly feel the need for something as the heat hasn't dissipated since I left the valley and I feel worn out.

Unfortunately, not even Pyrenean spring water has the desired effect and I toil up the rest of the climb in a way I've seldom toiled on a bike before. None of the elements that are inducing this suffering – the gradient, the length of the climb, the heat – seem overwhelming on their own, but put them together and it's a truly difficult situation.

I find myself riding at the speed of the also-rans, those occasional cyclists who try and ride some part of the various climbs on the Tour just to add a bit of spice to their experience of watching the race but without any aspirations of riding all the way to the top let alone all the way to Paris. As for the rest, the club cyclists, anybody not overweight, those who take their cycling more seriously and those against whom I normally measure myself, they are as far ahead of me today as the professionals are when I'm at my best.

I don't feel quite as bad as I did on the penultimate climb into Gap, mainly because I haven't got that terrible sensation of emptiness yet, but it's not far off. And it may well get worse, as with three miles to go I realise I've drunk all my water and I still feel parched. I say drunk – some of it was poured over my head in a misguided effort to keep cool, but either way I've run out.

It does get worse. At one point I have the distinct impression that something is actually pushing up against my feet as I turn the pedals. And it isn't only this subjective evidence that suggests I'm making painful progress. My speedometer has not just dropped below 7 mph, the usual benchmark for stiff climbs, nor even 6 mph, which is when you know it's really tough, but is now hovering at less than 5 mph – scarcely walking pace. I try and extract a Snickers from my pocket for extra energy, but at this speed and given the mush in there I can't manage so I grind to a halt. Without water to wash it down I almost can't swallow the chocolate.

This is without a doubt the nadir of the Tour so far – on the bike at least. The climb has just hit its steepest slopes and I start to consider how long it would take me to walk the rest, and if I could cope with the ignominy. I almost think it would be better to walk than continue this pathetic display of how not to ride up a hill, but I get back on – if all else fails pride will always give you an extra shove before allowing you to give up. Then, mercifully, and as if I've been rewarded for my stubbornness, the gradient eases and I can see the top. This is just the fillip I need to keep going, and I eventually reach the white line on the road and all the banners which mean no more uphill.

I wander around aimlessly for a bit until I spot a makeshift bar selling drinks. Two bottles of Coke and a bottle of water poured over my head later, I'm capable of sitting down – even this had been too much of a challenge immediately after I arrived. I begin to take in where I am.

The first things I become aware of are the vast crowds that I'd somehow blocked out during the climb. I also realise what a beautiful spot this is, with glorious mountain meadows spread on either side of the road and shapely peaks in the background. This cheers me up to some degree, but also makes me feel rather melancholy – I long for the chance to sit here in the breeze and appreciate the views for much longer than I know I have.

In fact I don't want to get back on the bike. Instead I want Catherine and Molly to be here with me so I can show them what a nice place this is; I want to stay and actually watch the race come through and enjoy the atmosphere and be part of the crowd; I want to go to some quiet, charming hotel with crisp, clean sheets and have nothing planned for tomorrow.

I stir myself from this unhelpful reverie and realise how long it's taken me to climb up here. It's nearly 2 p.m. already, almost four hours since I left Quillan, only 30 miles away (and it's not even an *hors catégorie* climb). I reckoned I needed to be at the bottom of l'Alpe d'Huez on Stage 8 at 1.15 p.m., whereas the earliest I'll be at the bottom of the last climb today is 2.30 p.m.

Instead of inspiring me to one last effort, this realisation almost makes me want to give up completely, but I have to keep going, if only to find Dad and the others who I've arranged to meet between the bottom of this climb and the last five miles up to Ax-3 Domaines.

With even less enthusiasm than a commuter going to work on a Monday morning I set off on the lonely, dispiriting descent. I try to impress upon myself a sense of urgency as not only do I have to ride up the last climb but I also have to come all the way back down again as well. It seems to take an age to reach the bottom.

When I get there I ride through the town, which is bursting with people and seems all the hotter for the noise and activity in comparison to the relative peace of the mountains, and reach the junction which signifies the start of the climb. At which point a gendarme blocks my way and says, 'No more bikes.'

And to be honest I don't know whether to break down in tears or hug him with relief. Fortunately for both of us I do neither, but I can't deny that a part of me is delighted at not having to ride up the hill. Then another part of me, obviously with more moral fibre, says I shouldn't accept defeat so easily. Wasn't I told to walk twice at the bottom of l'Alpe d'Huez?

I mull this over while sucking what used to be a boiled sweet, and watch a stream of cyclists being turned away or required to get off their bikes and walk. A handful do make it past but these are all intercepted by the next gendarme just up the road, who makes very ostentatious gestures for the benefit of his multi-national victims that no further cycling is possible.

It does still seem a bit early for an official road closure as it's only just after 2.30 p.m., but just as I'm about to chance my arm I remember the need to come back down as well. At the same time reinforcements join the frontline of gendarmes and I decide that I've had enough and that I definitely don't want to risk being stuck on the hillside in this heat, capable of neither going up nor down.

Not without a distinct feeling of shame I head for the car. As soon as I do I once again become aware of the incredible heat. I've only been down in the valley for ten minutes and I'm already getting that sort of panicky feeling that just says 'get me out of the sunshine', but the road out of town towards the meeting point is like a furnace and offers no shade.

When I reach the car Paul isn't there as he's already ventured part way up the hill on his bike to try and take some pictures of me. In fact Dad and Jon aren't there either for a minute or two. The prospect of having to fathom my mobile phone in this unbearable sunshine is just about to tip me over the edge when they appear from the campsite just round the corner. I leave Dad to put the bike on the car and head straight to the campsite bar behind Jon, who runs ahead and orders me a cold drink. As he promised, it's nice and shady and I begin to regain my composure.

Paul arrives soon afterwards, and he also has the decency to look hot and uncomfortable. He says he intended to ride as far up the climb as possible but only made it round two hairpins because of the heat. He then waited for me, and when I didn't come he thought maybe I'd had a blinder and had already made it to the top. He waited some more, not knowing where I was or what to do, when the decision to go back to the car was made for him by the gendarmes who started to close the road not just to those going up but also for those going down. In fact he says I stood no chance of making it up the climb, let alone back down, as he had to use his press card and his powers of persuasion just to ride the 400 yards down from where he was.

Hearing this is even more of a relief than the cold drink and the shade. To some extent at least it means that the reason for not completing the stage is not because I didn't want to, but because I arrived too late. The end result is the same, but the responsibility for it doesn't seem to be mine to the same degree – in effect, it was somebody else's decision.

The growing sense of despair from contemplating my own failure and inadequacies is replaced at least in part by frustration at the vagaries of road closures and the extreme heat. In the end my inadequacies have turned out to be more physical – of which I'm quite well aware already – rather than moral.

Once we're back in the car and heading blissfully away from all the hurly-burly and queues of frustrated supporters, these thoughts console me. They don't console me entirely, however, as I know that at least part of me was just looking for an excuse to avoid cycling the last five miles, but it does seem that it would in fact have been practically impossible. Perhaps sensing my continuing despondency Jon fills me in on yesterday's stage, in which it turns out Lance Armstrong suffered a surprising and surprisingly heavy defeat at the hands of Jan Ullrich. All sorts of explanations have been advanced, but the most likely reason for his below-par performance seems to have been the heat. After today, I can quite understand this. One report suggests he lost 13 lb in the hour it took him to ride the stage, which if true is incredible.

Jon's tactics, intentional or otherwise, have worked. I am indeed mollified by the implication that if Lance Armstrong can have his performance hindered by the heat, so can I, which is what I assume to be the cause of today's sluggish performance.

The irony is that I feel perfectly OK now. I'm tired and couldn't face another minute in the sunshine, but as long as I'm sitting down in the car with the window open I'm fine. There's none of the uncertainty about how I feel as there was when I arrived in Gap – I just couldn't go very fast on the bike today, that's all.

We arrive in St-Girons, the start of tomorrow's stage, and are just beginning to look for the hotel when we meet Louis. He didn't ride either the time trial or today's route, mainly because the logistics made it impossible for somebody without backup – it's just taken us an hour and a half to get here from the stage finish in the car. This goes to show the extent of the logistical demands that have to be factored in to the seemingly simple task of following the Tour from stage to stage. He's now planning to ride some of tomorrow's stage tonight so he's got a chance to keep ahead of the race. I ask where he's going to spend the night before realising that the answer will of course be a field – and it is.

We find the hotel, which has succeeded in keeping cool inside, and I have the best cold shower of my life. I start with just a hint of warm water to stop it from being too much of a shock to the system, but am soon on maximum power with gloriously icy water that feels as though it's just come straight from a Pyrenean glacier. I sleep deeply for a couple of hours before a band strikes up outside the window and continues its tuneless assault on the neighbourhood at high volume until we are driven from the hotel to find something to eat. On our way to the restaurant it becomes clear that the town is in full party mode, and we brace ourselves for a long night.

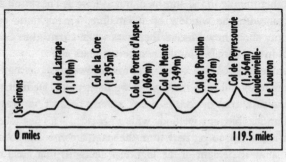

## Stage 14

# ST-GIRONS—LOUDENVIELLE-LE LOURON (119.5 MILES)

| Anquetil diet rating | 4/5 | Quality and quantity |
|---|---|---|
| Hotel opulence rating | 4/5 | Lovely |
| Quality of hallucinations | 5/5 | A bear takes some beating |
| Town en fête rating | 1/5 | 5/5 If you're a local and want a good night out |

It's a good job we did brace ourselves as last night proved to be one of the most trying of the Tour so far. The first problem we encountered was a considerable difficulty in finding somewhere to eat – most of the restaurants were full or booked-up even at 7.30 p.m. This lack of choice probably explains why our meal was one of the worst we've had. The pizzas were miserly in size and the service desperately slow – in fact it was difficult to decide which of these two elements was worse. The pizzas were so small that Jon and I ordered the same again, but the service was even slower second time around.

Hungry cyclists – or even hungry cycling fans and supporters –

don't take kindly to this kind of treatment and it meant we were already frowning upon the celebrations of St-Girons before we went to bed. I even cast aspersions on the baton-twirlers that led the parade of bands and entertainers up and down the streets: I don't understand what makes them want to do this, I mused, before Paul rightly reminded me that people might easily ask the same question of my current endeavours.

In spite of this moment of humility, the rest of the night did little to make us look more favourably on the town. I was relatively lucky as a combination of utter fatigue and earplugs allowed me to keep the window open while at the same time keeping the abominable noises from a town en fête to a background hum that only occasionally burst into a full-blown nuisance. Mind you, these occasions were certainly spectacular when they did happen, and we're not just talking about your average, drunken Saturday-night serenade. We're talking about a full civic firework display at midnight, followed by a battle of the bands at 2 a.m. (it was the spectators who lost).

What is it about towns that have names starting with St? St-Dizier has been the worst place so far for municipally inspired nocturnal disturbance and last night it was the turn of St-Girons. In spite of their names it seems a most unholy alliance.

Without earplugs and without the same urge to sleep, Dad, Paul and Jon, who were all in the same room thanks to the idiosyncratic arrangements of our host, had to choose between perpetual disturbance with the windows open or baking semi-quiet with the windows closed. They plumped for closed windows but this did them no good with the band or the fireworks, so they ended up hot *and* disturbed.

We all wake up rather frazzled from this experience and our fragile states of mind are then exacerbated by the behaviour of our host. Last night I'd spent ten minutes politely trying to impress upon him how early we were going to depart this morning – a 5 a.m. start was the plan – but he insisted he would get up and sort things out then rather than tie everything up while we were speaking. In particular he was adamant that he wouldn't give us hot water for our flask last night – instead he would provide it this morning – and no amount of gentle persuasion or robust insistence would change his mind.

This morning, of course, he doesn't surface until we are about to leave, at which point, grateful though we are for his offer, it's too late. It's a shame to leave on this sour note as he's been a friendly chap so far, accompanying Dad to the petrol station so he didn't get lost and very keen on what I've been doing. He was also remarkably impressed when I told him I was a journalist. In most cases this rather puts people off, but he requested a copy of my paper, seemingly indifferent to the subject matter. I decide against trying to explain to him that I write about construction machinery.

Maybe it's because I don't have my morning cuppa as a result but, whatever the reason, I find it very difficult to get going. The all too frequent routine of starting off on busy roads is followed once again and my lethargy makes them even less welcoming than normal. At least today I'm prepared to accept that the gradual incline along the valley floor will be more than just an easy run-in to the first climb. However, even though I'm prepared it doesn't actually help me to feel more awake or to ride any faster.

Once the main road has turned off to the left the imperative to stay alert reduces as the number of passing cars reduces. The effect of this is that it's even harder to keep myself awake. I end up almost soft-pedalling up the valley in a trance, with the conscious part of me wondering if it's possible to fall asleep on a bike. The subconscious part of me is asleep already, I'm sure. In some ways this makes me quite glad I don't have my bike computer with me (I must have put it down somewhere in my dazed state at the end of yesterday as I couldn't find it this morning). At least I can't see what speed I've been reduced to.

The only thing that stirs me is the sight of a bear in the middle of the river. At least it sure looks like a bear when I first see it, but as I idle past it begins to look more like a tree stump. Given my current state of semi-consciousness and the poor light I reluctantly conclude that it's more likely to have been a tree stump. Or could it be that I'm beginning to hallucinate? I'd prefer it to have been a bear.

Even this doesn't keep me on my toes for long, however. I try and take comfort from one of the legendary tales of cycling endurance involving none other than Jacques Anquetil, my dieting guru.

Having just ridden and won the week-long Dauphiné Libéré race, Anquetil then took on cycling's longest one-day event, the 348 mile Bordeaux–Paris, with less than 12 hours between the finish of one and the start of the next. Not surprisingly, Anquetil complained of being tired as he rode through the night from Bordeaux, and was on the verge of dropping out. Legend has it that it was only the goading of Anquetil's infamous pride by his directeur-sportif that kept him going: 'Drop out? Your name is Jacques Anquetil.' Needless to say, Anquetil went on to win.

Unfortunately, my name is not Jacques Anquetil, neither literally nor metaphorically, and this tale of true grit does little to inspire me. My name is Paul Howard – it just doesn't quite have the same ring to it, more's the pity.

To be honest, I'm lacking not just freshness but also motivation. No matter how I dress it up, I didn't manage to complete yesterday's stage, and that failure makes me feel like today is almost a pointless exercise. After not finishing the first day in the Alps I'd set great store by making sure I rode all the days in the Pyrenees. Yet this has already gone by the by for want of five measly miles yesterday, and my morale today is suffering as a result. If I weren't so tired maybe I could jolt myself out of this dangerously defeatist attitude, but so far I'm struggling. I'm not used to feeling so down on the bike – normally I'm enthusiastic to the point of singing aloud (except for Belgian TV). In fact the last thing I imagined was being chased all over France by a pessimism demon, which is what it feels like at times. *C'est la vie*, I suppose.

Finally I reach the village that signifies the start of the day's first climb and although hardly more alert I at least become a bit more focused. I also notice that this traditional, somewhat obscure Pyrenean spa resort is obviously not short of a marketing graduate or two if the sign at the entrance to the village is anything to go by: 'Aulus-les-Bains – *Centre Thermique de Cholestérol*' which roughly translated means 'cholesterol hot baths'. Whether there's any scientific justification for the implication that hot baths can reduce your cholesterol I don't know, but it suggests the sleepy little village is at least wide awake when it comes to tapping into the market for health tourism.

I embark on the climb and wonder if riding the Tour de France route on a bike would amount to health tourism. Halfway up I realise why it's seemed darker than normal this morning, and that's because it's actually overcast. Now that it's lightening up a bit I can see mist and cloud hanging on the hillsides, and it's a beautiful sight. Not just the subtle shades of green and grey that are missing when the sun's fully out, but the prospect of dampness and coolness that goes with them.

Not that this means I'm not sweating – it's pouring off me, which shows how close it is. Unlike yesterday, however, this sweat definitely gives the impression that it's cooling me down rather than just evaporating as soon as it appears. It doesn't seem to be stinging my eyes so much today either. In fact it seems an altogether more acceptable form of perspiration. I wonder if the chemical make-up of sweat changes as a result of changes to external conditions – the weather, what you ate for dinner last night, that sort of thing.

Shortly after this I realise that although the gradient is not particularly challenging I'm actually going better than I have been since I left the hotel. This is not saying much after my performance so far but I reach the top satisfied rather than relieved, weary rather than exhausted. The supporters are just beginning to wake up, perhaps stirred into action by all the noise that accompanies the installation of all the banners and barriers used to symbolise the top of a climb. They seem a cheery lot this morning, and greet my arrival with the usual array of cries including '*Vous êtes le premier*' (You're the first). Given that it's only 7.30 a.m. I'm inclined to believe them.

I ride down the other side and the coolness wakes me up a bit. In fact I almost feel back to normal until I arrive in Seix for my first halt, at which point I get off my bike and immediately feel tired and lacking in motivation again. This is made worse when I work out it's taken me just under three hours for not quite thirty-three miles. This is clearly below the kind of speed I need to keep up in order to finish today's stage, and once I realise this the effect on my morale is immediate. At this rate, and there's no guarantee I can keep up this rate as I've only done the easiest hill out of six today, I'm once again facing the prospect of a 4 p.m. finish.

I almost decide to call it a day there and then, especially when I take my first sip of tea and find it's only lukewarm (not only could the hotelier in St-Girons not provide us with water on time, he couldn't even provide us with hot water). I certainly assume the rest of the day is going to be a write-off, but I decide to keep going a bit farther, as much as anything else because Dad, Paul and Jon are so full of encouragement. I challenge myself to ride two more climbs, which would at least take me to halfway.

The next climb is the Col de la Core, which I've actually already ridden on a training trip with Jon at the beginning of June. It was cold and rainy at the time and I remember it being hard work, but I surprise myself now with how comfortable I feel going up it. It takes a while but I even get into a bit of a rhythm, something which was very obviously lacking yesterday. My speed isn't great but at least I'm feeling better. To add a bit of excitement the car keeps appearing with Jon and Dad cheering and Paul usually lurking somewhere nearby satisfying his photographic urges. It's still mainly cloudy and relatively fresh but every now and then there's a hint of blue sky and sunshine, which Paul always seems to manage to take advantage of.

The climb goes on for more than eight miles but I feel stronger and stronger the farther I go. At the top the sun comes out temporarily, although the temperature remains comfortable, and with all the spectators milling around against the dramatic mountain backdrop there's a healthy atmosphere of excitement which is infectious.

After another tea stop, this time with hot water, I begin the descent and make reasonable progress along the valley towards the Col du Portet d'Aspet, the next obstacle. It's noticeable, however, how much more lethargic I feel on this relatively flat section compared to the previous climb. My speed once again drops, and my morale is in danger of following suit, but the memory of how I felt on the climb helps me maintain some enthusiasm.

This is particularly important in the context of tomorrow's stage, which includes the Col du Tourmalet, a climb every bit as arduous and steeped in legend as those I've already ridden in the Alps. There are two other climbs as well, with the stage finishing at the top of the climb to Luz-Ardiden, which is very similar in profile and distance to l'Alpe d'Huez.

It strikes me that if I'm to have any hope of salvaging my pride in the Pyrenean stages I have to do well tomorrow, and to do that I need to be motivated, unlike this morning. So it comes as a relief when I hit the first slopes of the Portet d'Aspet climb and once again feel some strength in my legs. The combination of this and some positive thoughts running through my head means I veritably fly up. At first I try and hold myself back, worrying about the prospect of what's to come, but in the end I just can't resist the sense of enjoyment on a bike that I've been craving and that can only be found in feeling good on a climb. I get faster and faster all the way to the top, and on two consecutive occasions catch Paul by surprise as he's in the middle of setting up a shot.

He manages, nevertheless, to make it to the top in time to record my exhilaration as I cross the line. This is where I had set my sights on reaching when I left Seix, and I'm now feeling so good that I'm tempted to carry on. However, a look at the watch – it's already 11.30 a.m. – confirms the unlikelihood of being able to finish today's stage in its entirety. In spite of my recent improvement the damage has already been done: by my lazy decision to set off at 5 a.m. instead of 4 a.m.; by my tiredness after yesterday's stage; by the terrible drop in motivation I suffered this morning that compounded the damage caused by the previous two problems.

I decide to stop, and part of me feels uncomfortable with the decision simply because I'm quite all right to ride a bit more – for the moment at least. On the other hand, I know that a larger part of me thinks this is the right thing to do. I can't sweep away the very real fatigue I felt this morning and no matter how good I feel now, the longer I go on the more likely it is this will reappear tomorrow.

Nor do I want to risk damaging the fragile confidence that has just been restored by the last two climbs. If I overdo it today, instead of feeling enthusiastic about tomorrow I'll just feel intimidated again.

I actually ride down the far side of the hill in order to be able to pay my respects at the memorial to Fabio Casartelli, who died in a fall on this descent during the Tour in 1995. Once I've been rejoined by the others and we've put the bike on the car and set off again it becomes clear how near he was to the bottom of the climb – maybe only with half a mile to go. This seems to make his death all the more tragic.

I spend most of the journey to Bagnères-de-Bigorre vacillating between being disappointed for having stopped again, or rather for having let myself get into a position where I ended up stopping, and feeling delighted with my enthusiasm for tomorrow. In the main it's this latter sentiment that wins out, and it's probably thanks to this new-found peace of mind that I sleep like a baby once we've arrived at the hotel. I sleep for four unbroken hours, my most successful afternoon sleep yet. The only downside to this is that I once again miss watching the Tour on the TV. Once I do wake up I find out that I've missed possibly one of the most exciting days in recent Tours, with third-placed Alexandre Vinokourov, the revelation of the Tour, on the attack once again.

This inability to even keep up with what is going on is proving to be one of the biggest frustrations of trying to ride the Tour route myself. In some ways I feel so close to the event, and yet I'm able to follow it less than I usually do at home. Apart from the good fortune of sharing the hotel with the fdjeux.com team I've not even seen a single cyclist, let alone watched a stage live.

We decide not to eat in the hotel restaurant, which is obviously one of the more exclusive destinations in Bagnères, and instead decide to chance our arm in town. We end up in a very unprepossessing brasserie, mainly because it seems the likeliest place to be able to serve us before the early hours of the morning – Bagnères is also a town preparing to party. Unlike last night the meal is simple but superb and is served with an entirely unexpected efficiency. I have a hot goat's cheese salad followed by chicken and chips, a meal which sounds very dull but is sublime. Dad, Paul and Jon are all equally satisfied.

Over ice cream we have a discussion of the problems of coping with the heat, a discussion which is brought about by Armstrong's continuing travails – yesterday he too found the Port de Pailhères hard and lost more time to Ullrich on the last climb. Armstrong's perspective on the issue of hydration is reassuringly blunt: 'Well, the problem is when you drink water, all you do is pee a lot. Water's great, but you reach a point that you're just passing it through and if it doesn't contain the proper minerals and salts, it won't be absorbed. You can't just put it in your mouth; you've got to have IVs and a big bottle of saline when you lose 7 or 8 kilos in a race . . . What are you going to do, drink 8 litres of water at one go?'

Up until now I've been reluctant to accept that the heat, apart from when I was ill in Gap, has had a deleterious impact on my performance. Yet I suppose he's right about the water – after all, I drank nearly two litres in about eight miles yesterday, and that still wasn't enough. And if you're not keeping sufficiently hydrated I suppose your performance is bound to suffer.

Fortunately it looks as if the really hot weather has now broken, so I'm hoping for some more clouds tomorrow. I'm in bed by 9 p.m. and fall asleep dreaming of drizzle.

# BAGNÈRES-DE-BIGORRE—LUZ-ARDIDEN (99.5 MILES)

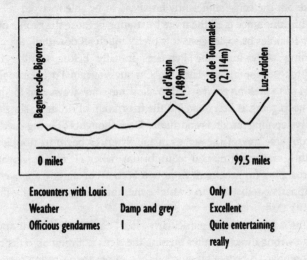

| | | |
|---|---|---|
| Encounters with Louis | 1 | Only 1 |
| Weather | Damp and grey | Excellent |
| Officious gendarmes | 1 | Quite entertaining really |

The air of civility and gentility that pervaded Bagnères-de-Bigorre was obviously not misplaced: they may not have had a party last night but if they did, it must have been a very civilised one. No raucous bands, no civic firework displays. In fact nothing from the list of 'Top six things to keep you awake at night when you really need to sleep to recover from a long day in the hills' that Jon was driven to compile yesterday after our experience at St-Girons.

The result is a fresh troupe that sets out at 4 a.m. prompt, the second-earliest start so far. Only on the stage to l'Alpe d'Huez did I start earlier (by four minutes) and that was longer by more than 35 miles, so I ride off confident that I should at least have plenty of time to complete the route today – fingers crossed.

Unlike the past couple of days this feeling of hope and expectation doesn't disappear as soon as I'm on the open road. Instead, it takes at least a quarter of an hour before I'm becoming nervous and downbeat, and for once the cause is more than just my physical or mental frailty. I am on a tiny country road with no lights and no traffic, and with the moon obscured by clouds I can't actually see where I'm going. Well, I can teeter along at maybe 10 mph, at which speed the feeble beams of the head torch just about allow me to make out the verge sufficiently far ahead to be able to avoid it.

This hindrance is all the more frustrating because the profile of the next 15 miles or so suggests it is pretty much all downhill, the route heading away from the Pyrenees initially before turning back towards the mountains later on. On such terrain I'd been looking forward to making good speed to allow me some leeway on the hills.

I keep going as best I can but the frustration of riding so slowly on this welcoming terrain is enormous. Dark thoughts of being fated not to complete any of the stages in the Pyrenees begin to trouble my recently restored mental equilibrium when I realise a car is approaching from behind. Although at first I'm slightly annoyed by its apparent reluctance to overtake me, the penny eventually drops that it's Dad.

This is a great relief, particularly after I earlier saw him disappear in the wrong direction after missing the signs pointing onto the road I'm on now. I'd been a bit worried that, rather than turning round to correct his error, he would carry on to the day's first meeting point and just wait for me there.

On the next straight bit he draws alongside and, after a cheery wave from the bleary-eyed occupants, gives the impression that he's about to head off – at which point I wave frantically and manage to make him concerned enough to stop. I explain my predicament, and in doing so realise how inadvertently beneficial it had been when Dad had been following me and I could see clearly as a result of his car lights. We decide the best thing to do is for him to continue to follow me and light the way – and this works a treat. The road is quiet enough for Dad not to be pestered by cars wanting to pass him all the time, and apart from the odd, twisty downhill section which I can negotiate faster on the bike than he can in the car, he manages to light up the road ahead of me admirably.

After the long descent there are half a dozen small climbs, three of which apparently merit the award of fourth-category status. I can't actually tell which of these is which but I succeed in forcing myself to keep up a good pace and before too long arrive in Lannemezan, the day's first stop.

Dad manages to locate some very appetising croissants and pain au chocolat and I wolf these down, keen to stock up before the real mountains. As it's still overcast and even threatening rain I also pack my cotton rucksack – a freebie from the last time I visited the Tour – with an extra top, cagoule and woolly hat. Given the weather to date this could well seem overly cautious, but I couldn't cope with the irony of now succumbing to the wet or cold having previously suffered so much in the heat.

After an unplanned detour via a petrol station a mile or so down the wrong road – which at least has the advantage of allowing me to use their toilet facilities – I set off on the part of the stage that I imagine will be the most boring. It seems that every stage in the mountains, whether it's the Alps or the Pyrenees, has to have at least one section on a main road in the valley, and this is today's offering. I suppose it's simply the topography of the area that dictates this route choice, and that also requires the largest valleys to be the principal communication corridors.

As it happens today's section is quite short and sweet, the large timber lorries with trailers that sway sickeningly from side to side and that carry very dangerous-looking implements mounted on the back being the only blight. I also see Dad driving back down the valley towards me, meaning that the climb is closed to cars and he'll have to take the alternative route to our next meeting point.

It takes me about an hour to reach the foot of the Col d'Aspin and I still feel fresh and enthusiastic as I start the climb. This feeling is only enhanced by the lovely countryside through which I'm cycling, and the wonderful peace and quiet after the busy main road. The crowds of people walking up the hill to find their preferred vantage point thin out quite quickly as it's still early and I'm left with a few bleary-eyed occupants of campervans and some fellow cyclists for company.

Although I ride within myself to start with I can feel that I have rediscovered my mountain legs and I begin to reel in the riders in front of me with some ease. Once again I find it difficult to resist the temptation to ride as fast as I can and towards the top I begin to hammer it.

This is the same sense of enjoyment and freedom as I had on the last climb yesterday. Everything is favourable at the moment. The climb is serious but the gradient not too stiff, the weather is ideal – clouds draped over the lush green hillside – and the scenery beautiful. And I'm feeling fit enough to take advantage of all this good fortune.

In the last half mile before the top I pass a familiar figure hunched over the handlebars on a bike laden with bags. It is, of course, Louis. I reach the top jubilant, and a minute or two later Louis joins me, equally pleased to be here on such a pleasant morning. The top of the climb is just below the clouds so we can see down both sides of the pass and appreciate the scale of our surroundings. We're at just under 1,500 metres, nearly 5,000 feet, and the wooded hillside through which we cycled is just being replaced by more open grazing and pastureland.

Louis tells me he too didn't finish yesterday's stage and has also been struggling to motivate himself to keep going. Given the haphazard nature of his journey so far I find this hardly surprising as I've found it hard enough even with very specific goals. He says he just wants some time to appreciate the mountains. He went off route yesterday at one point and says it was so quiet and peaceful he didn't want to try and get back on the route again. We agree how nice it will be once we can wake up in the morning without having our route or timetable set out for us in advance.

Nevertheless, I'm still feeling quite bullish about the rest of today's stage and I set off on the descent while Louis remains behind to contemplate the scenery. In spite of my cagoule and extra top it's quite chilly, which is in stark contrast even to yesterday when it was still very humid. Today it feels as though the heat that's built up over the past couple of weeks has finally dissipated.

The ride down to Sainte-Marie-de-Campan is charming, and the village – or perhaps more accurately hamlet – is packed with cyclists and pedestrians heading for the infamous slopes of the Tourmalet. It rapidly becomes clear that Dad won't have managed to get anywhere near in the car, and I'm about to set off again without having stocked up when I spy Paul. He looks rather out of breath and for good reason: he's just run about two miles from the car in order to bring me a bag of supplies.

What's more, he's been standing there for a minute or two wondering how on earth he's going to attract my attention in all this hurly-burly. The simple answer, as it turns out, is just to stand there looking slightly concerned until I cycle past, which I do. I very gratefully take advantage of his efforts, although I only need to refill one bottle, which just goes to show the difference between today's conditions and those of two days ago. I then set off again on one of the Tour's legendary climbs.

Part of its legend stems from the fact that it was first ridden as long ago as 1910, becoming the Tour's first climb over 2,000 metres and it's been the most frequently visited obstacle ever since; part from the incredible exploits played out on its slopes. None of these are more tragic, in a sporting context, than the misfortune that befell Eugène Christophe in 1913, who broke his forks on the descent to Sainte-Marie while leading the race. Showing incredible fortitude he shouldered his bike and ran the nearly nine remaining miles to the village where, following the very stringent race rules of the time forbidding any outside assistance, he mended them himself at the local blacksmith's. He even shrugged off being penalised more time for letting the stable boy pump the bellows for him and continued the stage and the race, in spite of losing over four hours, eventually finishing seventh overall.

Judging by the look of the village as it is now I'd say he'd have difficulty in finding a forge in which to effect his repairs, but that's progress for you. In fact he'd probably have more chance of buying a new pair of carbon-fibre forks like mine than mending his old steel ones.

I currently have a more mundane and certainly less heroic concern – an irresistible call of nature, which proves to be very difficult to satisfy given the hordes on the road. After a couple of miles I'm forced into using a very indiscreet location but at this point I can hold out no longer. No one bats an eyelid.

This is a great relief (in all senses of the word) and, fortified for the climb to come, I start picking off the cyclists ahead of me, the vast majority of whom are Spanish. There are plenty of them as well, so this is a very satisfying game, not that it's entirely fair as no one ahead of me actually knows I'm trying to catch them. Well, I say that, but I think every cyclist riding up a climb knows full well that they're fair game for anyone below them, while at the same time it's perfectly legitimate to chase anyone ahead of you.

I start off fairly steadily, even letting a couple of people come past me, but being careful not to let them get too far. I then begin to feel increasingly confident in my abilities and, even though I have the prospect of another long climb to come after this one, start once again to ride freely. I recatch those who had come past, and then move on to new targets, all the time checking the road behind me for likely rivals. What a delightful contrast this is to the self-restraint of the Alps and the terrible feeling of helplessness on the Port de Pailhères only two days ago.

Perhaps because of the Tourmalet's reputation, or perhaps simply because it's later in the day, the crowds don't dissipate at all on the way up. In fact they seem to thicken as I ride towards the ski resort of La Mongie, maybe two-thirds of the way up the climb. They are singularly encouraging today as well, and this helps me maintain my rhythm through the steepest section just before the resort.

Once in La Mongie it's almost impossible to avoid the spectators, but by now I'm far too focused on keeping going as fast as I can to worry about them. The last couple of miles are hindered by a gentle headwind coming over the top of the pass but, although it's stretching a point a bit at times, I manage to avoid both being overtaken and using my lowest gear.

Consequently I arrive feeling very pleased with myself, not to say smug, and I purposely allow myself to enjoy the moment. Once my ego has had a couple of minutes to deflate I also enjoy the magnificent views from the top.

Again I feel the temptation to stay and appreciate my

surroundings, although it's a less benign environment than at the top of the Port de Pailhères or the Col d'Aspin – the mountains are more jagged and it feels more exposed. I am also helped to resist this temptation to stay by the fact that I feel comfortable still and confident that I will have little problem completing the day's last climb to Luz-Ardiden. Even so I allow myself 20 minutes in which time I eat a cheese sandwich prepared from Paul's supplies.

I don my cagoule, as although the sun is now out there's still a distinct nip in the air up here, and set off on a descent that must seem perilous in a race situation. In fact it's a blistering descent as long as you don't mind the abyss at the side of the road, but in stark contrast to not having been overtaken on the way up any number of cyclists come shooting past me on the way down. I wonder if they really do feel entirely confident that they're in complete control or are just prepared to take some risks.

In what seems no time at all – compared to some descents that have been as interminable as the climbs – I arrive in Luz St Sauveur before the day's last obstacle. It's another hot, busy little town that seems to be overwhelmed by the people and paraphernalia of the Tour, and again it provides almost no opportunities for a discreet pee stop. In the end I just about get away with going behind a wall, but the proximity of an American family with two young children causes me no end of concern. I can't help imagining their puritanical horror were I to inadvertently become exposed and fear being sued for damaging the psyche of their offspring.

Fortunately this doesn't happen and my coarse, European behaviour goes unnoticed. I ride the first half-mile of the climb before deciding that the sun's presence and the renewed heat mean it would be prudent to once again refill my bottles. I stop at what appears to be someone's front garden where they have very enterprisingly set up a cold-drinks stall. I say enterprising, it could be seen to be profiteering at the price I'm charged, but I really have no choice and I don't care that much either.

I deliberately set off again while eating a banana, in order to ensure I ride at a sensible pace. I feel fine but there's just a hint of me beginning to run out of energy – perhaps not surprising after the past two climbs – and I decide that discretion is the better part of valour.

This is a shame as there are obviously a lot of cyclists who are riding up the climb at a very good speed, indeed some as fast as they can. It would undoubtedly have been a more worthy challenge to try and ride up here without being overtaken, but I decide I'm not going to succumb to the temptation.

As it is, my more moderate pace allows me to enjoy the spectacle afforded by the fans at the roadside who are already several deep. As at l'Alpe d'Huez, the colour that dominates is orange, but unlike the mainly Dutch crowds in the Alps the source this time is the proliferation of Basque supporters. Dressed in the orange of the Basque Euskaltel team and sporting Basque flags – a sort of green and red version of the Union Flag – this is by far the largest single group within the crowd. It's probably French followed by Spaniards and then Americans next (there are a lot of trans-Atlantic accents).

It's a real carnival scene and once again there are any number of weird and wonderful machines being propelled up the hillside to add some spice. There are several brave souls towing trailers containing one or even sometimes two children, and tandems are almost two-a-penny. My favourite, however, is the man riding steadily behind his lady cycling companion with a video-recorder in one hand, filming her every move. Given that they're riding significantly slower than me there will be over an hour's footage if he keeps recording right to the top. I wonder how many family friends or cycling club members will have this interminable home-made documentary inflicted upon them back in the States? (They are, of course, American.)

The last couple of miles see the road climb out of the trees and reveal the magnificent setting for the stage finish. I'm so intent on appreciating this that I almost ride straight into the wall of gendarmes forcing everybody to call a halt to their ride only 300 yards from the top. It's not yet 1.30 p.m. but I turn round and head straight back down before they try and tell me the road down is now also closed, as happened at l'Alpe d'Huez. Within less than a mile I see Paul riding up towards me. I make it clear that he should carry on and that I'll wait for him to rejoin me before heading back down together.

As I wait, however, the inevitable happens and an overly officious young gendarme takes it upon himself to stop riders going both up and down. He then proceeds to make a complete fool of himself as he tries in vain to stem the tide of cyclists – given that he can't watch both directions at once he's as effective as a sieve holding water. This only serves to make him increasingly irate, and the indifferent attitude of his colleagues up and down the road seems to drive him to distraction. At one point he even chases forlornly after a rider going downhill who has slipped the net – unsurprisingly he fails to catch up with him – provoking cheers of mockery from the vocally anti-establishment cycle fans.

Realising what's happening Paul walks amiably past the distracted officer and then ten yards farther down the road remounts. I join him and we make good our escape, leaving *Carry on Gendarme* to play itself out in our absence.

After a couple of hectic miles where the number of people on the road makes descending very tricky, we turn off onto the side road that Paul came up. We follow this all the way down to the valley – it looks like Paul had a steeper climb than me – and find the car within a few hundred yards of the bottom.

We pack away the bikes in high spirits – I'm delighted that I've completed the stage and feel in good shape, and Paul is delighted at having ridden his first Pyrenean climb. We then set off for Pau, marvelling at the number of people still walking up the main valley road in the full sunshine. They're obviously Tour supporters as they have all sorts of cycling paraphernalia with them, but the vast majority look singularly ill-equipped to cope with the demands of this kind of forced march. What's more, the human crocodile goes on for several miles, and apart from the arduous and unpleasant walk it's not even certain that they'll make it to the route in time to see the riders go past given how far they've got to go. It looks vaguely like a tide of refugees.

We arrive in Pau just in time to see Lance Armstrong's remarkable performance on the climb to Luz-Ardiden on the TV. In spite of being knocked off by a spectator – which prompts his closest rival Ullrich to wait for him in an act of great sporting chivalry – he launches a devastating attack not just to win the stage but to put himself back in the box-seat for victory in the Tour overall.

We head into the centre of Pau in search of dinner and apart from a moment's concern when the electric front passenger window doesn't close – prompting all sorts of incompetent attempts to fix it until it is finally mended by the simple expedient of slamming the car door as we are about to drive back to the hotel – we have a very pleasant meal. This is made all the more relaxing by the knowledge that tomorrow is another rest day. For once we're in no rush to get back to the hotel to be in bed by 9 p.m.

# SECOND REST DAY

| | | |
|---|---|---|
| Anquetil diet rating | 4/5 | If only for lunch |
| Duration of lie-in | 2 hours | Could have been better |
| (after 7 a.m.) | | |
| Size of bath | 4.5 feet | For large small people? |
| Hotel opulence rating | 0/5 | Truly awful |

The height of decadence! Not only did we stay out until after 9 p.m., it wasn't until the debauched hour of 10.30 p.m. that we were back at the hotel. The pleasant meal and the balmy summer's evening, sitting in an elegant town-centre square, combined to brush away the fatigue for an hour or two and allowed us to indulge ourselves. Paul and Jon even toyed with the idea of going to the cinema, but decided they'd better not overdo it.

I say indulge ourselves – the meal hardly scored highly on the Anquetil diet rating, but it did present us with another opportunity to debate the age-old dilemma of the Italian restaurant: whether to eat pizza or pasta. Given that you're undertaking some serious physical activity – such as cycling the Tour de France route, perhaps – pasta, with all its carbohydrates, would always seem to be the better choice. This is supported by cycling lore, as extolled by Lino and Guy at least, which has all the professionals eating pasta for breakfast and then again for dinner, it being the only food that can replace all the energy they've expended.

Yet this attitude never really reflects the reality of your average Italian restaurant, which is that pasta dishes are almost invariably half the size of any self-respecting pizza. Pasta may be better for you, but surely this is no good if it doesn't actually satisfy your appetite. What are you supposed to do – order two spaghetti bolognaises?

Last night Dad, Jon and I plumped for pizza and were delighted by both the quantity and the quality. Paul chose pasta and said it tasted lovely, which may well have been true but seemed only to exaggerate the disappointment that was written all over his face at the size of the dish. Another round to the pizza eaters, I think.

After such a relaxing evening, it's a shame that this morning we awake to discover just what an unpleasant hotel it is that we're staying in. We already knew from last night that it has a singularly grumpy and unwelcoming proprietor. We also knew that the outside was a challenge to the concept of beauty, and that the location – a mile and a half out of the town centre, on the main road to Bordeaux, opposite a supermarket car park – left a little to be desired.

Now we know a lot more – more than we would like, in fact. The garage, for instance, in which we parked the car last night, is a dead ringer for the multi-storey car park in *Manhunter*, the prequel to *The Silence of the Lambs*, where a burning body strapped to a wheelchair made a fleeting appearance. It doesn't inspire confidence.

Worse than this, however, as I discover when I go for my morning shower, is the state of the bathroom. There is such a variety of fungus and mould growing up the untiled wall at the head of the bath that were George W. Bush to know about it he'd probably declare war on France for harbouring biological weapons. It would certainly take more than a team of UN weapons inspectors to give it a clean bill of health.

The most disturbing aspect of all this is the fact that I had a bath last night without noticing – as a result of my head leaning against the offending wall rather than looking at it from the shower. Paul and Jon are equally disappointed with their room, although the bath does at least have tiles all the way round. Hotel Atlantic in Pau: not recommended.

This takes some of the shine off an otherwise relaxing morning – apart from our alarm going off at 3 a.m. and then Dad going out at 7.30 a.m. I slept undisturbed until after 9 a.m. To cheer ourselves up we decide to have breakfast in the delightful supermarket café over the road which, although open in the sense that you can walk in, turns out to be closed in the sense of them being able to provide you with something to eat or drink. All the staff are there, they're just waiting for the official opening time in five minutes.

This could be frustrating but in fact it gives us the chance to go to the supermarket next door and buy the croissants and pain au chocolat that the café doesn't provide. By the time we return the green light has been given and we manage to overcome our lack of tokens and obtain some coffee.

We mull over the fact that the caffeine in the coffee we are consuming is on the list of substances banned by the Union Cycliste Internationale (UCI). This is just another facet of the fact that cyclists – and those in other sports – are no longer trusted not to abuse otherwise normal, everyday substances in a bid to improve their performance.

This mistrust has led to the curious list of banned products – including caffeine – that has been compiled in an attempt to compensate for our lack of faith. But even this, essential though it may be, leads to confusion over what is or isn't a 'performance-enhancing substance', which is in itself a strange and misleading euphemism. After all, all competitive sportspeople try to enhance their performance, and I readily use substances that I think are going to enhance mine. It just happens that boiled sweets, malt loaf and black tea aren't on any list of proscribed substances (other than a dietician's, who would probably ban all of them for any serious competitor).

The problem is that some substances – like malt loaf and tea – are part of the normal range of products that people (well, some people at least) consume on a regular basis. Also, their purpose is not explicitly to improve the physical performance of an athlete (they may or may not do this) but first and foremost they nourish and provide the energy and vitamins required to live a normal, healthy life.

The bigger problem with defining what is and what isn't 'drug abuse' or artificial performance enhancement in sport is the fact that all practical, enforceable definitions inevitably result in an arbitrary line in the sand. One side of it is cheating, the other side of it isn't, even though it's only a question of degree.

This is the case with the coffee that we're now consuming with enthusiasm, and the performance-enhancing caffeine it contains. It is only deemed a performance-enhancing substance, however, above a certain concentration – presumably because it is accepted that some amount of caffeine is present in normal diets and therefore cannot be ruled out completely.

But where do you draw the line? How many espressos do you have to drink before you are over the limit? Will all Italian cyclists be able to drink fewer cups of coffee than their Belgian counterparts simply because their coffee is stronger? And would anybody consider it cheating even if you did drink ten espressos before or during a race? Wouldn't you be looked on instead with pity as the poor fool who'll make himself ill and not be able to sleep that night? I suppose the point is that you could boost your caffeine levels without the hassle of drinking lots of coffee, but its presence in a perfectly normal and legitimate substance – coffee – just emphasises the problems of drawing a line.

Then there's the different physiology of individuals and how they react to certain substances, which makes it hard to justify generalisations about permitted levels. There's no doubt, for instance, that consuming the same amount of coffee would result in different concentrations of caffeine in the blood of the three of us, just the same as how we can't all tolerate alcohol to the same degree. Would one of us overstep the limit and therefore be a cheat and the others not?

Or take EPO as another example. Until recently this was the drug of choice for cyclists (and other athletes, such as long-distance runners) who wished to artificially enhance their red blood cell count (and therefore the amount of oxygen the blood could transport, resulting in improved performance). Not many people would say this wasn't cheating. But what about spending some time training at altitude? This has the same effect of increasing the proportion of red blood cells – and unless you're born in the Himalayas and happen to pop home for the weekend for a bit of training it could be said that the process is also an artificial one. The cheating involved in using EPO is not the outcome, necessarily, but the shortcut taken to get there. Altitude training is much more time-consuming and hard work than having an injection of EPO.

The sad thing is that drawing up this kind of list – and creating these kinds of problems – results in even less trust in the riders not cheating in the first place. What's more, any number of banned substances can actually be used as long as you have a doctor's note. Which makes me wonder if I should have a doctor's note for the ibuprofen gel I've started putting on my knees again (not my right knee anymore, which is still miraculously cured, but the back of my left knee which is now starting to show signs of wear and tear).

The stuff I'm using is from Tesco, and although I recognise that it contains a performance-enhancing drug (the 'non-steroidal anti-inflammatory agent' ibuprofen Ph. Eur.), it doesn't seem to me that I'm cheating. But, were I to be racing and using this, would I fail a drugs test? For all I know it's just the kind of thing that might easily appear on the list of banned substances. Would I end up, like so many athletes, saying it was an 'honest mistake' and trying to convince a sceptical public that I really had just nipped into a supermarket to get something for my sore knee?

In fact the only reason I'm using this particular substance is because Dad remembered that he had it in his first-aid kit. But for this coincidence I might not be using anything at all. I don't even know for sure that it's having any more of an effect than simply as a placebo that makes me feel better – although this in itself would be performance enhancing.

All this rhetoric is enough to drive us into town to consume whatever food it is that we feel will allow us to enhance our relaxation this afternoon. This is the first opportunity since Paris to stay in the same place without any need to ride or drive anywhere, and it would be foolish not to make the most of it. On the last rest day we had to drive to Narbonne, and even though we spent two nights in Toulouse there was the little matter of the time trial (and getting up at 4 a.m.) to punctuate the day in between.

Relaxation through food – perhaps it should be called 'culinatherapy' – is a favourite pastime and one that's easy to indulge in France in general and Pau in particular, and now that time is on our side we choose our lunch spot carefully. In the end we select the cheapest and least pretentious option in another elegant, leafy square where we feast on good, wholesome fair – I have a very lovely and large salad with ducks' gizzards and bacon. Both the food and the surroundings are as conducive to relaxation as we hoped and it appears that Pau lives up to its reputation as an attractive place.

It also has a reputation for having a mild climate that enticed English settlers in the nineteenth century and that led to its being known as the most English town in France, whatever that means. Today, however, it's rather grey and muggy, although certainly not as hot as it has been.

The mugginess generates inertia and we turn to that other famous relaxation tool – the newspaper. Or newspapers, rather, for we've treated ourselves to *L'Equipe* and *The Times*, which, rather disappointingly, is the only English paper we can find. The English influence can't be that pervasive. After Armstrong's resurrection yesterday the majority of commentators, on both sides of the Channel, appear to make him favourite to hold off Ullrich and win his fifth Tour. The margin – only just over a minute – is not sufficient for certainty, however, and there is unanimity in the assessment that Armstrong has been pushed harder than ever, and that the Tour is better for it.

All this excitement tends to add to my sense of frustration at not having really managed to follow the Tour as closely as I would have liked. Even Dad, a cycling fan through circumstance rather than any inherent passion, is keen to see some of the Tour in the flesh. Maybe the last few stages will give us a chance to do this. They should certainly be a bit easier logistically as we're back to a section of the route in which the stages are flat (after tomorrow) and therefore I should arrive at the finish sooner and with more time to spare ahead of the race. As a result we might have a bit more of an inclination to find things to see and do rather than simply heading straight to the hotel for me to sleep.

Also, the drives between the end of one stage and the beginning of the next aren't so pronounced (until we head up to Nantes) so this should give us some more time. In fact Bordeaux hosts a stage finish and a stage start so that could be our best bet to see the real thing.

Another benefit of this more continuous route should be the rediscovery of the feeling of moving smoothly from A to B that has largely been lost as a result of the transitions between finish and start towns in the Pyrenees. For the first ten days the Tour followed an almost uninterrupted route, with only small transfers between stages. This meant that there was a very satisfying feeling of being on a genuine Tour – something that's a rare luxury for those like me constrained to spending most of their time cycling round-trips to and from home. Since before the Pyrenees, this has been lost to a large degree and the route has felt a bit contrived – as if it was looking for difficulties rather than just taking what stood in its way. It will be nice to cover some distance in a straight, or at least natural, line again.

Perhaps as a result of this feeling I'm succumbing to the temptation to think that it's nearly all over. I suppose this is all right as long as I remember that the finishing post is in sight rather than thinking I've already made it. In fact in some ways I welcome it, as I'm starting to get excited about reaching Paris and this in itself is quite encouraging.

First things first though, and tomorrow promises to be another tough day in the mountains. The reports from the *Etape du Tour* which covered this stage last week suggest that it lived up to its reputation as a real challenge, the Col de Bagargui in particular. I'm not exactly nervous about it but I am intrigued to see how I'll cope with the gears available to me, as a lot of people have suggested a triple-chainset would be necessary to ride up it.

Yet I just can't bring myself to believe it's that difficult. Even if it's as steep as some people have said it's not in the same league as some of the passes at home – in Yorkshire or the Lake District – which have pitches as steep as 1-in-3. I guess the difference is that they tend not to go on for seven or eight miles, but then if you average the gradient of the Col de Bagargui out over its length it's around 11 per cent (1-in-9). It can't all be steep. I suppose I'll find out for definite tomorrow.

I go back to the hotel for a doze while Dad, Jon and Paul explore the town and then we reconvene for dinner at the supermarket café.

It's a bit of a contrast to lunch and it's certainly not cordon bleu, but once again it's a question of convenience outweighing culinary preferences. Anyway, the food is perfectly edible, and it has the considerable merit of allowing me to be in bed by 8.30 p.m. I set the alarm for 3 a.m. – for what will hopefully be the last time.

## Stage 16

# PAU—BAYONNE (123.5 MILES)

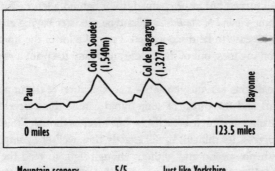

| | | | |
|---|---|---|---|
| Mountain scenery | 5/5 | Just like Yorkshire | |
| Officious gendarmes | 1 | It only takes one | |

I wake up with a sense of excitement that befits the fact that this is the last day in the mountains. I'm keen to get away, and after getting over the shock of being back on cereals and tea for breakfast we pack up and set off very efficiently. I suppose we're a practised unit in this respect now.

We have to drive out of Pau to find the beginning of the racing route – we even negotiate this with some aplomb – and it's at the entrance to the suburb of Jurançon that I start riding. By 4.15 a.m. I'm on the road again. Even though it's a main road there are insufficient lights for me to see or be seen clearly, and because it's a main road there's enough traffic to make being seen a priority. In fact there really is a lot of traffic, which I find hard to explain until I see a sign for Saragosse/Zaragoza – I must be on one of the main Pyrenean crossing routes into Spain.

The amount of traffic doesn't perturb me too much as the road is nice and wide, but it makes life very difficult for Dad as he tries to follow me at cycling pace in the car. While French drivers seem to have a good deal of tolerance for cyclists they seem to have none for their unofficial support vehicles.

Fortunately, I turn off after only a few miles onto a quieter road, which turns out to be a real switchback. Once again there is only one hill of category-four status, yet there are any number of ups and downs. There seem to be an unhealthy number of dogs about this morning as well. So far none of them have appeared on the road as they've all turned out to be chained up or behind a fence, but when there's some *Hound of the Baskervilles*-type monster baying at you in the dark it's easy to be disconcerted. I spend a lot of the time quite literally on my toes, out of the saddle and ready to sprint away from trouble.

Maybe it's this nervous tension – a combination of the impending mountains and the threat of some rabid canine that's developed a sudden dislike for English cyclists – but I feel as though I'm making good progress. It's difficult to tell exactly how well I'm going in the dark, with no speedo and without enough light to read the route description I've carefully folded and stuffed up the leg of my shorts, but I certainly feel good.

I am reassured when these apparently good sensations are given some grounding in reality and I arrive at the first stop of the day. I reach the appropriately named Arette – a French homophone of fishbone, ridge and, most pertinently, 'stop' – at 6.05 a.m., only 1 hour 50 minutes after setting off. As with the other mountain stages the stops today are dictated by the terrain as much as simply dividing the stage into four equal sections, with the result that I've only actually covered about 27.5 miles since Pau – but that's not bad going over such undulating terrain.

Maybe it's the pleasantly cool mountain air – in spite of the gloom of an overcast morning we can make out the proper mountains rising into the clouds only a few miles down the valley – or maybe it's just our hunger at another early start, but either way the *boulangerie* comes up trumps with possibly the best croissants so far (I liberated Dad from his task as chaperone a mile or two before the town so he could locate an open baker's). They are so good that I risk tarrying longer than I ought to, but I goad myself into action, once again carrying some spare clothes in my cotton rucksack.

Just as I'm about to set off, three cyclists speaking English to each other come past at a reasonable speed, and the prospect of an Anglophone group to accompany me on some of the route is the final catalyst to leave. I race after them and catch them just past the edge of the village.

I discover that my new companions – Dave, Rich and Pete – are old hands at cycling this route, having done the *Etape du Tour* last week and having been here on holiday since, which has given them a chance to ride some of it again on at least a couple of occasions. They must be gluttons for punishment as today's plan appears to be to ride as far up the first climb, which is fast approaching, as they can, before turning back at 7.30 a.m. to rejoin their families. At this point they will then cycle back up the climb to watch the Tour come past. As if that's not enough Dave, I think, will be towing at least one of his children in a trailer behind his bike. 'We'll try and bag a few normal cyclists,' he says with a glint in his eye. Before they turn back they add their own warnings about what lies ahead to those I've already heard.

First up is the Col du Soudet, a climb rarely frequented by the Tour. The initial slopes are very steep, although they only last maybe a mile before a more tolerable gradient is established as the road winds through alternate woodland and pasture. It's lovely and peaceful, not least because there aren't that many spectators, the probable cause of which is the fact that the police have already closed the road, considerably earlier than normal for such a little-known climb. It's also very still and the cloud is hanging on the hillside as there's not a breath of wind.

It's quite a contrast to the hectic scenes of most of the climbs so far, in particular to the heat, activity and crowds of the Alps. The higher I get the more peaceful it becomes, and every now and then I'm comforted by the smell of woodsmoke from a roadside campfire. I'm in danger of drifting off into a reverie and wishing I were a supporter watching somebody else ride past, but the climb carries on for long enough for me to need to concentrate on the matter in hand.

As I wind up and up, now surrounded completely by woodland, I actually reach the level of the cloud and start to cycle through it. Even though I'm continuing to work hard and the gradient is still significant, the damp makes it almost cold enough to want to wear an extra top. Nevertheless, it's a wonderfully refreshing sensation to have drops of condensation from the cloud coalescing on my brow rather than beads of sweat. This is the kind of weather I normally associate with mountains – or at least the hills of the Dales, the Lakes and Scotland – rather than the unrelenting sun of the past few weeks.

I'm still revelling in these familiar conditions when things get even better. I come through the clouds into bright sunshine and am privy to a cloud inversion. The valley below from which I've come is covered in cloud but above me the peaks are clear and bathed in morning sunlight. All of a sudden I'm in a different world made up just of mountain tops and ridges descending into a cotton-wool sea. The icing on the cake is provided when I come out of the woods onto a rolling limestone moorland even more reminiscent of home than the weather earlier.

I stop at the top of the climb to admire the fantastic views and to recover, as, although my legs felt fine on the climb, I feel tired (no surprises there then). Perhaps as a result of this tiredness I'm so intent on getting every morsel of energy from one of the last bits of Catherine's fruitcake that I absent-mindedly pick up a few crumbs that I dropped on the road. I don't usually worry about eating things that have been on the ground, but I should perhaps have been a bit more careful this time: as I stuffed the crumbs hastily into my mouth I bit hard onto a piece of gravel. To my relief I haven't lost any of the front tooth that took the brunt of the impact, but I can feel that it has a nice new serrated edge, sharp enough to cut my tongue on.

It's now quite cold – all the spectators at the top of the climb are in trousers and warm coats – so I don all my extra layers and my woolly hat for the descent. A descent which turns out to be every bit as hair-raising as any I've come across so far. The road seems much steeper on this side, and it is certainly much narrower – it's a genuine country lane, and not the kind of road you see the Tour using very often, even in the mountains.

This steepness and narrowness means that in the next valley the sense of isolation from the rest of the world is pronounced. I cycle past the sign welcoming me to the first village only to discover that it's not really a village in the usual sense of the word. There is no centre – instead the 'village' is just a collection of farmhouses dotted around the valley sides, the whole lot spread over two or three miles.

Apart from it being clear that this is a remote, infrequently visited area, the penny drops that I'm now actually in the heart of the French Basque country, as some of the place names would suggest – the Plateau Iratzordoky, for example, and the Col de Bagargui that's still to come. Then there are the French place names on signs that have been crossed out and replaced by their Basque equivalents (the language is so different I have to assume they're the Basque equivalents as I am unable to deduce this from any obvious similarity).

If this sudden linguistic shift weren't enough then the proliferation of signs and graffiti proclaiming ETA, the Basque terrorist movement (or freedom fighters, depending on your point of view), removes any lingering doubt. There are also calls to release all Basque prisoners, a demand that was brought to widespread attention a couple of years ago during the Tour. Three men with bikes, dressed up in the yellow, green and polka-dot jerseys of the Tour and wearing numbers displaying how many Basque prisoners there are, jumped over the barriers on one of the Pyrenean climbs and proceeded to ride up the hill scarcely a minute ahead of the race itself, throwing Tour commentators and race fans alike into great confusion.

These signs and graffiti also lend a rather sinister edge to the peace and tranquillity of today so far. Maybe it's the perennial fear of an attack by ETA – or just a demonstration by their supporters – that has prompted the police to close the roads so early, and this restricted access is presumably why the supporters are a bit thin on the ground. This is a shame as the Basque fans have been responsible for a large part of the atmosphere in the Pyrenees so far.

As I turn into the adjoining valley and begin the gentle pull up to Larrau, the day's second meeting point at the foot of the Bagargui, I suddenly feel very weak. I am worn out and hollow, and I realise that I may be in trouble. These are symptoms that every cyclist dreads.

The dread stems from knowing that you are on the verge of

'bonking', which for a cyclist is a very serious situation and, perhaps unfortunately, does not relate to any unlikely indulgence in sexual activity on a bike. Instead, in the cyclists' lexicon (the only other sport I know to use this term is fell-running), 'to bonk' means to suddenly run out of energy through a combination of over-exertion and lack of food. In terms of seriousness as a handicap to continuing a ride it's on a par with falling off or mechanical failure. Once you've bonked, as with the more carnal interpretation of the word, there's often no way back.

In this situation, only urgent action can save the day, so I immediately empty the remaining edible contents of my pockets into my mouth: a squashed banana, two boiled sweets and a Penguin biscuit. I have a swig of water and begin to soft-pedal the three remaining miles to Larrau. If only I had some malt loaf, one of the few things I've found to offer some guarantee of overcoming the 'bonk'.

As it is I'm on dwindling reserves and in a foul temper at my folly when I come round a corner halfway up the Côte de Larrau just before the village and see Dad's car parked at the side of the road. At first I'm cross because this isn't where he's supposed to be, and in my current state I don't want to get off the bike on a hill as I may not get going again.

In fact, so self-pitying am I that I'm about to remonstrate with Dad for changing the plan when I notice both he and Jon grinning widely at the side of the road. I then catch sight of Paul, ready with his camera trained on a spot just ahead of me and I look down just in time to see the immortal words '*ALLEZ PAUL HOWARD*' painted on the road before I cycle over them.

All at once I am smitten with guilt for how I was feeling and great pride at seeing my name on the road along with all the others. I'm also slightly baffled – perhaps as a result of having blood-sugar levels that are a bit awry – and can't quite work out how it got there.

The obvious answer is that Dad, Jon or Paul painted it, but for some reason I can't get it out of my mind that it might already have been there and they just came upon it by chance. It crosses my mind that both Martin and Chris from the cycling club at home rode the *Etape du Tour* over these very roads so maybe they'd painted it while they were here. Then again, the prospect of them cycling the route with a can of paint in their pocket and being able to write my name on the road while 8,000 other cyclists were riding by seems unlikely . . .

Dad drives past as I'm in the middle of this muddle and I eventually stop, as planned, in the village. Three croissants laced with myrtle jam and a cup of tea later and the worst of the bonk – and the apparent delirium it induced – has passed. This much is clear when I finally cotton on to the fact that it was indeed Jon who was the main culprit for my personal graffiti. He says he felt like a naughty schoolboy, although no one else seemed to mind. Apparently he bought the paint in Toulouse and there have been several frustrated attempts to use it already. I'm still too incoherent to express my appreciation fully, but I think that he gets the message.

While I'm finishing my recovery and making sure I've enough supplies to see me safely to the next stop, Paul sets off on his bike in order to take advantage of the last opportunity to take some pictures in the mountains. Five minutes later I set off as well, and almost immediately begin to feel the consequences of the rather mixed diet of the past half an hour. To put it simply, my tummy is in turmoil. I manage to ride up the gentle slopes at the start of the climb but it becomes clear that I'm going to have to find a secluded spot for a comfort break if I want to avoid the risk of 'effort-induced incontinence' on the steeper slopes ahead.

The only problem is finding somewhere secluded enough for my needs (and right at this moment I need more than just a tree to stand behind). The slopes at the side of the road are too steep to be safely negotiated by someone in cycling shoes, and every bit of flat ground is covered by hordes of supporters as a result. It's getting desperate when I spy a bramble-entwined route into the undergrowth. I decide that I'll have to sacrifice the skin on my legs for the greater good and a few minutes later emerge scratched but enormously relieved.

I can now concentrate on the rest of the climb, which straight away becomes much steeper (it also becomes much more open, making my sense of relief all the greater). The scenery is the lushest and greenest so far, and the overcast weather means I could quite easily imagine myself in the Lake District. The steepness of the road also encourages this perception, and I'm soon in my bottom gear (39 x 25) and nervous about what's to come.

However, the legendary steep slopes that make everybody want to get off and walk never materialise, and in reality it's reasonably comfortable. I say this – I'm out of the saddle in bottom gear for long stretches, but I never get to the point where legs and lungs are burning. It's also possible every now and then to sit back in the saddle for a breather and change up a gear once in a while just to vary the rhythm. I even manage to make an effort to look composed as I cycle past camera-toting Paul, who shouts encouragement before snapping away and then beginning the climb in his turn.

Towards the top the crowd is thick for the first time today and, as usual, seems completely ignorant of cyclists trying to use the road. There are also two new hurdles to my smooth progress. First is the van that sells copies of *L'Equipe* and that is almost as irritating and dangerous as the cars of the unofficial profiteers that pester everybody on the flat stages. In fact, judging by the prices they're charging for the 'official paper of the Tour', they're just as guilty of profiteering as well.

Second, and more endearing, is the wet paint on the road from all the exhortations and encouragements to the riders. I feel my wheel slipping on several occasions as I ride over recently completed works of art, and one beautifully crafted 'Lance is God' is almost smeared beyond recognition as I slide my way across it.

At the top I regain my composure and have a look to see if Paul is coming, but the hordes mean I can't see anything. I decide that, rather than waiting here and getting cold with another climb still to come, I'll wait at the top of the next climb instead. I set off and the far side of the col is as attractive as the climb itself. Then, almost before I know it, I'm at the top of the last serious climb of the whole Tour.

I eat a banana and wonder if it really is downhill all the way to Paris now, which is the impression I get as I look over the Pyrenean foothills descending gradually into the vast plains around Bordeaux. Paul joins me, and we fly down the beautifully smooth and sinuous descent feeling like it's the beginning of the summer holidays.

We arrive at the next rendezvous point at exactly the same time as Dad and Jon, who have been forced by road closures to travel into

Spain on a long detour before being able to rejoin the route. I've still got 37.5 miles to go and it's already after midday, so I don't stop long as I'm in a hurry to get to the finish. It also seems like the faster I ride the faster I'll be in Paris and it will all be over, even though I realise that I can't make tomorrow arrive any quicker.

No sooner do I set off than the notion of downhill all the way to Paris is quickly dismissed. In fact it's a real roller-coaster ride all the way, with the only advantage for a passing cyclist like me being the fact that the overall trend is downhill, meaning the descents are slightly longer than the climbs. In spite of the terrain I have the bit between my teeth now and I make good progress – to the delight of the vast crowds that make up for the relative absence of fans on the mountains earlier. They seem a knowledgeable rather than just enthusiastic lot, with one man enquiring after the gear I'm in as I ride past, although I'm unable to make the translation into French quickly enough to tell him the answer (39 x 21, as it happens).

At one point, with only eight miles remaining, I receive a massive ovation which turns out not to be for me but for the group of three Americans who've just succeeded in catching me. They're really motoring and I think twice before deciding to latch onto their wheels, but in the end I can't resist. It becomes clear they're taking it in turns to ride a kilometre on the front, and to my relief I find I can maintain the required pace when it's my shift. It's also clear that they're aiming to ride right to the finish, and that there's the prospect of a sprint for the line, which is like honey to a bee for me, starved as I have been of the excuse to let my hair down.

I quickly work out that I'll be off the front when it comes to the last kilometre, and decide to put my head down when it's my last turn to lead to try and draw the sting of the others, while I'll have a chance to recuperate at the back after my efforts. This probably explains why I ignore the half-hearted attempts of the gendarmes at the side of the road to stop us. I say half-hearted – they'd have to barricade the road to stop me. I just decide to assume they don't really mean it. Unfortunately they do and we are soon chased down by some very irate gendarmes on motorbikes, complete with flashing lights and sirens.

Perhaps carried away with my efforts, and frustrated at missing out on the sprint, I try to brazen it out, flashing my press pass to all and sundry and saying we're allowed through. This seems to be on the verge of working when a particularly obstreperous officer threatens to confiscate my pass if I don't comply with his insistence that the route is now closed. I'm forced to yield.

And so it is, somewhat with our tails between our legs, that we have to find an alternative route to the finish. This proves a bit awkward, and in spite of arriving at 2.15 p.m. (having covered the last section in only two hours, which I'm delighted about) it takes another half an hour to find the car, with the scope for my afternoon nap being reduced with every extra minute.

Nevertheless, we're quickly on the road for the hotel in Dax, which turns out to be as pleasant as the one in Pau was tawdry. An even bigger boon is that we arrive just in time to watch the stage finish, with the remarkable Tyler Hamilton, complete with broken collarbone, holding off the remnants of the peloton for a glorious solo victory. Not only this, he's covered exactly the same roads as me in precisely half the time I needed, if you include stops (which I couldn't have done without, so I suppose I should include them).

After a brief doze to recover from the ride and the shock of once more seeing how much of a gap there is between me and the professionals, we eat in the hotel restaurant. The simultaneous request for hot water for the flask and ice for my knee confuses the staff for an instant, but in the end they manage to provide both.

I retire to bed, confident now that I should make it the rest of the way to Paris with no more hiccups. The only cloud on the horizon is the deteriorating state of my left knee – which is very sore at the back now, hence the ice – and the general aches and pains that are taking longer to get rid of with every passing morning. Still, I shouldn't complain. I've got off lightly so far and I suppose that after 19 days on the road some degree of physical wear and tear is to be expected.

## Stage 17

# DAX–BORDEAUX (113 MILES)

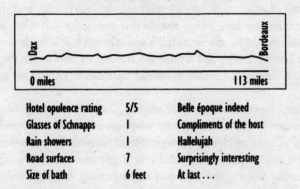

Dax

Bordeaux

0 miles                                          113 miles

| | | | |
|---|---|---|---|
| Hotel opulence rating | 5/5 | Belle époque indeed | |
| Glasses of Schnapps | 1 | Compliments of the host | |
| Rain showers | 1 | Hallelujah | |
| Road surfaces | 7 | Surprisingly interesting | |
| Size of bath | 6 feet | At last . . . | |

Even in the context of the trials and tribulations of previous mornings, today's start must rank as one of the most traumatic. In theory it should be nice and easy as our hotel is in the centre of Dax and, with the neutralised section being very short, there is no need for us to put the bikes on the car. Indeed, we start to ride straight from the hotel. This happy state lasts no more than a mile, however, as it becomes clear that Paul and I have missed a turning and are no longer on the correct route. To compound our error we then try and make our own way across the outskirts of the town to get back on track, rather than returning to the site of our original mistake.

The end result is that we get more and more lost until we eventually arrive on the slip road of a dual carriageway – even in our distracted state we realise that cycling down this in the pitch black would be a mistake too far. Fortunately, Dad has followed the same misleading course as us and we agree to put the bikes on the car once he can find a suitable place to pull over at the side of the road. Unfortunately, suitable places don't seem to exist on the slip road so we end up spending a harrowing couple of minutes on what passes for the hard shoulder, strapping the bikes on to the car as quickly as possible, in constant fear of an unobservant lorry careering around the bend towards us.

What's more, at this point – part way down the slip road – Dad can no longer turn round so we're in danger of going further out of our way before finding the route again. This development is only avoided thanks to a quick study of the road map and route instructions by Jon, which reveals that two miles down the main road we should be able to turn left and take stock at least. In this we are at last successful, and it turns out that we are now a mile into the stage, so Paul and I decide to offload the bikes again and get under way.

Then, in view of the time already lost this morning, we are confronted with one final irony when an automatic level-crossing closes in front of us and we wait several minutes while the world's longest goods train passes by at 10 mph. Eventually, at 5.30 a.m. and more than half an hour after first starting riding, we begin the day's stage in earnest.

All this distraction at least means that I don't have to worry about my sore left knee right from the start. Unfortunately, as soon as we are moving along at normal speed it becomes obvious that it's hurting more than yesterday. I try a variety of positions on the bike to see if these manage to alleviate the pain in any way, but to no avail. It's not enough discomfort to make me not want to ride, but it does feel as though rest rather than repetitive pedalling would be the most likely cure, and with 300 miles still to go I'm considerably less confident about the ease with which I'll reach Paris than I was last night.

At least the next few miles turn out to be spectacularly straightforward, even if they are through forests that are distinctly eerie at this time in the morning, and provide us with the chance to settle into the normal routine, sore knee notwithstanding. Not only are these first few miles straightforward, they're pretty much straight as well, which I think is a sign of things to come. The Tour guide describes today's stage as following the long, straight roads for which the Landes of Gascony are famous, while the profile shows hardly a blip – the day's high point is only 79m above sea level.

Dad follows in the car for the first hour until it's light enough for us to manage on our own, while Paul does another grand job of towing me along. The climbs of the past few days seem to have whetted Paul's appetite for the flat, and I benefit to the tune of riding faster than I normally would while at the same time expending less effort thanks to being in his slipstream. In fact, he's obviously enjoying himself as he raises the possibility of continuing for the whole of the day's stage, the only thing that's holding him back being the prospect of taking some more pictures with the endless woods as a backdrop.

I'm keen for him to keep riding, not for the incredibly selfish reason of wanting to follow his wheel all day, but for the still fairly selfish reason of being delighted at the prospect of company on what seems likely to be a slog on flat roads. He says it really depends on the weather and whether it's good enough for photos.

We arrive in Morcenx at just after 6.30 a.m., having covered nearly 25 miles in little more than an hour, which reflects the bowling-green flatness of the roads as much as any great effort on our part. Although flat, the terrain has once again dictated the location of our stops as the Landes appear to be very sparsely populated and the next town is not for another 12.5 miles.

My knee has improved slightly as we've gone on, so I feel quite pleased as we enjoy our break. However, as soon as we're off again the soreness returns, although in some ways I take this as a good sign, one meaning there is a definite link with being properly warmed up. I vow to stretch more thoroughly during the remaining stops.

Paul has decided to keep going, for the time being at least, and we've pencilled in an extra intermediate stop in another 15 miles or so for him to assess the weather again. At the moment it's difficult to tell if the greyness is a result of the early morning or a layer of high cloud. The one thing that is clear is a marked weather front out to our left, probably somewhere over the Bay of Biscay, as we can see the clouds and the heavy sky lit up by the sun that's rising on our right. We assume the flatness of the terrain means that we can see far enough for this to be tomorrow's weather rather than today's, but it's difficult to be sure.

The possibility, however unlikely, of rain urges us on, and we inadvertently goad each other into a continual increase in speed. This is great fun, and we're flying along at over 20 mph, but as we reach the extra stop at Trensacq I vow to try and tame our pace a bit if Paul decides to keep riding all the way to Bordeaux. Today's profile may make the stage seem like a walk in the park but memories of crawling to the finish of long rides after having let myself be carried away early on (and yesterday's near bonk) make me cautious. It would be unfortunate, to say the least, for a fit of over-enthusiasm on such a simple stage to scupper the rest of the ride, especially with Paris so close.

Paul does decide to continue and is quite happy to moderate the pace to look after his ailing, conservative riding companion. In fact he says he was already wondering if we were perhaps going too fast, and then unintentionally makes me responsible for the success of the rest of the day by saying he'll judge his pace by the speed at which I ride. Still, we ride well in tandem and it's not long before we pass through the village of Sore, which describes my knee admirably.

After another brief stop at St-Symphorien, Paul's calculation that today wouldn't be a good day for pictures is found to be sound: the farther we ride the more indecisive the weather becomes, with shafts of glorious sunshine penetrating thickening cloud. A few more miles and we're even confronted by the first rain of the whole Tour so far. It's no more than a five-minute cloudburst but it's heavy enough to give us a thorough soaking.

Although not something either of us would have asked for, this actually provides some welcome relief from the interminable, straight roads. To start with, for maybe the first 30 miles, these are quite interesting, or at least they have some novelty value. It's not often you get the chance to cycle along roads that are as straight and flat as these – six miles without a bend was not unusual this morning. The countryside that accommodates these roads is also novel to start with – apart from the odd area that has been cleared for cultivation it's a continuous mix of pine forests and heathland.

In the second 30 miles, however, these attributes can become a bit wearing and it's easy to pick holes in their charms. The forest, for example, is rather monotonous compared to the mixed, deciduous woodland of home; the heathland seems more like scrub than the attractive grazing land of the New Forest or Ashdown Forest, and so on.

By the time you reach the third 30-mile section, which happens to be a touch over halfway for our ride today and where we are now, things really get quite desperate. Not only do we almost welcome the rain shower for the distraction it causes us, we actually start keeping an eye out for changes in the road surface to bring some kind of variety to our riding – and it's amazing how much variation there is in the relative comfort of the different types of Tarmacadam and concrete.

I've never really paid much attention to this before, having always thought it was at best an irrelevant concern about something you couldn't change and at worst a distraction, but at times like this it's surprising what can capture your attention. We're fortunate enough to avoid cobbles, but apart from that seem to have pretty much every road surface on offer, from very smooth, new, state-of-the-art mixes that are all smart and black with crisp white lines, to old, uneven, gravely compounds that you'd hate to fall on as they look like they'd tear the skin from you in chunks. Sometimes there are even long stretches when we have two road surfaces to choose from as the road has been repaired in patches, or strips.

On occasion this prompts us to ride down the middle of the road if that is where the smoother option lies, which draws some peculiar looks from the spectators along the route. Not that there are many of them, which is probably a result of the terrain and the weather, and those few that there are seem like hardcore cycling fans. They also appear to belong to a special breed who are obviously devotees to long, flat races.

We make this assumption because their preferred position is standing facing towards the onrushing cyclists – even if there aren't any about to rush by for another four hours at least. They stand, stock-still, apparently intent on not missing a single second of the action, which is quite reasonable as on these flat roads it won't last long. To make the most of what does happen they are all equipped with very powerful binoculars slung round their necks, poised for the slightest blur of motion on the horizon. Once such motion has been detected the binoculars are raised and then trained on the source of this movement until it has come close enough to be observed by the naked eye.

However, at this point – the point at which Paul and I cycle by – the disappointed spectator has usually turned away in apparent dismay at our amateur efforts to replicate the real thing. He – for it's always a he – certainly never lets himself be drawn into the effusive encouragements so typical of the fans encountered so far. Instead it is left to the womenfolk to express such indiscriminate emotions.

With all this excitement it's not long before we reach Jauge, the last stop of the day. Just before we do a lone cyclist catches us from behind with apparent ease and I realise it's Alex – I think it's Alex – one of the two cyclists I met on the first day in the Pyrenees and who has also encountered Louis (I wonder where he is today?). He seems to be in fine form and is clearly riding faster than us, even in tandem, and soon heads off on his own again. Even just following him seems like too much effort.

Once in Jauge we don't take long before setting off on the final leg, which is quite tough to start with as we're immediately riding into a headwind that appears to have sprung up from nowhere. Then we finally turn a very obvious 90° corner to our right and begin the long run into the centre of the city.

We know that the finish is in the centre of the city today because Bordeaux has made a big thing about this since the debacle in Toulouse where hardly anybody turned up to watch the race finish in the suburbs. In fact Bordeaux seems to make a big thing about its long association with the Tour full stop (right from 1903, when Charles Laeser won the stage from Toulouse – 167.5 miles in 8 hours 26 minutes). It comes second only to Paris in the number of visits the Tour has made – 78 times out of 90, and it's also reputed to be the only city other than Paris that doesn't have to pay for the privilege of hosting a stage finish.

This familiarity with the Tour certainly seems to work in our favour as there's not even a hint of repeating yesterday's contretemps with a gendarme – in fact most of the roads right up to within a mile of the finish aren't even closed to normal traffic yet, let alone cyclists. We take full advantage of being left to our own devices and fly through the centre right up to the 100-metre-to-go mark. It's only 12.50 p.m., which makes for a good average speed (17.6 mph), and there is extra satisfaction today as it's Paul's first complete Tour stage (well, apart from the time trial, which was less than 30 miles so doesn't count).

Before we head off to find the hotel I ask Paul if he would mind if I look up the Eurosport commentary team to see if they fancy interviewing me about my exploits. My excuse for this incredibly vain notion is that a number of people at the cycling club suggested that Eurosport commentating guru David Duffield often spoke to people about 'quirky' things related to the Tour and he might be interested.

I rather tentatively approach the Eurosport van, where I'm met with an expression that says 'oh, another one', but am nevertheless ferried to the commentary studios where I'm told I can go in and see if David's around. He's not, but his co-commentator Sean Kelly is and I find myself going from vain to rather humble as I try to make what I've been doing sound interesting to somebody who's ridden the Tour fourteen times, come fourth overall, won four Tour stages and won the Green Jersey four times.

However, he does a very good job of humouring me and says that if I wait for David he's sure he'd like to speak to me. Encouraged, I wait outside and as Duffield arrives I hail him and again recount what I'm doing. Fortunately, before I get to the embarrassing bit of asking if he'd like to interview me the penny's already dropped and we arrange that I should come back and see him after tomorrow's stage, which is excellent news and should certainly give the cycling club something to talk about. In fact, I must ask Catherine to record it in case any of them miss it . . .

We find the hotel easily – Hotel Sèze – and in spite of the possibility of going to see the race finish I opt instead to take advantage of the excellent facilities. Indeed, the hotel seems far too opulent for our budget – all gilt-edged mirrors and large portraits.

There's also a garage, and even one of those old fashioned cage-lifts that runs up and down the middle of the winding staircase.

What's more, the room actually contains a full-sized bath. What luxury – no more contortionism, no more gymnastics, no more risk of serious injury. I indulge straight away and realise that the best thing is not actually being able to submerge my body with ease, although that's a big plus, but the fact that I can submerge both of my legs in their entirety and at the same time. In view of their increasing reluctance to pedal without complaining, this is bliss. Hotel Sèze in Bordeaux: recommended.

Only once I've finished does Dad arrive, he and Jon having had a more challenging journey than Paul and I to find the hotel. In fact he had to leave Jon guarding the car in an underground car park for nearly an hour while he found the hotel on foot and they've only just now returned with the car.

I manage to take advantage of finishing the stage early and sleep for nearly three hours – if only it had been this easy to sleep in the afternoons at the start of the Tour. Whilst I've slept Dad has effected a reconnaissance of dinner venues and, after exhaustive consideration of the options, we opt for Italian – there's one in the square just opposite and we know what to expect. This time it's Jon who falls for the temptation to have something other than pizza and ends up rather dissatisfied with his risotto.

Nevertheless, our host does his best to compensate for this by offering us a free glass of Schnapps. Seemingly this is because I asked for some ice in a plastic bag to put on my knee, which prompted him to come over and ask how far I'd cycled. Without even mentioning the rest of the Tour, the simple fact that Paul and I cycled today's stage was then enough for him to display this generosity. Mind you, in view of Jon's risotto perhaps we should have mentioned the whole Tour and tried to get the entire meal for free. After this it's back to bed, secure in the knowledge that there is now only one long stage remaining before Paris.

## Stage 18

# BORDEAUX—ST-MAIXENT-L'ECOLE (127 MILES)

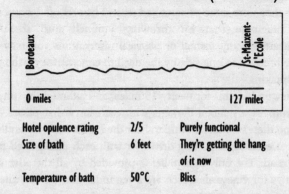

| Hotel opulence rating | 2/5 | Purely functional |
|---|---|---|
| Size of bath | 6 feet | They're getting the hang of it now |
| Temperature of bath | 50°C | Bliss |

It's a 3.30 a.m. alarm call this morning, not so much because of the length and difficulty of the stage (quite long, not that difficult) but in order to give us plenty of time to negotiate Bordeaux and its suburbs. The neutralised section is eight miles long today and whether on the bike or in the car it will take perhaps half an hour to cover, or avoid. One of the reasons for preferring the car is so that Dad, Jon and Paul don't resemble a bunch of unlikely kerb crawlers as they follow me. In the wilds of the Pyrenees this was not a problem, but in the seedy suburbs of Bordeaux suspicions could easily be raised.

As it is we set off in the car at 4.25 a.m. (not at all bad given the failure of Jon and Paul's alarm to go off) and by resisting the siren calls of the signs beckoning us towards the route itself we arrive at the official start, via the motorway, just before 5 a.m. I set off and almost immediately stop to put on an extra top as it's much the coldest morning so far. Once again I find myself riding along a busy main road that makes life uncomfortable for both me and Dad. There are a lot of lorries even at this early hour, and the road isn't quite wide enough for them to pass the car without having to slow down first. This seems to make them lose their normal respect for cyclists and I feel as though I have several close calls with wing mirrors.

The good side of this is that I put my head down and ride pretty much flat out with the aim of getting off the main road as quickly as possible. This also has the unlikely benefit of curing me of my morning aches and pains much more quickly than yesterday, even though they were more pronounced when I first set off. I suppose it's often the case that by throwing yourself into something wholeheartedly any mental or physical reservations you may have had are brushed to one side by the need to concentrate on the effort you're making.

I carry on like this for nearly 15 miles, and although my physical self improves my mood darkens with each lorry that passes. It's a good job there's no one around to hear the curses I mutter under my breath at each unsuspecting driver, or with each unexpected bump in the road. The only light relief is provided by all the advertising hoardings for vineyards which are a reminder that we are, after all, in the world's pre-eminent wine-growing region.

At one point I become aware that Dad has stopped and is flashing his headlights, with the implication, I assume, that I should go back to the car. Having to turn around while dead set on getting this leg over as quickly as possible almost sends me into a fit of apoplexy and, muttering an unrepeatable range of expletives, I arrive at the car some 100 yards back down the road. My attempts to keep a civil tongue in my head succeed to the extent that I utter a curt 'What?', when I really mean: 'Don't you realise I've got 127 miles to ride today, this better be good.'

Not answering, Jon leaps out of the car and picks up a scrap of paper which he hands to me. I'm chastened to discover that it's my route description, which must have fallen out from the leg of my shorts. Up until this point I've found having this description invaluable for my morale as it means I can work out how far I have to go to the next stop, or how much ground I've already covered. I should be delighted not to have lost it, and indeed I am but, still recovering from my Mr Angry mode, I manage no more than the briefest of expressions of gratitude before setting off again.

I ride off wondering if this is the sign that says my cycling shorts have finally had it. Paul has already commented on the need for care when he's taking pictures so as to avoid making me look indecent. Now the lycra and elastic around the legs appear to have worn enough for this to no longer be a safe storage space for route details (either that or my legs are getting even thinner, which is unlikely even if the rest of me may be fading away with all the effort).

Given that I've had these shorts for more than three years and they've been subjected to almost constant use, and probably more than 20,000 miles of cycling, I suppose it's hardly surprising that they're showing some signs of wear and tear. In fact, I have to admit that the only reason I'm still wearing them is the fear that a new pair might engender saddle sore, something I've managed to escape, by and large, during the trip (Clive's recipe of Vaseline and surgical spirits has worked well). 'If it ain't broke, don't fix it'; maybe I'll treat myself to some new ones when I reach Paris.

The main road section doesn't last much longer and then I'm onto lovely, quiet country roads. As the sun comes up it becomes apparent that the countryside itself is very pleasant, much nicer than yesterday, and I spend the next hour riding between alternate patches of meadows and mixed woodland. The meadows are particularly charming as they're draped in mist which is made golden by the first rays of the sun. The sight of cows apparently wallowing knee-deep in cloud adds to the otherworldly appeal.

The first stop comes and goes quite quickly as I manage to maintain a good speed even once I've turned onto the quiet roads. With the sun fully up, but a partially cloudy sky, I'm even keener than the past couple of days to complete today's ride as quickly as possible in case of bad weather. It's also almost impossible to think of this stage as anything other than the final hurdle, and the excitement that's building as a result helps me to maintain my momentum.

The countryside has become a bit more mundane now – rolling, undistinguished arable land – and it's with some relief I find that this section of the road has more than it's fair share of messages painted on it. Not just the rider's names, of course, although these are still present: Virenque remains the most frequent, and he has long since won this unofficial popularity contest, although his compatriot and erstwhile rival Jalabert, even though now a TV commentator, has come a close second. The current best-placed French rider, Christophe Moreau, doesn't seem to inspire such affection, however, with one message even accusing him of jealousy over the amount of publicity given to Virenque.

I wonder how all these messages affect the riders and if they pay any attention to them? It must be quite something to receive all the adulation Virenque does, but what if the messages are critical rather than encouraging? This must make a hard task even harder.

More interesting than the names, however, are the non-Tour related messages, and the potential for influencing spectators through the shop-window that the Tour has become is obvious. Nowhere more so, in fact, than the point at which I ride past a municipal road gang making the final preparations for the Tour's passage through some obscure village. Not content with installing barriers, sweeping up leaves and generally trying to look busy, this bunch of unwitting apologists for fast food and globalisation is painting over the by now familiar 'LIBEREZ JOSE BOVE' pleas. The local mayor must be a shareholder in McDonald's.

What makes this even more pathetic and unseemly is that in the next village, and indeed in the previous village, these messages are simply ignored. Perhaps it was the repetition of the provocative 'BOVE A LA MAISON – CHIRAC EN PRISON' that prompted the local authorities into action (I wonder if anyone else has noticed the striking resemblance between Chirac and an ageing James Garner)?. Or maybe the catalyst was 'NON AUX OGM' (No to GM crops). Perhaps the local mayor is a shareholder in McDonald's *and* a GM farmer. Either way it doesn't seem to be a wise investment of tax-payers' money.

After this controversy there are then a succession of messages relating to issues of more local importance. 'Yes to the TGV, no to the landfill' seems a reasonable compromise position, although maybe it's a question of having your cake and eating it. I bet the campaigners in Horsted Keynes near home who are currently waging a vigorous campaign against a landfill 'on their doorsteps' that will ruin a tranquil corner of Sussex (or provide an essential civic amenity, depending on who you listen to) would like the Tour to pass through so they could convey their message this publicly.

I delight myself by arriving in Cognac faster than I expected, but then realise this is more down to the impact a growing tailwind has had on my ride so far than any sudden discovery of great form on my part. Nevertheless, it's great to think that this is likely to continue for the rest of the day. It's not often I have the privilege of riding from A to B *and* having a tailwind all the way.

I see Dad parked at the side of the road a little way into the town and stop for the morning's first croissants; we couldn't find a baker's that was open at our last rendez-vous. As if trying to compensate, this time Dad has parked just about as close to the baker's as he can manage, which is great except that it presents me with no opportunity for a pee stop. In the end I'm forced to visit the café that Jon has just emerged from. He tells me to keep an eye out for the regulars who appear to be strict adherents to the Anquetil diet — they're eating oysters and pâté on toast while drinking either white wine or cognac. I see what he means and I wonder if I should join them, but decide this is a bit rich for my tastes, especially at 9 a.m.

The rest of the ride turns out to be fairly uneventful, apart from a couple of villages making a late run on the 'best-decorated village on the route' award, which just goes to show that the competition seems only to attract any interest when the terrain or the race don't. Then there's a crash apparently involving an elderly spectator and the windscreen of a passing car. The unfortunate victim is being tended to on a stretcher as I ride past, while the car that hit him suggests it was a pretty heavy collision given the extent of the damage to its front.

This is not the only accident we've seen, either. Yesterday Paul and I rode past a car upside down in a ditch with families having picnics only 20 yards to either side. Worse than this, a young fan was killed in 2000 by a car in the official publicity caravan. The caravan is now subject to fairly stringent rules and limits on the number of vehicles allowed. However, little seems to have been done about the period before the roads are closed and the official race entourage arrives. The density of the crowds on some of the low-lying stages like today, combined with the volume of the traffic on the roads that are almost invariably still open as I ride down them, combine to create the impression that there's a crash waiting to happen.

It's difficult to know who's more to blame for this unnerving atmosphere: the spectators who behave as if they own the road, and who oblige me to cycle with my eyes peeled, or the drivers. Half of these are Tour fans in hot pursuit of a parking spot, which apparently gives them the right to ignore normal driving conventions such as paying attention to other people who may be in the road; the other half are not Tour fans and are driven to distraction by the behaviour of the half that are. If you add in the role of the unofficial caravan – the profiteers – and unwitting cyclists then you have a heady mix. I have a distinct feeling of 'there but for the grace of God go I'.

With 20 miles to go before the finish I'm feeling great; with 15 miles to go I feel like the wind has gone from my sails. It's similar to the feeling I had on the last day in the Pyrenees when I was on the verge of bonking, but today it feels less serious. Nevertheless, I'm grateful for a pocket full of malt loaf and a series of long descents that allow me to maintain my momentum. These descents come as a bit of a surprise as I didn't realise I'd done any climbing. Such is the benefit of a tailwind, I suppose.

I recover, and cut a reasonably healthy figure as I ride along the last mile or so, which is already packed with supporters, even though it's at least four hours before the race will arrive. St-Maixent-l'Ecole has never hosted the Tour before and the locals certainly seem keen to make up for lost time.

I arrive at 12.50 p.m., and that's the last long stage of the Tour completed. Tomorrow's stage is a time trial and only 30 miles long, and then the stage into Paris is quite short, if you discount the circuits of the Champs Elysées, which I assume I won't be able to do, at least not in their entirety. I find Dad and the others quickly, and after the standard, if somewhat perfunctory wash with water from my water bottle, I settle down for a doze before going for my interview with Eurosport. When I arrive Kelly and Duffield are already commentating and they beckon to me to sit in between them.

After I've had my earphones and microphone explained as well as what to do if I'm talking just before the adverts, I'm introduced seamlessly and find myself on air.

Apart from forgetting to say, 'Hello, Catherine and Molly', I manage, I think, to sound reasonably articulate when fielding Duffield's suitably gentle questions. The highlight is not actually being on air but seeing Kelly strive successfully to ignore twice Tour winner Laurent Fignon flicking water in his face while he's making a point about this being a very fast stage thanks to the tailwind that's helping the riders. Not only does this display admirable concentration from Kelly it also portrays a beaming Fignon in a different light to the more usual perception of him as being a bit serious and dour.

And then that's it and I'm back out in the real world again. It's beginning to drizzle as I make my way back to the car and the long drive to Pornic is a trial for all of us. It takes 3.5 hours, which is a long time for four people to be packed into a car full of food, bike gear and spare clothes. I manage to avoid cramp everywhere except for in my buttocks, which are possibly the most difficult part of the anatomy to stretch in a car, especially one full of food, bike gear and spare clothes . . .

Jon succeeds in overcoming the by-now-ferocious wind and rain and ignoring the distractions around him – Dad trying to play a Rod Stewart tape, Paul reading the newspaper, me kicking out as cramp once more sets in – and delivers us to the hotel in Pornic in one piece. This is more than can be said for the victims of another crash, which we drive by on the edge of the town. This time it appears that a car has driven head-on into one of the many white campervans already lining the route for tomorrow's stage to Nantes. Maybe it's the drivers who are worse than the pedestrians after all.

The hotel is another one that fits into the functional rather than charming category, but its merits (right on tomorrow's route, clean and welcoming, full-sized baths) far outweigh its bad sides (situated right opposite a McDonald's, of course). After I have my first *hot* bath of the trip we decide against a Big Mac (or '*Le Royale*' as John Travolta once said in *Pulp Fiction*) and drive into town, which is a sort of Breton equivalent of Weymouth, if a bit smaller. The combination of normal tourists and Tour tourists means it's choked with people, but we manage to park and find a restaurant with a table – an Italian restaurant, of course.

This time it's me who is the fall guy who chooses something other than pizza and is terribly disappointed as a result. My lasagne is small, bland and late, and although I know I just couldn't have faced another pizza I do regret the decision not to eat moules frites. The consensus is that I really ought not to chance my arm on shellfish so close to the finish; what I should have done, and what I'm sure Anquetil would have done, is say that I shouldn't miss the chance to eat shellfish so close to the sea.

In spite of a large if nondescript pudding, I'm still hungry but more concerned to get to bed than hunt for extra food as the pursuit of my five minutes of fame and glory on Eurosport meant that I missed my afternoon sleep today. We return to the hotel under grey skies, and I ice my knee for hopefully the last time – the next two days shouldn't put too much of a strain on it. The last thing I do before going to bed is watch the weather forecast for tomorrow, which can be summed up in one word: rain.

## Stage 19

# PORNIC—NANTES (30.5 MILES)

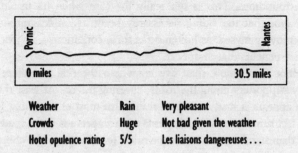

| Weather | Rain | Very pleasant |
|---|---|---|
| Crowds | Huge | Not bad given the weather |
| Hotel opulence rating | 5/5 | Les liaisons dangereuses . . . |

I'm up at 5 a.m. and away before 6. It's grey and overcast and looks like rain so I'm keen to get going as quickly as possible. There's also a noticeable tailwind which should make for fast times when the real Tour riders complete the stage.

Perhaps because of the wind at my back, I'm half-tempted to try and ride the stage as if I were racing. I've had this in mind ever since I saw the route, thinking this would probably be my best chance to do so. In this respect the fact that it's short and there's only one day left to go are it's most important attributes.

This doesn't last much more than half a mile, however, with my general sense of achiness and fragility triumphing over my ego. The cool, wet weather – it's already started raining – is very welcome, but these don't seem like the best conditions in which to subject my muscles to the intensity of effort required by competition (even if the competition is only one I've contrived).

Instead, I content myself with maintaining a brisk pace like yesterday morning, which once again has the effect of loosening my muscles satisfactorily without encouraging them to deteriorate further. The rain gives the impression of easing off for a minute or two but then begins to come down more heavily again. Another reason to try and keep the pace up.

In fact I've always found that riding in the rain is quite a good thing in terms of being able to concentrate on riding quickly. I suppose it's because the distractions of a nice day have been removed. When it's sunny it can be very pleasant to stop for five minutes to admire a view, or simply to ride along slowly and soak up the surroundings. This is not really the case when it's tipping it down. Not that the riding necessarily becomes unpleasant – I'm quite enjoying myself, as I often do in these conditions – it's just the ancillary benefits that disappear.

I'm not much more than five miles into the ride and there are already supporters lining the roads, cheering me on. At least this is how it appears at first, but then I realise that most of those that I see are in fact running between the tents and campervans at the roadside rather than standing waiting for the riders to come past. The cheering seems to be purely by coincidence, a result of the shared misfortune of being cycling fans on a rainy day, but either way it's well received.

Even more indicative of the hardiness of the average Tour fan than these furtive appearances from last night's arrivals is the behaviour of those who are just arriving for the day. Even at 7 a.m. in the pouring rain whole families, from grandparents to grandchildren (and the obligatory dog), are struggling gamely with picnic equipment designed for fair weather outings, intent on spending the day celebrating the Tour come what may. As I cycle past I receive the full gamut of reactions, from grim, blank-faced looks suggesting despair and mutual folly, to warm-hearted encouragement implying 'we're all in this together, so why not make it fun'.

In addition to this varied response there is equally great variety in the clothes people have chosen to wear to ward off the inclement conditions. In fact, there's a clear distinction between the French/Italian/Spanish and other supporters from 'southern' Europe and those Brits/Scandinavians/Germans/Dutch who represent the northern half of the continent (the Belgians seem to have a bit of both camps in them). Those from the 'south' are recognisable by their brightly coloured raincoats, all yellows, reds and pinks, while the more stolid northerners wear dark colours apparently designed to blend in with a rainy day rather than stand out from it.

Maybe this is because it only rains infrequently in the south, so there's no harm in putting a brave face on it and keeping things jolly with bright, vibrant colours. In the north, on the other hand, it rains often enough for such apparent jollity to become a bit wearing and seem a little forced after a while. Or maybe not.

I ride on, still wearing my head torch and backlight in an attempt to remain visible to cars in spite of the greyness and all the spray. Just as I come out of a small town I notice the first message painted on the road today – presumably the rain has deterred other attempts. As I ride over it I have to turn round to make sure I'm not seeing things, but sure enough – there's no mistaking it – the phrase outlined on the road is as unusual as I'd first thought: *'ICI – UN HERISSON TUE'* (a hedgehog was killed here).

I've become quite used to the esoteric references of some cycling fans to obscure riders or races from the past, as well as the politically motivated messages of local inhabitants, but this takes the biscuit. I know that the death of hedgehogs can provoke deep feelings – I remember the fight to save hedgehogs from a cull in the Outer Hebrides that made it onto the national news – but I admit that I'm struggling to make any connection between this unfortunate incident and the Tour de France.

While I'm thinking about the possible link – maybe a bunch of 150 cyclists is as perilous to a hedgehog intent on crossing a road as motorised transport – I'm left in no doubt of the seriousness of the situation in these parts: I ride over four more messages indicating the untimely demise of a relative of Mrs Tiggywinkle.

I'm none the wiser as to the motivation for this public-spirited display of sympathy for our prickly friends when I finally come across the apparent purpose of the demonstration: *'TROP D'HERISSONS MORTS'* (too many dead hedgehogs). I'm not in a position to disagree with this statement, but do wonder how many is too many. I suppose the obvious answer would be five, as this is the number who've apparently already met their end on the route so far.

After this last, doleful declaration I see no more references to hedgehogs, deceased or otherwise, and am soon on the outskirts of Nantes. Instead of enigmatic messages to ponder I'm confronted with the more immediate problem of negotiating any number of roundabouts and junctions made treacherous by the water that's now standing on the road surface.

In an unfortunate twist of fate these conditions are made worse by all the attempts to make Nantes a more cycle-friendly place. By this I mean all the painted lines on the road indicating a cycle-lane – now very slippery – and the cobbled humps at the entrances and exits of roundabouts. Presumably these are designed to ward off drivers from unwittingly cutting up cyclists (a regular misdemeanour at home). Nevertheless, with the road closed, these simply create a decidedly unwelcome obstacle that lies right in the middle of the natural line for a cyclist to negotiate a roundabout. I suppose it's fair to say that the needs of everyday cyclists en route to the shops are about as far removed from those of the Tour riders as Formula 1 is from the school-run (although . . .), but it would be ironic if the outcome of the stage is determined by these 'cycle-friendly' devices.

I arrive at the finish and am by now quite chilled after nearly two hours of rain. Even though it's not a cold day, I'm now soaked to the skin, having eschewed a cagoule, and I stand shivering in a shop doorway wondering where on earth Dad and the others are.

Just as I'm struggling with cold fingers to untie the knot on the plastic bag that contains my mobile phone, Dad wanders past. It turns out he's been here quite a while but didn't know where in the unfinished 'finish' area I would arrive. The car isn't far away but it takes me some time to manage to find a way to change into warm, dry clothes without in turn making these wet in the incessant rain.

We drive out of Nantes, intent on settling into a nice warm café (it's an unusual feeling finishing a ride cold and damp) to allow me a chance to catch up on breakfast, but the town appears closed. The only food outlet open between the city centre and the beginning of the motorway to Paris is a bakery, so we stop here instead. Slices of warmed-up pizza and croissants in the car washed down with tea from the flask isn't quite what I had in mind, but it'll do, and I'm soon feeling cosy and replete.

We also buy *L'Equipe* to read on the journey and find it is full of the contest this afternoon between Armstrong and Ullrich. With yesterday's weather forecast having accurately predicted rain and a tailwind, the majority of 'expert' opinion is now clearly in favour of Armstrong. Not only does he have a reputation for performing better in the rain, but most commentators also conclude that the tailwind will make it unlikely that the time gaps between the two will be big enough for Ullrich to overtake him.

With this in mind, Armstrong is already being pencilled in to join the Tour greats as a five-times winner, the record for the number of victories. Only four other riders have done this – Jacques Anquetil, Eddy Merckx, Bernard Hinault and Miguel Indurain. The paper contains profiles of all four riders, and apart from Indurain – rather unimaginatively labelled 'Big-Mig' – it's clear that you need a catchy nickname to succeed as a Tour legend.

In this respect, at least, Armstrong – somewhat reluctantly labelled 'The Boss' by the papers – has some distance to make up on his rivals: Jacques 'The Master' Anquetil, Eddy 'The Cannibal' Merckx and Bernard 'The Badger' Hinault (maybe all the hedgehog graffiti was a reference to a badger's ability to eat hedgehogs in spite of their spiny defences, and was therefore a campaign against Hinault?).

This practice of awarding nicknames dates back to the very first Tour, when overall victory went to Maurice 'The Chimneysweep' Garin, who also won the stage into Nantes in 1903 – covering the little matter of 266.5 miles from Bordeaux in 16 hours and 26 minutes.

In the light of all this I suggest that I ought to have had a nickname to encourage me on my ride. I'm thinking of something along the lines of Federico 'The Eagle of Toledo' Bahamontes, the first Spaniard to win the Tour and six-times winner of the King of the Mountains competition. In fact, such was his climbing prowess, and a reluctance to put himself on the line in the overall competition, that he is reputed to have sat at the top of one climb during the Tour eating an ice cream and waiting for the others to catch him up.

I may not share such a fine cycling *palmarès* (record), but it's clear that my preference is also for the mountains so I think it's a perfectly justifiable suggestion. Paul, however, thinks otherwise, and reminds me of 'The Camel', which was a somewhat unfortunate epithet I acquired in a previous life as a fell-runner. He reassures me that this was the result of my sometimes obstinate desire to keep going in adverse conditions rather than any physical resemblance (or any reputation for spitting and kicking), but I'm not entirely satisfied. To be honest, it's not quite as romantic as I'd hoped, and I try to dissuade him by pointing out how much trouble I had in the heat – surely 'The Camel' would now be inappropriate. Unfortunately, Jon steps in and dismisses this concern, saying that doing as much as I have done is quite enough to justify the title. I make one last plea for something with a little more panache – Paul 'The Mountain Lion' Howard sounds good to me – but this falls on deaf ears. In the end I vow to let the whole idea drop quietly.

After four hours in appalling driving conditions we arrive in Paris, and locate the hotel – within 500 yards of the Arc de Triomphe – with scarcely a hitch. The only problem as we arrive is that the Hotel Résidence Chalgrin is as plush as Hotel Sèze was in Bordeaux, but is a good deal less enthusiastic about accommodating our bikes. I explain that I called in advance to make sure it was not a problem as we can't leave them on the car, but the receptionist is unmoved, especially when I suggest putting them in the rooms: 'There is furniture worth several thousand pounds in the rooms. We can't risk damaging it with some bicycles.' This is my moment, however, and I point out that our bikes are also worth several thousand pounds. Once he's overcome his disbelief he decides to let us store them in a room behind the reception, which is perfectly adequate, and a great relief.

The bedrooms themselves look designed for passing diplomats on secret assignations rather than weary cyclists: more gilded mirrors, although this time the pictures are of scantily clad maidens rather than pre-revolution aristocrats. We have writing desks and high-backed chairs, and the room Dad, Paul and Jon are sharing even has an anteroom.

Paul and Jon find the prospect of comfortable beds to lounge on and being able to watch the Tour live on the telly irresistible, but my tummy's still trying to make up for last night's meagre rations so Dad and I head to the nearest café for lunch. The waiter immediately picks me for a cyclist – it's the tan line on my legs that gives it away, apparently – and I tell him what I've been doing. He's full of congratulations, and this temporarily goes to my head until he rushes over to tell his colleague, who turns out to be not in the least bit impressed or even interested.

Lunch, especially the delicious, made-on-the-premises strawberry tart, just about gives me enough energy to make it back to the hotel to go to sleep, and I manage a very welcome couple of hours. I wake up and watch the climax of the time trial with Jon and Paul. In our predictions of the likely outcome I've made the rash assertion that Ullrich will thrash Armstrong by two minutes and win the race overall. This quickly reveals itself to be impossible, giving both Jon and Paul the satisfaction of having been right to have made the more obvious, and let's face it sensible, choice of siding with Armstrong. We'd all have liked Ullrich to win, simply because he's come second so often already and was the underdog. Nevertheless, no one begrudges Armstrong his victory. It would just be nice if Ullrich would win at least one more Tour.

After all the excitement of the stage, culminating in Ullrich's crash (fortunately not caused by the 'cyclist-friendly' street furniture), I can't quite work out whether or not if I feel excited about having reached Paris. I *am* excited – I've been striving for this for the past three weeks – but I also know that I've still got tomorrow's stage to ride before I can actually say that I've finished. What's more, I'm not sure how much of tomorrow's route I'm going to be able to ride. I can't imagine that I'll be able to do ten laps of the Champs Elysées like the riders in the real race, so it might all end in a bit of an anticlimax. I hope not. I hope I can at least make it to the Arc de Triomphe, at which point I'll happily call it a day. In fact I'm not sure I'd ride down the Champs Elysées even if I could, as it might feel all too much like stealing the limelight of the real Tour, so maybe a low-key finish is the best thing.

Low-key won't last long tonight, however, with the arrival of my sister Caroline and our cousin Kay. Indeed they arrive in a bit of a state having just negotiated the Metro all the way from Charles de Gaulle airport *with bikes* as they're en route themselves for a week's cycling down near Biarritz. This remarkable feat encourages the receptionist to react kindly to their requests to store their bikes inside as well and he adds them to the two already there, making the hotel entrance look temporarily like a bike shop.

Catherine is also due to arrive soon, so we leave my mobile phone in the room with instructions to call Dad so that we can provide her with directions for how to join us in the restaurant for dinner. We enjoy a cheap-and-cheery meal before I head back to the hotel, slightly alarmed at not having received a call, only to find Catherine already there. Even though she's the more technologically minded of the pair of us, she hasn't managed to fathom how to use the phone, with whatever combination of French and British prefixes she dialled seeming to make no difference. Fortunately, I've only left her waiting on her own for about half an hour even though the journey from the airport – by coach – was as quick and efficient as Caroline and Kay's was long and arduous.

In a very selfish way I'm relieved to hear that Molly isn't quite crawling yet and has only cut one more tooth in my absence. She's also been helping her to follow my progress on a map that Catherine has drawn on the wall at home, moving a picture of me to the appropriate location every day. I can't really believe I've only been away for just over three weeks – it seems a lot longer.

I check with Dad what time we're planning to set off in the morning – 6 a.m. – and then it's early to bed for the last time. I find it difficult to go to sleep since, without a doubt, I *am* now excited about the prospect of finally finishing tomorrow.

## Stage 20

# VILLE D'AVRAY—PARIS (95 MILES)

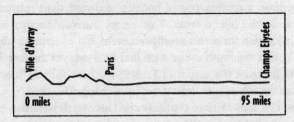

| Cases of mistaken identity | 1 | No harm done |
| Glasses of beer | 4 | It is a special occasion |

I wake up with the alarm and disaster strikes immediately: I realise I've left my wet cycling kit in a plastic bag in the boot of the car. When I retrieve it, the combination of 24 hours of dampness in a confined space and three weeks of continuous wear (even if I have been rinsing it out most nights) is as potent as you might imagine. It's clear that I'm going to have to resort to my spare set.

In practice this is not such a bad thing, as it's all perfectly functional and it has the distinct merit of being clean and dry. However, this practical approach doesn't account for the fact that putting on the same jersey and shorts every morning has become part of the routine, a ritual almost. It's quite upsetting for this routine to unravel now, on the very last day.

Nevertheless, I put on a stiff upper lip as I don't want to get emotional in front of Catherine, and am soon ready to face the outside world. In fact my new, clean, dry pair of shorts means that

I'm probably more acceptable to the outside world than I have been at any time on the ride so far. I'm also quite keyed up about setting off, although this is mitigated by the sight of Catherine snuggled up in bed having already gone back to sleep. Still, one more day and I'll have all the time in the world to lie in with my wife – until we're back at home with dear Molly, of course.

Even though there seems little point in them trying to follow the route today, given the likelihood of road closures, Dad, Paul and Jon are all accompanying me to the start. We don't actually know where the start is but, apart from somehow managing to miss the périphérique, a combination of hunches and road signs delivers us successfully to Ville d'Avray. This sleepy Parisian suburb is an unlikely location for such a prestigious event, but its claim to fame is that it hosted the finish of the sixth and final stage of the first Tour in 1903 (because the mayor of Paris at the time forbade sporting events in the city proper; how times have changed).

In the first Tour Maurice Garin clinched his overall victory in style, winning the last stage – 287.5 miles in 18 hours and 9 minutes – to add to the two he'd already won. He arrived in the town at 2.09 p.m.: 'Shouts went up and a fantastic roar greeted the end of the race. Women brandished their parasols and men waved their hats. I saw spectators cry. There it was for all to see: the pure emotion of sport,' reported Alphonse Steinès of *L'Auto*, the paper belonging to Desgranges, the Tour's organiser.

Apart from the usual suspects putting up crowd barriers and erecting advertising hoardings, it's a good deal quieter this morning when we arrive, even if the sight of a car stopping to unload a cyclist threatens to stir some of the sleepy-eyed gendarmes into action. Fortunately they continue to succumb to their lethargy. We arrange to meet at the Arc de Triomphe in two or three hours' time, depending on how far I manage to cycle. Then, with some final words of encouragement from my three stalwart supporters, I set off.

Almost immediately I feel strangely nervous. In some ways it's similar to how I felt in anticipation of the Prologue, but rather than being worried about not being allowed on the route I'm now concerned about being turfed-off. Once again I have the impression of trespassing, although this feeling gradually fades away as I ride out of the town and enter into a wooded section en route for Paris. There are fewer people about,which makes me seem less conspicuous.

The first port of call after Ville d'Avray is Versailles, but I don't manage to see the chateau as the route just skirts the town before heading off to the next suburb. In fact it's just a succession of suburbs of greater or lesser degrees of leafiness for the next few miles. The villas at the side of the road are imposing, suggesting a sort of Parisian stockbroker belt, although perhaps one that's a bit jaded since the roads that run past seem quite big and I can imagine them busy. Not so busy at this time on a Sunday morning, mind you, and far from seeming conspicuous anymore I feel like just another urban cyclist taking advantage of the quiet roads before they become clogged with people off to worship at the nearest DIY superstore.

Actually, I'm probably cycling slower than most cyclists out for a Sunday jaunt and am more like somebody riding home with the Sunday paper. It all seems rather genteel and the slow pace afflicts me until I spy a cyclist ahead. There are so few people out and about that in itself this is quite exciting. More exciting still is the fact that it might, just might, be Louis or Jeremy; it would be nice to share the last few miles with either of them. I soon catch up only to find out that my quarry has a beard, which rules out both Louis and Jeremy. I cycle past my pannier-laden companion and try to disguise my disappointment as we exchange brief greetings.

As I ride on I try to work out what it is that rings a bell about him. He certainly looks like he's covered a fair few miles, so maybe I have seen him somewhere earlier on in the Tour. Then it dawns on me that it's the beard that I recognise. Well, not recognise as such, but I do recall that the legendary Skippy is supposed to be as heavily bearded as this fella. I wonder if this might finally be him.

I slow down to allow him to catch up and brace myself for at last meeting this mysterious Australian who has, according to the rumours I've picked up so far, ridden the routes of the Giro d'Italia and the Tour de France for the past five years. If this is true it strikes me as though it would be quite a privilege to ride the concluding part of my first Tour with him, although I'm not sure I'll try and emulate his record.

By now I've convinced myself that this must be Skippy, so I hail the slightly puzzled-looking cyclist in English, asking him how far he's ridden. He now looks even more bemused, so I try again. After a few seconds he replies in broken English with a strong German accent, and once again my hopes are dashed. Out of a sense of embarrassment at having twice spoken to this unsuspecting character and twice seemed disheartened at his replies, I try gamely to maintain conversation, but neither his English nor my German are up to it, so I pedal off again feeling distinctly silly.

At least I have a reason to keep riding a bit faster now, lest he catch me up again, and I ride through a succession of more modern and somewhat less charming suburbs. Using my limited knowledge of London I'm struggling to work out which borough or area this most closely resembles, when I see a sign which in some ways answers the question for me: '*Suresnes – ville juméllée avec Hackney*' (Suresnes – twinned with Hackney). Not knowing Hackney, I can't work out which of these two towns should be more pleased with the association. Suresnes seems tidy enough but little more than functional, whereas although Hackney doesn't conjure up visions of great prestige like Kensington, I've always assumed it has a kind of earthy charm that is distinctly missing here.

I continue my unofficial tour of the Paris suburbs and begin to climb up a hill. I check my route description and realise this must the category-four climb just before the town of St-Cloud. It's not a particularly demanding climb, although it does afford a striking panorama of Paris – everything from the Sacré Coeur on the left to the Tour de Montparnasse on the right, with the Arc de Triomphe and Eiffel Tower in between. Below me is the Bois de Boulogne, and all in all it's a very pleasant surprise on this slightly grey day. This panorama also provides me with the excuse to feel excited again about having made it to Paris. What's more, I now feel as though I've actually cycled into Paris, rather than our sneaky arrival in the car yesterday.

I then ride through St-Cloud, the site of the first official, recorded, bicycle race on 31 May 1869 (won by an Englishman, James Moore). How close I am to the route used that fateful day I don't know, but I'm sure it's no coincidence that the Tour has decided to visit in its centenary year. I'm soon back in Ville d'Avray – the route does a sort of P-shaped loop before heading into Paris proper – and then get temporarily lost as I arrive in Versailles for the second time as the signs indicating the alternative way out of town on the second lap are still obscured. A friendly gendarme puts me straight and then points out that I'm cycling the wrong way down a one-way road before shrugging his shoulders and letting me carry on.

I reach the Seine but don't cross it straight away, turning right instead and riding through a very run-down, former industrial area. I'm in sight of some of the grandest monuments of Paris, yet this is really quite grim. Nevertheless, it's not long before I cross the river and pass a sign saying 'PARIS'. Now I really feel that I can say I've done it. There's nobody around with whom to celebrate, but this is the moment when I feel justified in saying 'I've made it'. I may not have covered the entire route since setting out three weeks ago, but I have at least managed to keep going all the way to Paris and this sign is the proof.

No sooner have I made it into Paris, however, than a phalanx of gendarmes indicates that I can't cycle any further on the route along the river embankment. I confidently pull out my press pass, indicating that this should allow me through, but they remain unimpressed. They're perfectly amiable, but regardless of what I say, they're not going to be persuaded. Maybe it's their special uniforms – all-white raincoats, gloves and hats – but they have an air of authority that means they're quite prepared to tolerate my attempts to persuade them without giving the slightest suggestion that I'm having any effect. Even the l'Alpe d'Huez trick of offering to walk with the bike cuts no ice: the route is now closed to pedestrians as well.

At this point I remind myself that the success of the trip so far has been based on recognising when it's best to stop banging your head against a brick wall, so, with a reluctant sigh, I ask if they can direct me to the Arc de Triomphe by an alternative route. I say reluctant, I'm not that bothered really and I'm certainly not disappointed. I've made it to Paris, and I'm quite happy for that to be that. I fiddle my way through the Paris streets until I reach the Trocadéro and then I ride up the wide, empty boulevard that is Avenue Kléber, one of the less famous spokes that radiate from the Arc de Triomphe. There's hardly any traffic, and certainly no cycling fans lining the road, so I have one final opportunity to savour the moment before I reach the Arc de Triomphe itself.

In fact I'm quite pleased not to have been confronted with the opportunity to ride down the Champs Elysées – it saves me the problem of deciding whether or not I really wanted to ride along it. This would have been a glorious end, there's no doubt, but I find something very satisfying arriving at the finish on a road that runs perpendicular to that which will be used by the real race. I suppose it should be a parallel road, as I've sort of been riding the Tour in parallel, but Haussmann's carefully planned layout of Paris obviously didn't take this into account, so perpendicular will do.

I also think I would once again feel a bit like a fraud if I rode along the Champs Elysées, especially with the number of fans I can already see lining the pavements. I haven't tried to ride the Tour seeking the adulation or even admiration of others, I've done it simply to see if I could. Perhaps because of this I'm glad that my arrival passes unnoticed.

I cycle once round the Arc de Triomphe as a sort of full stop, and then spot Dad scanning the road for my arrival. In spite of the Parisian traffic I manage to make my way to the edge of the roundabout where he's standing. He's on his own because the others have gone to look for me at the top of the Champs Elysées, assuming that I'd arrive from that direction. Dad says well done, and I thank him for all the support and encouragement I've had over the last three weeks – and during my preparations. It's clear I couldn't have done it without him, and it's quite fitting that it's just the two of us, as it was at the start.

The others arrive, having seen me cycle past, as well as Darren and Kirsty from V.C. Etoile back home, who've come over to watch the final stage, and it's congratulations and a sense of relief all round. And then that's it. It's all over and I climb off the bike for the last time.

# EPILOGUE

I suppose in the main I feel relieved. There is a distinct sense of satisfaction, although I suspect that there hasn't really been time for this to take hold yet. I'll also admit to a good degree of elation, and there is a smidgen of disappointment, yet the single biggest sensation is relief.

I'm relieved that I don't have to concentrate on what we're doing and where we're going tomorrow, that I don't have to think about whether I have enough bananas for the ride, or to remember to pack my bag and not leave anything behind.

I'm also greatly relieved – physically – to be able to stop. I could keep going, and maybe the more you keep going the more you get used to it, but right now I feel as though my body could do with a rest. All the little niggles normally associated with riding a long way have been magnified by having to do it almost day-in, day-out for three weeks. Instead of them getting better and being replaced the next time by something else – one day your left calf, the next your right shoulder – they've all persisted. Now it's my left calf and my right shoulder and my left knee and . . . Individually none of these are serious, but cumulatively they make me feel a bit worn out. It's clear that a few days off would do them, and me, the power of good.

Even more than this, I'm relieved that the sense of obligation to do something has now stopped. I'm back to the real world in which there's variety in what you do and where you have to make choices; where the days are different, or at least can be.

Nevertheless, in some ways I'll miss the strict routine that we've been following for the past three weeks. There's no doubting that it has had the distinct advantage of making life very simple – if not always on a practical level then at least philosophically. In effect the parameters of our lives were set. The route was laid out for us and all we had to do was follow it. There may have been times when it turned out to be quite tricky to achieve, but the aims remained clear.

What's more, because trying to follow the Tour turned out to be such an all-consuming activity – the Tour is a demanding mistress – it affected almost everything we did, not just the bit of each day when I was actually cycling. Everything had to be done according to where and how far I had to ride.

This dictated the time we set the alarm in the morning and therefore the time we went to bed at night. It dictated the type of food we ate – just look at the breakfasts and some of the places we had dinner in the evening. It dictated the clothes I wore – no dilemmas over which shirt or which trousers to wear (should I wear the jumper I was bought as a present or the one I actually like?). Fitness for purpose was the only criteria when getting dressed in the morning.

Trying to accommodate these demands so as to give the best chance of success while not letting them dominate was perhaps one of the hardest challenges. It seemed important to make an effort to keep doing normal or mundane activities – cleaning my teeth, washing out my clothes – so as to keep the ride in some sort of perspective.

This may not appear to be the type of focus for which people who set out to take on major undertakings are renowned. Yet, even after doing what I did under the intensity of competition and with the world scrutinising every move it's a rare professional cyclist who doesn't manage to step back from the race and indulge the press or talk to the fans. If a professional can do it, surely it was incumbent on me to try as well, even if it was simply talking to Dad in the evening (even if he didn't want me to).

As for the rest, well, the sense of satisfaction is quite profound. I was realistic enough during my preparations to know that there was a distinct possibility that I wouldn't be able to manage to ride the route in its entirety – which I don't think is the same as admitting defeat before I'd started. In this light the amount that I did ride makes me pleased.

I'm delighted to have ridden the stage to l'Alpe d'Huez, which on its own made the whole trip worthwhile, and I'm also pleased to have kept going after the disappointment of the first two days in the Pyrenees. In particular the last four stages seemed quite a chore after having completed all the more obvious difficulties of the mountains, and the amount of time and effort required to ride the last two stages, although both were only 30 miles long, made them in some ways the most difficult of all. I suppose a large part of the challenge was in fact keeping going for the whole three weeks, and I'm pleased to have succeeded in that.

There's still a hint of disappointment, however. I came close enough to doing it all to remain convinced that I could – although obviously not this time. I don't feel as though I can blame this on the conditions, either, even though by all accounts it was an exceptionally hot year. On balance, I think the weather was more favourable than anything else, at least to me as a lone cyclist. I would have struggled more, I'm sure, if I'd been confronted on the flat stages of northern France with the kind of wind and rain I had on Stage 19 from Pornic to Nantes. Heat affects a lone cyclist no more than it does a group, whereas a headwind would have made a massive difference and perpetual wetness would have been as hard on the morale as continuous heat.

Nor did I really have any physical problems that affected my ride. At different points I thought that both knees might cause me to stop, but just as they were at their worst they started to get better again, and apart from that I got off very lightly.

Instead, I think it was my mental frailties which let me down a bit. In particular it's the Pyrenees that were a bit galling, whereas I'm not so disappointed at missing the amount I did in the Alps. The rest I had after stopping on Stage 7 from Lyon to Morzine was essential, I'm sure, to making it to l'Alpe d'Huez the next day. As for not riding from Gap to Marseille on Stage 10, at the time I had little choice. I think it was my mistakes – complacency on the day, eating too much afterwards – that made me feel as I did, but once I felt ill I could do nothing about it.

In the Pyrenees the disappointment is slightly greater because some of my failure to complete all the stages was down to weaknesses of the spirit rather than of the flesh. I let myself get too down after not finishing Stage 13 to Ax-3 Domaines (five measly miles) and it was this that really scuppered the following day. I'd admitted defeat almost from the previous evening when I settled for a 5 a.m. start instead of 4.

In fact, that is probably my only real regret – along with not realising how important rest was earlier on. I think if I had made more of an effort to ensure we were at the hotel as soon as possible and I had as long to sleep in the afternoons as possible I would have stood up better to the challenge in the long run.

I suppose I also regret to some degree not having had the competitive imperative to keep going for as long as I could, rather than thinking about keeping going for the whole three weeks. I had the opportunity to drop out on one stage and then start again on the next, which I did and which ensured I reached Paris having done as much as I did. But it would have been quite nice to have had a different focus – simply to try and keep going for as long as possible. As it was, there were maybe only two occasions during the whole ride when I was at the edge of my abilities on the bike – the penultimate climb on the day into Gap (Stage 9), and the Port de Pailhères climb (Stage 13) – and both times I managed to keep going.

Apart from that, I'm delighted and elated at finishing. I'm particularly delighted at the prospect of being able to watch the last stage live, having until now been so close yet so far. I wonder how the riders in the real Tour will feel once they've finally crossed the line. I imagine it will be a similar mix of emotions for most of them, only much more intense. I imagine relief will play a big part for them as well.

Mind you, they'll mostly be racing again within a week, whereas I'm not planning to be back on the bike for some time. Having said that, even during the last couple of days, when I felt pretty much worn out, I've had the urge to see how much benefit I'll have gained from this intensity of cycling, so hopefully the appetite for riding will come back soon. After all, it's not often you get the chance to ride some 2,000 miles in three weeks. Once I've recovered I'll surely be as fit as I've ever been on a bike.

Maybe I should do it again, then, to take advantage of this wonderful training? Not on your life . . . except, except . . . I think I would like to do it again, but only if all the planning and logistics were taken care of by someone else. I don't mean the driving to and from hotels and that sort of thing, which Dad did admirably. I mean everything, like a package holiday: all the hotels booked in advance and guaranteed to be cool, and clean and quiet, all the food prepared for you and available at whatever time you fancy, not just restaurant opening hours. If all I had to do was start cycling from point A in the morning and keep going to point B in the evening, I think it could actually be quite fun. Anyone else fancy it?

The final thing, I suppose, is to decide whether I achieved what I set out to achieve. The most obvious answer is 'no' because I didn't cycle the whole route. Nevertheless, once this became a fait accompli I did at least manage to keep going for the whole three weeks and eventually make it to Paris. Perhaps more importantly, I think that in doing so I threw some light on what an extraordinary undertaking it is to ride the Tour de France. If nothing else, hopefully this will encourage fans to once again invest some faith in the achievements of those who ride it in earnest.

## Appendix

# SOME FACTS AND FIGURES

## HOW I FARED AGAINST THE PROFESSIONALS

*Prologue: Paris (individual time trial)*
Bradley McGee – 6.5 km in 7 m 26 s
Paul Howard – 6.5 km in 20 m

*Stage 1: Montgeron–Meaux*
Alessandro Petacchi – 168 km in 3 h 44 m 33 s
Paul Howard – 168 km in 6 h 18 m

*Stage 2: La Ferté-sous-Jouarre–Sedan*
Baden Cooke – 204.5 km in 5 h 6 m 33 s
Paul Howard – 204.5 km in 7 h 28 m

*Stage 3: Charleville-Mézières–St-Dizier*
Alessandro Petacchi – 167.5 km in 3 h 27 m 39 s
Paul Howard – 167.5 km in 6 h 31 m

*Stage 4: Joinville–St-Dizier (team time trial)*
US Postal Service – 69 km in 1 h 18 m 27 s
Paul Howard – 69 km in 2h 44 m

*Stage 5: Troyes–Nevers*
Alessandro Petacchi – 196.5 km in 4 h 9 m 47 s
Paul Howard – 196.5 km in 7 h 17 m

*Stage 6: Nevers–Lyon*
Alessandro Petacchi – 230 km in 5 h 8 m 35 s
Paul Howard – 230 km in 8 h 30 m 20 s

*Stage 7: Lyon–Morzine-Avoriaz*
Richard Virenque – 230.5 km in 6 h 6 m 3 s
Paul Howard – *d.n.f.* (127.5 km in 5 h 27 m 10 s)

*Stage 8: Sallanches–L'Alpe d'Huez*
Iban Mayo – 219 km in 5 h 57 m 30 s
Paul Howard – 219 km in 9 h 10 m 12 s

*Stage 9: Bourg d'Oisans–Gap*
Alexandre Vinokourov – 184.5 km in 5 h 2 m
Paul Howard – 184.5 km in 8 h 16 m 26 s

*Stage 10: Gap–Marseille*
Jakob Piil – 219.5 km in 5 h 9 m 33 s
Paul Howard – *d.n.s.*

*Stage 11: Narbonne–Toulouse*
Juan Antonio Flecha – 153.5 km in 3 h 29 m 33 s
Paul Howard – 153.5 km in 5 h 58 m

*Stage 12: Gaillac–Cap' Découverte (individual time trial)*
Jan Ullrich – 47 km in 58 m 32 s
Paul Grogan – 47 km in 1 h 44 m 28 s
Paul Howard – (*as above*)

*Stage 13: Toulouse–Ax-3 Domaines*
Carlos Sastre – 197.5 km in 5 h 16 m 8 s
Paul Howard – *d.n.f* (189 km in 9 h 5 m)

*Stage 14: St-Girons–Loudenvielle-Le Louron*
Gilberto Simoni – 191.5 km in 5h 31 m 52 s
Paul Howard – *d.n.f.* (107 km in 5 h 15m)

*Stage 15: Bagnères-de-Bigorre–Luz-Ardiden*
Lance Armstrong – 159.5 km in 4 h 29 m 26 s
Paul Howard – 159.5 km in 7 h 46 m

*Stage 16: Pau–Bayonne*
Tyler Hamilton – 197.5 km in 4 h 59 m 41 s
Paul Howard – 197.5 km in 8 h 40 m

*Stage 17: Dax–Bordeaux*
Servais Knaven – 181 km in 3 h 54 m 23 s
Paul Grogan – 181 km in 6 h 20 m
Paul Howard – (*as above*)

*Stage 18: Bordeaux–St-Maixent-l'Ecole*
Pablo Lastras – 203.5 km in 4 h 3 m 18 s
Paul Howard – 203.5 km in 7 h

*Stage 19: Pornic–Nantes (individual time trial)*
David Millar – 49 km in 54 m 5 s
Paul Howard – 49 km in 1 h 50 s

*Stage 20: Ville d'Avray–Paris*
Jean-Patrick Nazon – 152 km in 3 h 38 m 49 s
Paul Howard – 50 km in 2 h

*Overall Classification*
Lance Armstrong (winner) – 3,427.5 km in 83 h 41 m 12 s
Paul Howard – 2,910 km in 117 h 40 m 36 s

*d.n.f.* – did not finish
*d.n s* – did not start

## PERFORMANCES IN THE ORIGINAL TOUR, 1903

*Stage 1: Paris–Lyon*
Maurice Garin – 467 km in 17 h 45 m 13 s

*Stage 2: Lyon–Marseille*
Hyppolyte Aucouturier – 374 km in 14 h 28 m 53 s

*Stage 3: Marseille–Toulouse*
Hyppolyte Aucouturier – 434 km in 17 h 55 m 4 s

*Stage 4: Toulouse–Bordeaux*
Charles Laeser – 268 km in 8 h 46 m

*Stage 5: Bordeaux–Nantes*
Maurice Garin – 425 km in 16 h 26 m 31 s

*Stage 6: Nantes–Ville d'Avray*
Maurice Garin – 460 km in 18 h 9 m

*Overall Classification*
Maurice Garin (winner) – 2,428 km in 94 h 33 m

> *Note*: For the sake of consistency with official Tour statistics,
> in this appendix metric measurements are used for all
> distances and heights.

## THE RIDE

For no reason other than to make myself feel better all the above
times have been calculated on the amount of time I spent on the
bike rather than the total elapsed time for each stage. If I included
all the pauses when I met Dad to replenish my supplies this would
add around an hour to the long stages and therefore about 15
hours overall. This would reduce my average speed from a
respectable 24.732 kph (15.5 mph) to a painfully slow 22.045

kph (13.8 mph). In doing so it would also mean that I would have been slower than all the Tours to date – the slowest ever was in 1919 when Firmin Lambot covered 5,560 km in 231 h 7 m 15 s at an average speed of 24.056 kph. If I allow myself the luxury of discounting breaks and using my average cycling speed as the comparison then I beat the average speed of the 1919 Tour and seven others:

> 1906 René Pothier – 4,367 km in 189 h 34 m at 24.463 kph
> 1920 Philippe Thys – 5,503 km in 228 h 36 m 13 s at 24.072 kph
> 1921 Léon Scieur – 5,485 km in 221 h 50 m 26 s at 24.724 kph
> 1922 Firmin Lambot – 5,315 km in 222 h 8 m 6 s at 24.196 kph
> 1923 Henri Pélissier – 5,386 km in 222 h 15 m 30 s at 24.233 kph
> 1924 Ottavio Bottecchia – 5,425 km in 226 h 18 m 21 s at 24.250 kph
> 1926 Lucien Buysse – 5,745 km in 238 h 44 m 25 s at 24.273 kph

Given the advances in bike technology between 1926 and now I find it amazing, and humbling, that these are the only Tours with a lower average speed than mine (and that there are none of these at all if you count the actual amount of time I took). What's more, the only reason even these few Tours had a slower average than mine was because of their total length – 1926 was almost double the distance I cycled – and the length of their stages. In 1926 there were only 17 stages, from 1919 to 1924 only 15 and in 1906 there were 13 stages. This means that the average length of the stages in these Tours was considerably longer than even the longest stage that I rode. In 1919 the *average* stage was 371 km – 232 miles – and the longest stage (joint longest ever in the Tour) was 482 km (301.5 miles) from Les Sables d'Olonne to Bayonne. This, no doubt, explains why it was the slowest Tour on record. I don't like to imagine what my average speed would have been if I had undertaken to ride this route on the types of bikes and roads they had to cope with.

The 1926 Tour remains the longest Tour on record, both in terms of distance covered and time taken. Two Tours share the shortest route – the first two Tours in 1903 and 1904, in fact, when the route covered 2,428 km. These are the only two Tours to have covered less distance than I rode. Only four other Tours – 1905 (2,994 km),1988 (3,286 km), 1989 (3,285 km) and 2002 (3,278 km) – were shorter than the distance covered by this year's event.

Nevertheless, to put the distance covered in a different perspective, this year's route is still over twice the distance between Land's End and John o' Groats (the shortest officially recognised distance is 849 miles), and the distance I covered more than doubles this. The total distance I rode (1,819 miles plus the extras to and from hotels etc.) is also about the equivalent of riding from Canada to Mexico.

Last year Lance Armstrong won in the shortest-ever total time – 82 h 5 m 12 s. This year he set the fastest-ever average speed – 40.954 kph (25.6 mph).

## THE ROUTE

The longest stage this year was the 230.5 km (144 miles) Stage 7 from Lyon to Morzine-Avoriaz, although several Tour guides said the stage the day before from Troyes to Lyon – measured at 230 km – was actually longer.

The Tour's highest point was when it passed over the Col du Galibier at 2,645 metres (8,730 feet) on Stage 8. The lowest point was only 3 metres above sea-level at the entrance to Bayonne at the end of Stage 16.

According to official Tour measurements the longest climb was the 34.3 km (21.4 miles) Col du Lauteret on Stage 9, although this includes 4 km when the road actually went down and the average is only 3.8 per cent (1-in-26). Even if you only count from the last of the downhill sections it's still the longest, however, with 23.3 km of consecutive climbing. There should also be a special mention for the climbs of the Col du Télégraphe and Col du Galibier which, when combined, go uphill for 30.4 km (at an average of 6.8 per cent – 1-in-14.5) with only a 5 km descent in between.

The Lauteret also wins the competition for the most ascent, coming in at 1,303 metres, with the Tourmalet (1,265 metres), the

Galibier (1,244 metres) and the Port de Pailhères (1,214 metres) all having more than 1,200 metres of climbing in one go. It's interesting to note that neither the Lauteret nor the Port de Pailhères are hors catégorie climbs. The relatively easy gradient of the Lauteret may well explain this, but the Port de Pailhères is steeper than both the Tourmalet and the Galibier – and as I found to my cost is very difficult as a result. For my money, whether on subjective or objective criteria, this could easily be recategorised. It comes as no surprise that the stage with the greatest amount of climbing was Stage 8 to l'Alpe d'Huez – 3,892 metres.

The steepest climb was the category-three Côte de Larrau on Stage 16 which had an average gradient of 10.5 per cent (steeper than 1-in-10), although this only lasted 2.4 km. The steepest climb of any length was on the same stage – the much feared Col de Bagargui, which averaged 9.2 per cent (steeper than 1-in-11) over 8.8 km. The official Tour guide says that the Bagargui contains one kilometre at an average of 11.5 per cent; unless I was hallucinating as a result of the effort, the roadside signs said the steepest section averaged 13 per cent (about 1-in-7.5).

The total amount of climbing in the Tour is very difficult to calculate and there are no official figures. However, the total height gained on the all the climbs that merited a category (or were hors catégorie) was 23,028 metres (76,000 feet). This in itself is over two-and-a-half times the height of Everest and of course falls considerably short of the actual amount climbed as it excludes all the false-flats up to the foot of the climbs in the Alps and Pyrenees, as well as myriad ups and downs not deemed worthy of category-four status. It's impossible to know how much more to add, but another 5,000 metres (16,500 feet) wouldn't strike me as unreasonable. This would make it more than three times the height of Everest – in three weeks.

## MY BIKE

The bike on which I rode all this was a Giant TCR Composite – which means it was almost entirely made from carbon-fibre, including the forks and the handlebar stem. It was lent go me by the manufacturer especially for the ride. My gear ratios were 53 x 12 to 39 x 25, which proved entirely adequate for even the steepest slopes. The only time I struggled to turn the lowest gear (as opposed to just struggled) was on the Côte de Saint-Appollinaire, the penultimate climb on Stage 9 into Gap, and this was because I'd almost completely run out of energy and no gear would have been low enough. Even on the Port de Pailhères in the Pyrenees, where I was in similar trouble, I could turn the gear, I just couldn't turn it very quickly.

All the gear-changing mechanisms were Shimano Ultegra, giving me in theory 18 gears to choose from. The saddle was a Selle Italia Trans Am and the wheels were Mavic Cosmos (24 spokes at the front, 28 at the rear). For the first five stages I rode Michelin Pro Race tyres, and then changed to Continental DuraSkins for the rest. I had no punctures throughout the whole duration of the Tour. I used Wellgo pedals and wore lace-up Shimano trainers – old favourites.

## CLOTHING AND ACCESSORIES

Almost without fail, I wore nothing more than bib-shorts and a short-sleeve top. I also carried a cloth cycling cap, which I wore frequently, as well as sunglasses from Stage 11 (I had some originally but I broke them on the first stage and didn't replace them until the first rest day). On only two mornings (Stage 2 and Stage 18) did I wear an extra layer at the start of the day, and I needed extra clothes in the mountains only on two days in the Pyrenees. Most mornings I wore a head torch and a back light clipped to my vest pocket.

The longest unsupported section of my ride was the last 98 km of Stage 8, finishing at l'Alpe d'Huez, so I managed to carry all the food I needed in my pockets. Along with this I also had two water bottles, a small saddle bag with a multi-tool and two spare inner-tubes. The only time I took any more than this was on Stages 15 and 16 in the Pyrenees, when there was a hint of rain, although none came. On these occasions I carried a cotton rucksack containing a cagoule, a spare top and a woolly hat.

In terms of spare clothes I had everything I could think of ever needing on a bike (in Europe in summer anyway). I had a Gore-Tex cagoule, a windproof pile jacket, waterproof trousers, long-john cycling shorts, thick socks, neoprene over-boots, thick gloves, waterproof over-mitts, a woolly hat, a windproof top, three thermal tops, a long-sleeved training top, spare shoelaces, an extra pair of bib-shorts and an extra short-sleeved top. Of course, I needed hardly any of these, but if hadn't had them it would surely have been the coldest and wettest Tour on record.

I was perhaps less well equipped when it came to bike spares, and tools, but as I'm no mechanic there was little point in me carrying things I didn't know how to use. I had two spare tyres, five spare inner tubes, a puncture-repair kit, spanners, pliers, some brake and gear cable, some oil, a spare pair of cleats for my cycling shoes and a track pump. Fortunately I used hardly any of these either.

## FOOD AND DRINK EN ROUTE

On most days I ended up carrying more food with me than I needed, through paranoia at running out of energy and not being able to complete the stage. I certainly ate more than anybody racing the route would have done as a result of riding at a much slower speed. Basically, I was riding slowly enough to be able to digest food as I went along.

Standard fair included bananas, maybe four a day on average, Catherine's home-made flapjacks and fruit cake, boiled sweets, chocolate bars – anything from Penguins to Snickers – and the inevitable malt loaf.

At stops with Dad, I would eat a croissant or two on the first and probably a sandwich – usually Camembert and tomato – at the second. I also often ate something savoury during the ride, anything from flans to BabyBel mini-cheeses. Without these I could never avoid succumbing to a ravenous hunger that would not be satisfied, regardless of how much sweet food I consumed.

Until becoming ill after Stage 9, I drank almost nothing but water, apart from tea at the first stop of the day and Coke whenever I needed something extra/cold during the ride. After Stage 9, I took to using isotonic drinks for at least some part of each day, although one bottle would always contain water. In the main I assumed that by eating such a variety of food as I was during each stage I was not going short on the salts necessary to avoid dehydration.

## MISCELLANEOUS

Between the four of us we used seventeen rolls of film: me three, Dad three and Paul eleven.

We stayed at 19 different hotels.

The route ventured into 38 of France's *départements* and only once crossed into another country – 16 km of Stage 14 in Spain.

I used 1.5 bottles of sun cream – a combination of factor 8 and factor 30.

Dad drove 3,096 miles while following the route, and the total driven in France, including driving between Dieppe and Paris and back again, was 3,382 miles.

I consumed 11 malt loaves.